Dedication

To my grandmother Lorraine, my mother Janice and my daughter Jillian: thanks for sharing your love of books with me.

To my sons Nathan and Liam: thanks for half listening when I read my book aloud. Your silence was affirmation that it was moving along nicely.

To my husband Mike: thanks for believing in me and making this dream a reality.

Contents

Foreword

Anyone reading this novel will wonder about the location of this place called Ballinhassig. Situated on the bank of the Owenabue River, the village is almost central to Cork, Bandon and Kinsale in Southern Ireland.

It was here that I met Ellen Alden for the very first time, and I was very impressed with her enthusiasm, as she outlined her proposal about writing her first novel, which included Ballinhassig, and the effects of the famine on its people.

Indeed, Ballinhassig suffered greatly as a result of the famine, and many people emigrated to England, Scotland, and America. In 1846, 2000 people prayed on their knees on the road outside the Mountain Chapel, in the Northern end of the parish. They were appealing to God, to the government, and to the landlords for help. Sadly, help never came and many starved to death shortly afterwards.

They say there's a book in everyone. If so, I'm hoping this is just the first book from Ellen Alden. It's a fascinating story of hunger, suffering, emigration, death, lost love, war, peace, and above all survival. Ellen has weaved together a vivid account of the Potato Famine with a story of two lovers who are caught between the loyalties to their country and their loyalty for one another. She tells a real-life story of Irish immigrants struggling to adjust to life in Massachusetts at a time when their adopted Nation has become divided. The Irish were not welcomed with open arms as they entered America. They struggled and fought for respect-and some took extraordinary gambles.

I congratulate Ellen on her noble efforts to capture the essence of these unsettling time periods on two continents as well as creating a riveting story of survival, endurance and personal triumph.

Congratulations and good luck to all its readers from your local historian in Ballinhassig.

John L. O'Sullivan

Part One

"God Sent a curse upon the land
because her son's were slaves;

The rich earth brought forth rottenness,
and gardens became graves,

The green crops withered in the field,
all blackened by the curse,

and wedding gay and dance
gave way to coffin and hearse."

Anonymous poet, 1849 Ireland

Chapter 1

Florence Burke
January 1864
West Springfield, MA

"It's done." Knowing I'd settled my fate with a few strokes of a pen, I sit back in my chair and weave my hands through my thick, dark hair. A single droplet of sweat glides down my cheekbone and lands smudging the signature of the legal document set before me. I remove my handkerchief and dab at the widening, inky stain, hoping I can wash it all away. The heat from the woodstove in the lobby has seeped into this small office, and as I ball my soiled handkerchief into the quivering palm of my hand, I feel my chest rise as I gasp for breath. While I attempt to ease my constriction, I forget I am not alone in this confined space.

"Mr. Burke, you are an official volunteer of the Union Army. You will report to Boston Harbor immediately and join the men at Camp Long Island under the leadership of General Devens." Mr. Parsons reads my orders without looking up from his papers. "There at the camp you will be equipped and trained before joining the 37th Regiment in Virginia." I can hardly concentrate as this intimidating gentleman I've know as Treasurer stands before me sealing my fate with the official conscription papers. In addition to his duties as Town Councilman, he is mandated to find recruits for the war, and he's done just that.

As I look into Mr. Parson's tired, creased eyes I see no hints of compassion or even appreciation for this stumble towards Mr. Lincoln's battlefield. The Treasurer's glossed hair, finely tailored clothing and stubby, callous-free hands hint at a life much different from mine. A new, sudden cold shiver streaks down my spine. The sound of stiff pen to paper is all that is audible to me, and my mind races almost as fast as my heart. I notice the afternoon light has now found an entry into the miniscule office through a narrow window, and its beam has fallen upon Mr. Parson's face. He squints and looks older as the lines on his face wind down his cheek, like an ice pond newly cracked by a heavy weight. Mr. Parson's benign countenance conceals his eagerness, nay, his relief, to enlist another Union soldier.

Although my years are not as advanced as the Treasurer's, I am not a young, green boy going to war for strong political principles or for the hero's mantel. I am 35 years of age, a father of three, and a husband to a woman I dearly love. I have worked my whole life as a farmer tending land for wealthy landowners, in Ireland, and in my new country, and now I am making a bold move to realize my dreams.

"My land," I mutter, "My land…" My voice rises to an audible level as I've finally recovered from a state of shock. I clear my throat and begin to speak again when Mr. Parsons raises his gnarly face toward me. He sighs and takes a moment to replace his quill to the inkwell.

"Is there something else you require, Burke? I still have a day's business to complete so if you have further inquiries will you please post them to me from Camp Long Island…"

"Mr. Parsons, Sir, may I have the deed to my land? If I'm to leave straightaway I must have the deed in my possession. I want to see the boundary lines and the farmhouse for my wife and children and I want to know there is a roadway to the house as well, Sir, as Mr. Day assured me that one would be made when the deal is done. Please, I want this to be made right before I depart."

My desperate tone and wilting posture did not seem to move the old man. With both hands on the clasp of his leather case, he looks to me and I notice his eyebrows change significantly. They were slightly arched and poised to aid in his heavy concentration one moment, and then suddenly they are provoked and standing to attention, falling in line with the many deep wrinkles that have formed across his forehead. He raises his face to me as his eyes rake across mine.

"Burke," Mr. Parsons hisses, "may I remind you, you are an Irish man volunteering to go to war in place of Mr. Day's son in exchange for an allotted parcel of farmland? You will be granted your land as soon as the elder Mr. Day has signed your deed and his lawyers have drawn the boundary lines. I advise you to leave my office and swiftly collect your personal items, for your duty begins tomorrow at 3 p.m." Mr. Parsons finishes and flutters his hand back and forth waving me out of his office, as if I were a fly buzzing around his head.

What? My head starts to throb. How can I be expected to leave immediately? I grasp onto the edges of his desk and start to plead,

"Tomorrow at 3, so soon? Sir, I'll hardly have time enough to find a lawyer for this trade, not to mention saying a proper good-bye to my family. I've a young wife and three children who must have help moving house before I depart. It's the dead of winter. I need more time!" The last of my words are sounded in a loud, desperate plea. I release my hands from his desk and stand erect, although my knees feel weak and I fear I may topple over.

"This is the way it is done, Burke. Why are you here wasting time when you have so many items to attend to? Report to the

Town Hall tomorrow at 3 o'clock or your deed will be destroyed and another man will surely take this land. Good day." With that Mr. Parsons begins tidying up his desk. He straightens the loose papers and opens his drawer to remove a pipe from his desk. He carefully empties the contents onto a shabby handkerchief, banging it several times to deplete the remaining ashes.

"Thank you Mr. Parsons." I am resigned to leave with questions unanswered. He rises and offers his hand to me, although I notice his eyes are fixed upon the timepiece sitting squarely on his desk. I hear the strident sound of its ticking, and I wonder for a moment if it is indeed the pocket watch which is beating, or the sound of my own heart pounding loud enough to be heard through my winter layers.

I am going to war, yet I can hardly believe it is true. I suddenly think of James, my wife's brother-in-law. James was drafted into the Union Army and fights in a Massachusetts regiment in Virginia. He's been a soldier for one year's time, and thankfully, has not suffered wounds or been struck with an illness. His letters describe marches and drills, but he has yet to see the truly heavy fighting our newspapers report. His last letter mentioned a victory for the Union at the battle of Mine Run, and if he has felt the terror a man must feel while standing down his ground, he has not spoken of it. Surely James is writing to us with Ellen and the children in mind as recipients, a rose-colored field stripped of war's atrocities. James is brave, a true soldier. I pray I will join his regiment when I am mustered to Virginia.

I think of the gamble I've made and I worry that perhaps I've been rash in my decision. I thought it was a good risk at the time, but now I'm not nearly as confident. The North far outnumbers the men it can send into battle, but the Rebels are wily, their commanders fierce, so it's a game of men and minds.

I feel a lump in my throat as I recognize that I am being sent to war to replace someone who has fallen, an unlucky corpse left to rot in an open field. As an Irishman, I am expendable, a face without definition, needed to wave a rifle and charge the Johnny Rebs. The Army cares nothing for my real motivation or for the loving family I leave behind. The Union wants its other half back; I want desperately to own land in my name. This is the only way I see it will happen.

I exit the Treasury office dizzy and unsatisfied. "Lord, give me strength," I can't help thinking as I make my way through the West Springfield Town Hall. I pause a moment as my gaze catches a glimpse of a wooden cross in the foyer near the exit of the building. I slowly traverse the hall and stand before the cross, observing its subtle carvings and ornamental gold-plated engravings. I trail my finger down its indented border and across to the statue of Jesus. I leave my hand there for a moment as I lower my head and pray to the Almighty Father.

I have many items to attend to before I depart, yet I hardly know where to begin. My mind keeps drifting to Ellen and the children and I have to shake their images away if I am to plan my departure readily. I have a signed trade by Mr. Day and Mr. Parsons, but no official Deed as yet. Ellen will move house without me, which means she will need to borrow a wagon and enlist our neighbors for help. Oh, I can't make lists and organize details just now because I'm dreading her reaction to my news. I'm not confident that Ellen will ever forgive me. How will Jerry, still a boy, manage the farm? Michael's even younger and although he's helpful with the farm animals and looking after the baby, he's high-spirited and easily sidetracked. And, then there's my darling baby Grace. She's as delicate and pink as a rose petal. How can I leave them? Have I erred unalterably in signing this deal?

As I exit the Springfield Town hall, the chill of the early January air sobers me, temporarily easing my anxiety. I look across the cobblestone road and try to settle on a path to take home. I must collect myself and try to be as resolute as I can. With this trade I have made a move to improve our future and to give my children a chance at success in this country.

One final internal torment surfaces from deep within my soul. The thought of my father, and the contemptuous words he last spoke to me in Ireland. He hates me for deserting him, for deserting his farm, and for deserting Ireland. I can't bear to hear his wretched voice in my head any longer. He is my last motivation to join this war and attain my own land. My life thus far has been a risk. First I left Ireland, now I'm leaving behind Ellen and our children. I imagine my father, willing me to fail, to go under in this cold and distant land. That would please him.

My mind reels back to the events that brought me here to American soil.

Chapter 2

16 years earlier...

Florence Burke
September 29th, 1848
County Cork Ireland

What a shock, seeing Ellen, my dear sweetheart, come bounding
into the Relief Works building. This dilapidated building, with its
broken windows and cold, dim interior is generally accustomed
to occupying weary, half-starved men who wait patiently as their
petty wages are distributed. I can't recall a time a woman has ever
appeared through its somber doorway, and I am aroused with
concern. However, as I watch her move through the crowd, I am
overwhelmed with pride and affection, and my fears wilt. Ellen
Malloy is delightful, her freckles dance around her small, elegant
nose and her wide blue eyes display a brilliance and liveliness that
I have never seen in any other woman. She has fair, lengthy ginger
hair, which she commonly sweeps into a neat bun, and her body is
long and lean, strengthened from long trips to town and working on
the farm. She looks like a beautiful angel coming towards me, and I
watch the sea of pale, wasted men part to allow this beautiful young
woman to approach. What a contrast she is in the foreground to the
gruesome background of emaciated Irish men crowded together like
a pack of mangy wolves. The light she brings into the building is
a reminder of what Ireland used to be, its goodness and promise.
Today, Ellen's long red hair gently falls around her wool cape, and

her small waist sways back and forth as she makes her way through the men. I am initially so stunned to see her here that I fail to notice her troubled state.

The day is a Friday, and I am queuing with other village men to collect my thirty pence for a week's work here at the Relief Works Programme. The Brits established this programme here in Ballinhassig after the third year of spoiled potato crops. It is supposed to supply aid and offset our lost farming wages, but at eight pence a day, it does little to support us. My seventeen-year-old brother John works beside me, digging, hauling-- and trying to provoke an Irish rebellion. His words, however, arouse no one, as most men are too tired and hungry to entertain thoughts beyond the day's struggle for survival.

John towers over most lads his age and he, like everyone in our town, has grown so thin that his bones protrude from under his thin sheet of skin. Before the blight, John was naturally slim, but hard labor and lack of sufficient nourishment has made him look like a skeleton topped with a wild mane. John has never made an effort to manage his full, messy mop, and I have to say I have always envied the way it flows and curls, as if it decides daily which arrangement it will shape. Despite John's physical changes he has not lost his confidence or his outspoken convictions. I worry that John's idealisms will get him into trouble with the British police or the Relief Works officials. John and I have been working at this program for six months and we want to return to our farm to help our father or we fear we too will be evicted by our landlord for lack of profit. We can't bear another misfortune; our family is already crippled by the loss of my dear sister Louisa, just nine years old. We are desperately trying to survive this famine even as starvation and disease sweep into our village wiping away all in its course.

I shake my head removing the dark images of this unthinkable state, and take in the startling sight of my love walking towards me. She's close enough for me to clearly see her eyes and I sense fear in them. I knew there had to be a reason for this unexpected visit. Ellen looks pale, bilious, as she ignores the salutations of those she recognizes and passes. This is not like my plucky girl who is commonly full of smiles and sweetness. She is not herself and I am certain that something had occurred to cause her distress.

She charges towards me so fast that she knocks into my mate Patrick, nearly shoving him straight from the queue. Patrick smiles and leans into my ear, "Florence, I think Ellen is eager to do business with you." I feel my cheeks redden but wave Patrick off with a flick of my glove. Patrick tosses his head back and turns toward my brother to share his witticism.

When Ellen finally reaches my spot in the queue I place my hands on the damp shoulders of her coat. I feel her body trembling. Immediately I take a step back and search into her misty eyes, looking for a clue to her misery. I want to draw her into my arms but I know this is not the place. By now the folks around me can sense something is off too; they turn away whilst the mood in the queue grows quieter and darker. I lead Ellen ahead, firmly, lovingly until we reach the clerk and collect my pay, and then we head out the back way. I can feel her crumbling beside me.

Ellen cannot wait until we are out of doors; she bursts into tears and fitfully spews out the words that all of Ireland has feared for the past three years, "The blight, it's back!"

"Shite, we are done," I say through clenched teeth. We reach the door and I push hard through it, desperate to relieve some of the anger I feel. The cold rain falling from the dark, lurid clouds seems fitting at a time of such horrific news.

As I wonder when the incurable suffering will end, Ellen suddenly pauses. She raises her head and I see her pretty face twisted in a wrath of despair. She takes a deep breath then her mouth seems to involuntarily release words fast and carelessly.

"My father's decided to leave Ireland and we're to depart in three days. We're sailing to Boston and travelling to Western Massachusetts to stay with my sister Mary. Florence, I had to slip from my house to speak with you because my father's distraught and his mind is made up. He's determined to leave this dying land and its vanishing populous. As you know my mother's fallen ill and my young brothers are withering away from hunger. I'm frightened Florence… and I don't want to leave you here, but what choice do I have? Please, please help me. What shall I do?" The last of Ellen's words emanate in a choke, and she grasps onto me so tight that I feel the braces beneath my overcoat dig into my chest.

I am crushed, blown soberly still by her news. I struggle to release myself and take her face into my hands, "Ellen," I look into her eyes, flooded by worry. "I'm sure your father is disheartened by the news of the spoiled crop. Perhaps he will change his mind in a few days' time…" Ellen shakes her head wildly in my hands releasing them from my grasp.

"No Florence, you're wrong! He will not change his mind. Today we sold our jewelry and silver in order to purchase tickets, and my father has penned a letter to our landlord informing him of our departure. I've been told to clean and iron our linen so we may pack them in our trunk. For God sake's Florence, we are leaving, and I need you to tell me what I should do."

I raise my eyebrows, "What do you mean Ellen, what should you do?" I search her crumpled face for understanding. Ellen's distress seems to have halted for a moment and a new look of exasperation has taken its place. She sighs and raises her hands in the air.

"Florence, I don't want to leave you, I can't bear it. I love my family but I love you as well. If I leave Ireland, don't you see, it will surely be the end of us…" Ellen's words fade. I pull her close and feel her body shaking from the tips of her full lips, to her thin, bony knees. The rain has soaked her hair and her cape is shining and clinging tightly to her small frame. I lower my head and realize she has been standing in a muddy puddle, the water covering her boots to the ankles. I gently guide her over to a dry hill of loose stones and lift her hood onto her cold head. Now all I can see are the dark shadows of her tiny features, her grief-stricken face hidden within her wool cloak. How I want to take her hand and lead her off into the night, safe and protected. But, I am not capable of it at this cursed time. That is the terrible truth of it. I can hardly even look out for myself. I must convince Ellen to leave this country, it is the only way I know she will be safe. My frustration at this situation mounts and I feel my jaw tightening and my fists clenching as I begin to speak to her.

"You must go, Ellen. Your mother's ill and needs proper medicine and food. We cannot find that here, it no longer exists in Ireland. You've got to care for your brothers and help your folks with the new house. Most of all I want you to leave so you will be safe and remain well. Go to America and reunite with your beloved sister, your brother-in-law and their new baby. Write to me about Boston, Western Massachusetts and all your journeys and adventures. We shall remain close through the reflections of the written word." I pause and feel my throat tighten from within as if a valve is slowly closing. Before my words become choked away, I swallow hard and look into Ellen's dark blue eyes that look as deep as a well. "Go Ellen, now, please. I release you from our relationship." Right away I know this is too direct and unfeeling, but my throat mutes and will not permit me to say more. I take a step away from her and feel my shoulders sag with resignation.

Ellen looks up into the falling rain and shakes her head in disbelief. The brief movement forces her hood from her head and

I capture the full look of shock on her face. She readjusts her hood and spins on her heel towards the dirt path. "No, Ellen, wait," I call out, but then pause and wrap my hands around my head. Let her go, I say to myself. I close my eyes tight and force myself to remain still and not pursue her.

When I finally open my eyes I feel a panic swelling in my chest and I sprint along the muddy roadway only to find an endless tunnel of brown mud and leafless trees with no sign of Ellen. She's gone.

Suddenly I hear the sound of hooves behind me and whip around to see Patrick veering his horse in my direction. He slows and I tread towards him as the rain continues to fall like tears surrounding me. I look to him and it seems obvious that he, too, has heard the grim news of the spoiled potato crop.

Patrick grimaces and dismounts his horse. He's wearing his work clothes, and he looks ragged and drenched. He takes his horse by the reins and pats the shoulder bag he's wearing around his neck, as if checking to be sure it is still on his person. The moon is casting a glow on his cropped, red crown.

When Patrick turns his gaze toward me I can see his face is blotched and his eyes are bloodshot and droopy. He wraps one arm around me roughly and I smell the drink on his breath. "Ellen's leaving me." I say and wiggle out of his headlock.

"Bloody hell Florence! We are in a desperate state in this God-forsaken village, and it seems leaving or dying are the only options. I could only buy two onions and some Indian corn at the mercantile...but I swiped some pricey whiskey from a nodding English policeman. Lots of good they are doing here protecting and aiding our country! At least I got myself a drink, courtesy of His Majesty." Patrick takes an unsteady step backward and waves his arms in the air as he continues.

"The English are fuking with us, Florence, they don't give a damn if we live or die. Did I tell you I rode to Kinsale last week and watched a cargo ship being loaded with cattle meat and vegetable crops? Our harvest and meats are being sent to England to be distributed to those in Turkey and Europe. How bloody cruel of the English Government to demand we export our precious crops when the food is needed here. I'm telling ya, mate, those rich English bastards are not trying to save us, they want us dead. I'm collecting my family this evening to propose a plan I've made to travel to Canada for a time. I wish I'd have the coin to journey to America, but it costs more than I have, and I want to leave before this cursed famine abolishes Ireland." Patrick belches and pants for a moment, worn-out from the day's work and the affects of the whiskey.

Finally, he shrugs his shoulders and grins with the scatter-tooth, resilient smile I have known since my childhood. "We'll both find a way to make it Florence, you'll see. I'll make my fortune in Canada and you'll get over your girl. Just be patient." Patrick takes a clumsy step toward me and extends his filthy, blistered hand.

Not Patrick gone too, I think in my head. I exhale a deep, remorseful breath and shake my best friend's hand. I try to steady my voice and conceal the fear I have in my heart.

"Take care of yourself, Patrick. Steer away from the terrible whiskey in Canada, and may we reunite in Ireland one day." Patrick nods and turns toward his horse. He heaves his leg over the unsaddled horse, and pulls himself up slowly, steadying himself with the reins.

I raise my hand to bid farewell, and watch him slap his horse's backside propelling him forward into the grey-black, ominous evening. I look to the starless sky, rain still falling relentlessly on my face, and I search for a sign to guide me through this plight.

Chapter 3

Ellen Burke
October 2nd, 1848
Cobh, Ireland

I never dreamed I'd be leaving my country at seventeen years of age. Yet, here we are at the docks of Cobh queuing to board this massive sailing vessel, leaving our home and those we love. I've packed two trunks containing a collection of our most valuable possessions, but it doesn't seem real to me because it has been so sudden. I feel a cool breeze blow against my back, and my hair flows forward and around the hood of my wool cape. I remove my hand from my cloak pocket and tuck in the long straying locks, raising my gaze into the distance. The ocean looks unwelcoming with its deep blue swells crashing against the docked boats, and the receding water is rippled with streaks from the strong northwest wind. My mouth has gone dry, but I am not going to let my nerves get the best of me today.

I've been trying to be brave for the sake of my two young brothers, but my strained smile and false optimism have not helped them thus far. At ages six and eight, Phillip and Daniel don't understand the severity of the state of Ireland, and they both look weary, thin and their eyes are puffy and red-rimmed from their tears and whimpers. They are saddened to be leaving our home, especially distraught because we have to leave behind our family sheepdog Rudy.

I hardly slept all night, and this morning I prayed Florence would come to the docks to claim me, or to at least bid me farewell. But, as the minutes passed, and our departure time draws nearer, I concede that Florence isn't turning up. He's released me and must carry on here, working at the Relief Works program until he and John can return to the farm. With utter grief, I leave Florence behind, fearing the worst for his future, shaken that we are really done.

I am interrupted from my thoughts by Father; he looks dashing in his best travel coat and Irish cap. His grey scarf is blowing in the wind and his handsome face is turned down so all I can see is the tip of his smart nose, and the brim of his cap. He is distributing our boarding papers and tickets. I take mine holding it close to my body to keep it from the wind as my hands are shaking. Mother is sitting in a pushchair in front of Da. He built it for the journey from furnishings in our house and wheels from our oxcart. Mother looks pale and thin, and her neck is red with some sort of oozing sore. She turns to me as if she can sense my uneasiness, and gives me a brave, reassuring smile. My eyes moisten as I try to return a cheerful look. I swiftly turn and wipe the stray tears, as I will not reveal my desolation, not now.

I grasp my brothers' small hands, give them a little tickle, and tell them to prepare for a great adventure aboard the ship. My brother Daniel raises his pale face to me and asks if we may see pirates on the journey. I lean down and pull my brothers close, whispering in their ears that they should be wary of pirates and ghosts. They both flush and look into each other's wide eyes. They pass the next few minutes pointing to the ship, speculating on where they will find spirits and thieves.

At last I notice the queue is truly progressing as we near the loading dock and Emigration stand. I watch as Father confidently presents the Emigrant Master with our documentation, and signals to each member of our family to turn over our tickets. I notice the

Master's eyebrows knot and his lips curl as he clicks his tongue against the roof of his mouth. He has been scrutinizing Mother in the pushchair and scrawling notes on his ledger. "What is it?" Father demands. The Master ignores Da and calls over to a man wearing a doctor's robe. Then, we are led out of the queue to a makeshift tent where the Immigration Master tells Father that the ship's doctor must examine Mother before we board.

"Father…" I whisper. Da turns to me and places his finger to his lips urging me into silence.

We gather under a large tent and straight away the elderly doctor enters, adjusts his spectacles on his crooked nose, and begins. "I am obliged to inform you that this ship cannot transport emigrants in wheelchairs. We are not equipped for this and it could prove dangerous to the user and to the other passengers on board. Those passengers that cannot walk on their own accord are strictly prohibited from boarding this vessel. I hereby recommend…"

"Oh, thank heavens, Doctor, Doctor Baker is it? I see it written on your badge," Mother interrupts, raising herself off the chair and stands with her hands firmly on her hips. Her face has a strong, confident look, and her voice has an authority I've never witnessed before. My mouth opens in shock, and I can see Dr. Baker is stunned as well as he takes a step back and raises his eyebrows. Mother continues, "You see Doctor, my husband made this pushchair for me because he feared I'd be weary from the journey as we travelled here by foot. But now I'm quite refreshed from the ride and desperate to walk about until it is time to board your fine ship." With that, Mother gives a small kick to the chair, sending it rolling down the dirt path, and cocks her head to the side, "Are we all right now?"

Doctor Baker gives Mother a quick examination focusing on the sores on her mouth and throat and the swelling around her abdomen. He finally sighs loudly and pauses to think. When at last he turns his attention toward Father, his face slackens and his eyebrows part with certainty of his conclusion. He quietly mutters that he will impose an extra charge on Mother's ticket because she is considered infirm. "However," he adds with a hint of kindheartedness, "if you, Mrs. Malloy, are able to walk up the ramp and onto the boat unassisted, then you may carry on and take your place in the hold with the other passengers. Good luck, Ma'am, good luck to you all." Father shakes the doctor's hand and Mother beams as she somehow slowly but steadily leads our way up the ramp and onto the ship. We've made it on board and this must be a sign of a turn in our fortune. We are sailing to America, and Mother has regained her strength!

We are on our way, together, and I feel optimistic for the first time in ages. After we enter the vast ship, we are ushered across the bow and then down several flights of stairs to a steerage room where about seventy-five other emigrants are gathering and talking softly. I don't recognize anyone, but I notice many children, and I am pleased my brothers will have companions for the journey. I wonder where we'll eat, sleep and use the toilets, but I know Father has made the arrangements, and everything will be sorted out. I try to keep from thinking about leaving Florence. I am deeply disappointed that he did not come to see me in our final days here. In my dreams I imagined him running to me; begging me to stay in Ireland. I would have said yes straightaway. But he didn't and now, if he has turned up to see me off, I won't be able to wave to him because we are so deeply down in the boat's belly. So I'll never know.

I sit on the hard wooden floor and observe the family members around me. Father's eyes are scanning the space and he seems to be trying to deduce how we will live here for the next six weeks. Mother is leaning on him, and although she holds her head high, her face is pale and I know she is trying to be brave. How I admire her! Daniel and Phillip sit with their knees tucked firmly to their chests. I am pleased to see their eyes are full of excitement as they wait for the adventure to begin.

I look into the faces of the many men and women crowded in this steel cell-like space and read appearances of relief, hope and optimism, but I also note some with downcast looks of fear, shame and utter abandon. Finally, a loud whistle blows from somewhere above. The moment has come, we are setting sail for America! My heart lurches suddenly as I think about Florence. This is really the end of it then. A hot tear runs down my cheek and once again I swiftly wipe it away. No, I will have no more of that. I must carry on with my family and my past will remain in Ireland. I feel the ship moving slowly now, and I give a silent prayer to the Almighty Father that he will take pity on us and allow our safe passage to America over these next six weeks.

The journey, however, is more miserable than we anticipate. The most difficult part for me is the tight quarters and the wretched odor. I assumed we were placed in a steerage room for departure, but it seems this is to be our main living quarter, dining room and sadly, our toilet. Our only other space is through a narrow alleyway to the bunkroom, which contains closely packed bunk beds made of planks. Since there are not enough beds for all the passengers, my father and brothers, as well as many others, sleep in the holding room cramped together with only their jackets as blankets. Mother, and the others suffering from illnesses are the first to be offered bunks, and they rarely move from these beds except to use the toilet. This makes the conditions in the bunkroom and the steerage rooms deteriorate fast and soon we are overpowered by the all-consuming stench of human waste and sickness. We try to divide the tiny holding room into small sections; one for clean water and food, one for dining, one for eliminating, and one for gathering and resting. However, because there are too many people and not nearly adequate space, these sections become blurred, then nonexistent.

As the number of days pass, many become ill and need to be transferred to the bunkroom. I gladly give up my bed in there because I cannot bear to hear the groans of the sick, the sight of human waste violently spewing from their bodies, and worst of all, the foul smell emanated by their ghastly conditions. An elderly woman next to me has been crying out in her sleep as she writhes around to find a more comfortable spot amongst her bed sores. I pity these poor invalids and feel guilty leaving them.

Out of necessity, a few men have become leaders and my father is among them. This group tries to organize the emigrants and to make food rations equitable, make living conditions as clean as possible, and to manage problems as they arise during the journey. To deal with the sick, the leaders declare that some kind of quarantine must take place in order to halt the spread of the diseases. After only three weeks of travel, more than 25 folks are suffering from more than the usual symptoms of seasickness, and they occupy the majority of bunks. Father proposes that because of this ever-growing problem, we should entertain the idea of placing the toilets in the bunkroom where many of the sick need them anyway. The hopes are that consolidating the waste with the infirm will reduce the number of new patients. So, we move the toilet buckets to the bunkroom and we plead with a few crewmembers to borrow disinfectant to scrub the holding space.

The crew is impressed with our diligence and amazed at our cleaning skills. The captain is too, and he sends a cabin boy to fetch volunteers to remove the rust and filth from the ship. The cabin boy looks to be about ten, and his face is green and bilious with seasickness. I beg Father to allow me to join the men and women volunteers. I'd give anything to get out of this stifling space and have a look around; perhaps I'd even have a chance to see the blue ocean! After much pleading, Father relents and gives me a stern but loving nod as I trot off with the others to receive my assignment.

I'll never forget the feeling I experience when I first arrive on the deck, the sky is azure and I have to shield my eyes from the stunning sun. I feel the ocean breeze blow through my thin coat, and although I am chilled, I know it is brilliant to have fresh air in my face and abundant space around me. I take in the scent of clean, salty air and notice my nose instinctively inhales, deeply and fully to capture this familiar aroma. The washing is hard work, but the seamen are kind and respectful to me. They caution me to be wary of the crashing waves near the bow and advise me to be certain I'm secured to a cleat before commencing work. I scrub and shine with care and meticulousness, and although I am soaked from the sea's spray, I am exhilarated to feel clean, alive and productive once more. I shiver as I finish polishing the railing on the main deck and nearly gasp when a crewmember suddenly stands before me pointing to the sky where the sun has disappeared and dark grey clouds have replaced the day's light.

My smile fades as I place my rags and polish into the pail and begin the descent to deliver the cleaning supplies to the cabin boy on the lower deck. My spirits droop even lower when I enter the holding room and am assaulted by the familiar stench and by the sounds of murmuring, singing and complaining. Even with the thorough cleaning of the dining hold, the horrible odor from the bunkroom invades our living space. After experiencing clean air on deck, I feel consumed by the putrid air and I have to place a flannel sprayed with perfume across my nostrils in order to remain in this room and find Father and the boys.

My eyes search though the sea of folks gathered in small groups, mostly sitting on the floor or laying flat on their coats. I spot Father in the corner, standing and speaking to a slight woman named Charlotte. She's been aiding the infirm on board and has taken a special fondness to Mother. Charlotte worked as a midwife in Ireland, and her medical experience and kindness have been a blessing to the many ill passengers in the bunkroom.

As I draw nearer to them I notice Father is shaking his head and they both look solemn. When he looks up at me his eyes widen but his mouth remains fixed and taut. Charlotte's eyes glance quickly at Father and she can sense that he does not know what to say, or how to say it, so she is the first to speak, laying her slender hand on my shoulder. "Ellen your mother has taken a turn for the worse. It is believed that she and several other passengers are suffering from a condition called typhus."

I remove my flannel as I gasp, "What can be done for her?" My eyes dart from Father to Charlotte while my throat turns bone dry. Father's eyes are red and his face is lined with worry. He looks older than when I left this morning, and his arms sag. He clears his throat and forces the words from his mouth, "Ellen, your mother's not improving and I'm afraid she's slipping from us." He turns and raises his face to the low ceiling.

"But Father!" I wail, "No! We have but a few weeks before we reach America. You haven't given up on Mum? You said we could save her by leaving Ireland, you said she would make it to America. You promised!" Father steps towards me and wraps his long arms around me. I can feel his heart beating fast against my temple. He slowly releases me and takes my face into his hands. "Ellen, your mother is too weak now to travel to the deck or leave her bunk. We're just too late, Ellen. Too late." His words fall off. Father raises my chin and I look into his grief-stricken eyes. "We must prepare the boys for the sad truth that your mother will be taken from us. My dear daughter, your mother fought bravely to make this journey and keep our family together. Go now, and say your good-bye."

"No Father," I repeat, shaking my head frantically, "I will make her eat the broth and drink water, and tell her she must hold on a few weeks more until we arrive in Boston." I turn away, "Charlotte," I plead, "can you please ask the ship's doctor for help. We must do something!"

I feel the heat of frustration in my face and in my veins and I violently extract myself from my Da's grasp and turn running toward the bunkroom. When I arrive I see Daniel trying to read to Mother, but she's motionless; ghost white as she sleeps in sweat-stained sheets. I give his blonde curls a gentle tap as he rises to leave the room. Even he seems to understand that Mother is gravely ill.

I find a pitcher of water and take a rag and place it on her head. She is burning, and the nearer I come, the more red splotches I see on her pitiful white face. I place the rag in the pitcher and squeeze some water onto her blistered lips. Mother chokes and the water drizzles from the corners of her mouth. Her eyes open, waking with a start. She attempts a weak smile as she recognizes my face. I see that her sunken eyes still have brilliance in them. Mother tries to speak but her swollen tongue makes it garbled and difficult for me to understand. A moment later, she lifts her hand and reaches toward my own. I open my palm and see that she has placed a small, delicate handkerchief in my hand. I recognize this handkerchief and remember when she proudly displayed it to our family one evening at dinnertime. She had taken on work as a seamstress in Blarney, and this was her first piece made at the woolen mill. She loved and cherished this handkerchief, and now she is passing it to me.

"For you," she struggles. She tries to say more but she is too weak. Then suddenly Mother begins coughing and gasping for air, and I pull her into a sitting position. Her body feels light and fragile.

"Mother, please hold on, you're going to be all right. Charlotte is fetching some medicine for you. You'll get better; just hold on a bit longer..." Mother's gasping turns into heaving and blood spurts from her mouth. I turn my head to avoid the explosion but feel her warm, sticky blood dripping down the side of my hair and cheek. I want to run away and find help but my arms refuse to let her go, so I hold her close and whisper words of love, as tears blend with drying blood, releasing tiny pink droplets onto her gray sheets.

At last the coughing subsides and I place Mother gently on the hard bunk. "Rest Mother, rest, you'll need your strength in America." I place my hand on her chest and my head down on her fragile hip. Where is Father? After a few minutes pass, I suddenly become aware that Mother's chest is not expanding. I holler for Father, for Charlotte...for anyone! I reach down to her and cry, "No Mother, don't go, don't go! Don't leave me, please!" All I experience after this is a slow, hazy picture of people moving, women consoling, brothers crying and the ship's hold becoming smaller and more constricted. Mother is gone and I feel empty and cold in her absence.

The next morning a funeral service is set for her on the top deck. It is a clear day, cool, and the ocean obligingly calm. The chilly air feels different to me today, just raw and cruel. I stand by Father dressed in his travelling suit and cap and hold my little brothers' shivering hands. When Mother is blessed by the ship's chaplain and sprinkled with holy water, I feel a brief warming sensation in my soul. Perhaps this is a sign assuring me we'll meet again in heaven. The last memory I have of this day is watching Mother's body pitched over the railing and into the vast ocean. I recall observing this scene in horror as my fingernails dig into my sweaty palms. In between my left palm and fingernails is a crumbled, white handkerchief slowly receiving its first red stain.

Chapter 4

Florence Burke
November 3rd, 1848
County Cork, Ireland

I can't stop thinking of Ellen. She is lost to me, perhaps forever. What a fool I was to release her without a written note or even a farewell kiss. I couldn't bear to see her off; instead I hid under the dock, like a cowardly cat, watching her ship's mast sail over the horizon. That was four weeks past.

Now as I trudge home from another miserable day at the Relief Works, I'm feeling tormented here without her. She was my greatest joy, fiery and passionate, and by far the most beautiful woman I have ever known. How did I let her go? How can I find her? Blood drains from my face as I realize what I must do. But how? With what money? Questions surface to the forefront of my mind without rational answers, but I feel a surge of hope and excitement swelling in my chest.

As I consider my future, I tramp along through thick mud, rain is pounding me, and my overcoat is becoming drenched. Darkness is falling like a heavy curtain and fog has billowed in, eerily resembling the shapeless form of ghostly spirits. Could these be the souls of the starved and sickened in Ireland? Is this a sign that I should go? I leave the main roadway, and follow a grassier path to my home. I have quickened my pace, spooked by dark, ominous thoughts, and the unnerving atmosphere enveloping me.

As the path narrows I see in the distance that the heavy rain has rolled a four-foot log down along the steep knoll to my right. As I approach and veer left to walk about it, I am suddenly struck by the realization that this is no log, but a young boy who is curled into a ball with only knickers and a muddy jumper on his emaciated body. I remove him from the ground and take him in my arms. He is icy cold; his body lifeless with lumpy bones protruding from every limb. He has no shoes on his grayish-blue feet, and they are wilted and shriveled like the skin of a suckling pig.

Suddenly the lad lifts his head from my chest and tries to speak, but no words are audible. His head flops back down as his tiny, frozen finger points in the direction of town before he goes limp once more. I am shivering now and uncertain where to bring this frozen, starving lad. Will he make it if I journey back to town? Are his parents alive and searching for him? Shall I carry him home?

I search to my left and right but see no sign of folks on the tight pass. The black night and thick fog will thwart my efforts to travel a great distance. I moan in helplessness, and swiftly remove my wet coat and wrap the warm, wooly liner around his icy body. I make certain his head is covered but not before noticing his face is aged with wrinkles and elderly features, and tufts of hair are missing from his tiny, golden head. Oh, dear God. He might be a little boy, but his starving condition has left him looking like an old man, withered and hardened. Poor child. I have a sudden inspiration on whom to call, and I begin running down the slick grassy path towards our neighbours, the O'Sullivans.

Siobhan O'Sullivan is an elderly woman and a midwife in the village of Ballinhassig. She is a recluse, and has become more solitary since her husband and eldest daughter died last winter from Cholera. Her only remaining daughter worked as a nurse in Cork, but I vaguely recall my mother mentioning that Brittany or is it Brita, is no longer working but at home tending to her grieving mother. I pray they are here and will aid this unfortunate lad.

When I finally arrive, I knock loudly on her splintered door and peer down at the worn and rusty door latch. My arms are burning and sweat and rain saturate my entire body. Despite the heat emanating from my forehead and underarms, I am trembling with little bumps emerging all over my exposed skin. I have not felt any movement from the boy, but I feel his cool, uneven breath on the nape of my neck. Something is willing this child to live.

I become anxious while waiting and I trot around the tiny house looking for a burning candle or any hint of life inside. I run to the window and peer in, but all I see is a dark reflection and streaks of rain gliding down the thin pane of glass. The streaks are in perfect, parallel lines and look like wrought iron bars on a jail cell. I see myself through the lines and suddenly panic at the thought of being locked behind them, isolated with this emaciated boy, forced to remain in this dying village. I look away from the window quickly and take a step back. I am truly frightened by this thought, and I feel my heart quicken and my breath contract. I am starting to panic but I must collect myself and find this boy shelter and food. I stomp back around to the door and begin pounding on it with my left fist, yelling for the O'Sullivans at the top of my hoarse voice. Oh, it is useless.

I lower my head and reluctantly turn toward the dark, menacing trail. One step later I hear a door screech open and I spin around as Mrs. O'Sullivan emerges with a lantern in one hand and a large ring of keys in the other. She is wearing a woolen shawl over her tiny shoulders and her long tangled hair falls in her face. Her sunken eyes peer through the gray locks and reveal a moment of recognition. "Sorry son, I'm here. You woke me with your pounding and I was fumbling around in the dark looking for my oil and keys.

Follow me Florence, Brita is at the back." Mrs. O'Sullivan leads the way with her lamp casting dim light on the rough footpath. She doesn't speak another word but silently leads me to a tiny, squalid bunkhouse. We enter and I find to my horror that there are four more children in there, sickly thin, with weeping sores on their mouths, distended bellies and old, wrinkled faces like that of the boy I am carrying.

"We have another one, Brita," Mrs. O'Sullivan says solemnly as she searches for a place to put him in this crowded hovel. "We'll make room over here." Mrs. O'Sullivan points her bony finger to a tiny, hay covered space, and I carefully tread over and around the starving children and place the boy on the filthy straw next to a little girl holding her belly. Mother and daughter exchange somber glances. Brita heaves a sigh as she removes my coat from the boy and scrutinizes his face and body. She asks several questions about his condition and how I happened to find him, and then she wraps him tightly in the blanket and surrounds his body with hay.

"Can he be saved do you think? Can any of these starving children be saved?" I ask with my voice trembling. Brita casts her eyes toward the ground for a moment but does not answer. Instead she begins mixing herbs with water and prudently spoons the ointment onto the open sores around the boy's mouth. I'm stunned at how calmly and steadily she works while treating these children, and I can't help but watch in silence as she swiftly moves from one child to another, applying ointment, bandaging sores and bundling them tight. Brita is a plain woman, with light brown hair, a narrow, pretty nose and small, round brown eyes. She is also alarmingly thin and pale like her mother, but she moves with a sense of purpose and I see her jaw is set as if determined to save these orphaned children.

Mrs. O'Sullivan places her wrinkled hand on my arm and whispers softly near my ear. "Brita brought these children from the hospital in Cork. They're orphans and have no one to look after them; left for dead. She's made them comfortable and uses what we have on our land to ease their maladies, but we can't save them. They're too wasted. We can do our best with the simple remedies and broths, but it is likely they will die and join their parents in heaven." Mrs. O'Sullivan kneels down and lovingly caresses the spiny back of the little girl. She looks like my dear sister Louisa. I lower my head, praying for the children, for Louisa, for the boy I had the sense to bring here, who may yet have a chance. As I pray for Ireland tears slide down my face.

I suddenly have to get out of this wretched place. The low roof line and rotten wooden walls feel like they are closing in on me. Dark shadows are cast around the small bodies and the smell of wet, soiled hay is making my stomach churn. Hastily I thank the O'Sullivans for tending to these children and reach deep in to my pocket to pull out my wages from today. I offer them fifteen pence, half my week's wages. I beg them to keep fighting for these children, and then run as swiftly as I can until I reach home, which now seems like a sanctuary from this appalling night.

Before I enter the orange-lit house, I remove my wet clothes, and hold them in my arms. I open the door and the warmth of the cozy cottage wraps around me and I draw comfort from it. I gingerly make my way to the opposite end of the house, just five steps, and open the back door to deposit my clothes into the wash bin, located cleverly under the roofline. I find a dry towel in the linen drawer and make my way to my bedroom, which I share with my brother John. He is not yet home, but my folks are here because the house is warm with a large fire, and I smell some sort of meat soup cooking on the fireplace. I dry my aching, trembling body and dress in warm, woolen pants, and a black jumper. What a miserable day. I hear Mother talking quietly to Da, but I don't feel prepared to join them and share my account of the day's troubling events. Too much has happened too quickly and I've hardly had time to sort it out. I can hardly think about Ellen, or how to tell them of my plan. Suddenly I am aware of footsteps coming toward my door, and then a pause,

"Florence, are you home darling?" Mother calls from the other side of the door.

"Yes Mother," I reply, "My clothes were sopping wet and I wanted to dispose of them quickly. I shall be out in a moment." I run my hands through my slick hair and lean over pressing my elbows onto my knees. Reluctantly, I begin to pull on my woolly socks and find my old tattered slippers. Ah, the first good feeling I've felt this long day. I breathe a long sigh, straighten my knees and head toward my bedroom door.

I open the door and nearly collide with John who is as soaked as I was tonight but who nonetheless seems high-spirited. He gives me a quick smile and swiftly glides into our room to make ready for dinner. The smell of the soup is all I can focus upon as I make my way towards the living area where we have an old wooden table neatly set for dinner. I see Ma near the fireplace and walk to her and kiss her soft, warm cheek. Her long auburn hair is pinned at the front and flows past her shoulders in the back. Her light-blue eyes shine in the lamp light and her thin lips stay pressed together. Ma takes several moments to scrutinize me, and raises her eyebrow as if she can sense my anxiety and pain. She pats my hand and her tired eyes soften. Her face still hints at the youthful, pretty girl she was, but age and grief have carved a new landscape that minimizes her favorable features.

I take in a deep breath and ask her if she'd like me to fetch some fresh milk from Marigold, our cow. She tells me it is already done but to please collect Father and John from their rooms for dinner.

Da and John arrive at the table at the same time and we remain behind our chairs and clasp our outstretched hands in a circle. I stand next to my mother and gaze at John and my Da on the opposite side of the table. I never noticed how similar their facial features are, especially their long, straight noses, large, sea-blue eyes and wavy, raven-colored hair. Age though, sets them apart as I note the harsh, deep lines that thatch across Da's face, earned by years of working in the severe climate and toiling on the rough land. John, in contrast, has fair, freckled skin and soft features. His face used to be round and full, but now, his cheeks are sunken like the rest of us. Looking at my underfed family makes the misery of today wash over me anew. They've no idea what I've experienced or the haunting signs I feel certain I have witnessed. Da bows his head and we follow.

Da begins grace by thanking the Almighty Father for the health of his wife and sons, for the pot of beef stew and for the comforts of our home. He asks God to be merciful and to spare us from eviction. He raises his voice and his eyes lower as he asks the Almighty Father to end this famine and to assist our family, friends and neighbors. Finally he closes with a soft, affectionate prayer to my sister Louisa, whose birthday would have been celebrated in one week's time. We bow our heads, and I feel my mother's hand tremble. "Amen," we say in unison.

After Ma takes her first spoonful, the rest of us hungrily dig into the stew. No one speaks for several minutes, savoring the flavors and appreciating the texture of the tender meat. Finally, Da breaks the silence by asking about our day at the Relief Works.

Still unable to voice my muddled feelings, I just shrug and reply, "Fine." John looks across at me and tries to catch my eye. He isn't aware of all that has transpired, but John can clearly see that I am not myself.

To deflect any further attention to me, John begins a wild recitation about his day at work, digging with a rusty shovel, heaving large stones, and laying wide, metal rails. "We still can't understand the need for a bridge in the middle of an abandoned potato field. We're not working with the most clever of Englishmen I'm afraid." John looks around the table then continues, recounting his journey home after work. He tells us he saw many ill villagers along the roadside, and offered one poor woman and her baby two pence of his own wages.

Da looks up from his bowl obviously pleased with John's generosity, turns his mouth upward on one side, and gives an approving nod. Then he says confidently, "You see boys, if folks in Ballinhassig share what they can with their neighbors, then we will survive this famine and come out all the stronger."

I can't suppress a low snicker. Although I dare not voice my resolution to emigrate, I have regained my confidence and feel compelled to question his optimism. "Father, surely you've heard the potato harvest turned up blighted again. Things are not getting better here, they are getting worse."

Father raises his spoon to his lips, nods, and with the last of the beef still stored between his teeth and cheek, replies, "Yes, of course. It's miserable news but we must be patient and wait out this famine. You'll see Florence." He swallows the last of his food and his plum-sized Adams apple jumps up and down his throat.

At that simple response I can't contain all that's occurred today and words spill from my mouth like lava erupting from an active volcano. "Father, do you truly believe the state of Ireland will improve? Ellen's family fled because her brothers were starving and her Mum fell terribly ill, and Patrick's sailed off to Canada because his family could no longer afford to feed him. The Gallivan's are fearing eviction any day, although they're hanging on and trying to sell their beloved farm animals, one cow, one chicken at a time." John gasps and opens his eyes wide. I nod to him, acknowledging his surprise, but continue. "Folks are frightened, they're worried about sickness, starvation and removal from their cottages and farmland. Our beautiful green Isle is wasting away, Da."

I lay my spoon on the table and feel my throat go dry as I conjure up the images of the bunkhouse in the woods. I gather strength from a deep inhale through my nose and continue, "Something terrible happened on my way home this evening. I stumbled upon a starving boy on the ground and carried him to the O'Sullivans's place. He scared me Da, because he looked pale and thin like Louisa and I think he's going to die. I am disgusted by the present state of our village and I want to discuss..." Father raises his hand motioning me to stop and slices through my unfinished thoughts.

"Your sister died of relapsing fever, and many from her school suffered as well. It was a miserable disease, caused by the lice trouble in town, and its advanced stage left us without treatment options!" Father's eyebrows furl and his eyes narrow with a despondent, punitive look.

"But, Da," John suddenly chimes in, "that's because our village doctor left for America himself three months earlier, and there's no place left to buy decent medicine in Ballinhassig." Father growls at this comment, not sure how to respond. Mother turns to me and lays her warm hand on my arm.

"I'm shocked to hear Patrick's left Ireland, Florence, and I know you adored your Ellen and thought, perhaps..." her voice drifts off, unwilling to say the obvious. That ours was more than a simple courtship, and that I'd intended to someday bring her into this family.

"Yes, Ma, I still adore her." I gently place my hand on hers and give it a loving tap. Father rakes his fingers through his wavy black hair and steadies his voice as he speaks. His eyes are creased and the line etched between his eyes is more pronounced. I know this look. My father is using every ounce of his energy to control his temper.

"Florence, son, never mind. We need you here fighting for the survival of the farm, fighting for the survival of our country. We're fortunate this livestock farm remains profitable, and we will keep working to diversify crops and grow what we can."

When will my Da understand that this land is not even ours, that we are mere tenants tending land for the wealthy landlords in England? We own nothing. We are given a pathetic cottage and some rocky fields to sow. We're forced to pay high taxes to absentee landlords, and tithes to the Protestant Church, and above that, we must export the majority of our crops and livestock back to England. How does he think we are fortunate? I know he's at the breaking point but I must challenge his thinking.

"Da, what good is any profit we make here if there is no food or medicine to buy?" I didn't mean to upset Mother, but she's already grasping for a handkerchief and blessing the rosary she wears around her neck in Louisa's memory. Father leans his long body forward and I see his back has a slight arch and a wide lump between his wide shoulders. He has always been a burly, ox-strong man, but I see that years on the farm have altered his build and perhaps impaired his intellect as well. Before I can begin to ponder this, Da speaks again.

"Florence, I have lived my whole life tending land for greedy English Landlords, but I think things are changing here. I read an article in the *Cork Examiner,* and it said that new land owning laws are inevitable. You see with so many Irish folks leaving their farms or being evicted because they can't pay their taxes, land is laying barren. Absentee landowners are consolidating small plots of land, and putting their interests into profitable crops like livestock. That is what we have here. If we expand we may be able to afford a parcel of land when new laws are amended. I've waited for this chance my whole life and I refuse to walk away from this dream." I feel my shoulders droop with submission. How could Da not see what is happening here? Is there any way to get through to him? I look across the table at John, my eyes wide and I shake my head in exasperation. He nods and I know he will have a go at talking sense into Father.

"Father," he pleads, "folks are not planning on departing forever. People are frightened and trying to make preparations to save themselves from what seems to be a worsening situation here. What do we do if we can't find cornmeal or vegetables in town? We can't eat our livestock and corn and butter or there'll be none to ship. The English haven't done enough to aid the starving people now with three years of failed crops. Worse yet, they're still expecting us to export what we make, even though the meat and produce are so badly needed here. I'm worried for Ma and our family, and I think we must discuss some plan for ourselves. Please Da, listen to us."

"I'm listening and I'm becoming disgusted. John, for God's sake, I thought you would have more sense. Why can't you see that I am not leaving and that we will be safe here on this farm? We will manage if we remain calm, use our resources and stay together. You can trust me on that."

I heave a sigh of frustration, and slide back resting my back against the hard, wooden chair. I turn my head to my right until I find Mother's moist eyes, and she knows I am willing her to speak. She reaches for my hand.

"Boys, your father has always protected and provided for us. We must put our faith in God now. Please, with Louisa gone, I can't bear to lose any more of my children." Ma turns away as a steady stream of tears fall from her eyes. I want to comfort her but I must reveal my plan even though I know my words will be the knife that tears my family apart.

"Ma, Da, I am leaving Ireland to find a farm of my own in America." There, I've said it. The words I've been meaning to say all evening. I haven't had such conviction or clarity in any decision in my entire life, but this I am sure is the right course for me. As expected, Da's cheeks inflame, and John blanches with shock. Da is the first to recover,

"You will not leave Ireland and abandon her just as she is at her weakening point. You must have faith in the resilience of our strong nation and remain here to rebuild her when our potato crop returns. You are weak, Florence, have you no faith in our Lord?"

"I do have faith, but I believe my destiny is not here in this wretched place. We'll all die of starvation or disease. Don't you think God wants us to save ourselves? Shouldn't we travel to a place with fertile land and vigorous crops? Where we won't have to depend on the bloody potato? Ellen's family is settling in Massachusetts where diverse crops grow in abundance…"

"God damn your soul to hell! That's it, your true reason for wanting to abandon your home, your parents! You're a foolish, lovesick boy." Father shakes his head, clearly ashamed of me.

"Yes, Da, that is part of it. I fear I will either perish here with you and the others staying on, or I will survive knowing I lost her. I can't live with that."

I push my chair back and look Da in the eye. I gently release Mother's warm hand and momentarily clasp my hands together. "Father, I beg you to join me, for our family to leave together and return when the blight is over." Father's anger unleashes itself.

"Damn you, Florence, you coward, not another word!" He pounds his massive left fist on the hard, wooden table. Mother gasps and gives me a desperate look but rises and moves towards Father to comfort him. John lowers his head. I know he can't bear to witness the rupture in the seam that has held our family together but says nothing, caught between us. I remain stalled in place, staring at Father in desperation. He grits his teeth and points a gnarled finger my way.

"Unless you're remaining in Ireland, please don't address me or even look my way," he thunders.

Without hesitation I respond, "I'm leaving."

With that, Father heaves his chair back, detaches himself from my shrinking mother, and stomps in front of me. I am sure he is going to punch my face so I retract my arms and cover my head, but instead he takes his giant left hand and clasps the front of my jumper with his fist. He pulls me up toward his red face and I can smell Ma's sweet, beef stew still on his lips. His eyes are now even with mine and I see all the hatred and disgust surging in them.

"Leave Ireland then, because you're not worthy of our name. America has nothing to offer you except shame and misery, do you hear me? You will not better yourself there, but be cursed with poverty and unhappiness. That's what I see in your future." With that Da drags me to the door and heaves me out onto the cold, wet grass. The rain has stopped, but my world becomes blackened when Da slams the door, seizing the last of the light. I am suddenly filled with anger and I pound my fist on the hard mud. How have I lost everything? Is Da right, am I running because I'm frightened? Am I a coward? Am I chasing Ellen or my own ambition? I don't know now; my world is upside down and what I thought was right now is unclear. Dear God, please help me.

Slowly, I lurch forward and stand erect. I look down at my feet and realize I have been tossed out with slippers on my feet, and that the wet grass is already dampening my socks at the ankles. I cautiously step on small pebbles as I make my way to the shadowy path. I hope Patrick's folks will take me in for the night. I suddenly hear footsteps behind me and I whip around hoping to see Da, but it's John approaching carrying a heavy sack over his shoulder. Although the dark night hides his face, I see it is glistening in the moonlight, revealing his troubled state. He pauses for a moment to catch his breath, and wipe his eyes. When he collects himself he somehow manages to produce an elusive, wry smile. "Florence, if we are to journey to America together, you'll need your boots and coat."

Chapter 5

Florence Burke
November 4th, 1848
Cobh, Ireland

"How much money do you have, John? I'd never have guessed we'd be drifters tonight." I walk side by side with my brother, my lone companion. We're both feeling the sting from my father's harsh words, and at the same time we're trying to sort out an immediate plan.

At least the rain has temporarily halted and the fog has lifted. I can see the moon as we walk towards town, and it casts a faint light across the sky. The shy stars seem hesitant to come forth and show their brilliant sparkle; the dark grey clouds are keeping them veiled. We tread carefully through the steep, muddy path until we meet a wider roadway that is level and easier to negotiate.

"I have the payment from today, minus the money I gave to the woman on the road, plus ten quid that Mother slipped me. Not nearly enough for two tickets, not even for a place on a cargo ship. I wonder if we could sneak on board as stowaways?" He is walking slowly, a few paces behind me, apparently deep in thought. I slow my pace until he is even with me and reach a hand across and knock him in the shoulder.

"For God's sake, John, try to think clearly! Your plan is foolish and shortsighted. Even if we could get on the ship, we wouldn't have money for food, we would have to stay hidden from everyone, and we wouldn't have money in New York to support us. How would we pay for lodging? Most of all, do we want to begin our new lives as criminals?"

"Florence, you're the one not thinking clearly. Your problem is that you think too much. We have to act! We have little money so we need to make things happen. We need to be clever. I've got some ideas."

I see a faint shadow cross his face. It appeared so quickly I couldn't tell if it was a look of fear or deception. I let it go and tried to move forward, "Well, John, where shall we sleep for the night and deliberate our next move?" Inexplicably I'm reminded of the sickly children staying in the O'Sullivan's bunkhouse. I feel a pang of guilt that I am strategizing a way to leave and abandoning the sick and dying souls left in Ballinhassig. Is Da right; am I unfaithful to my Nation? I shake my head removing the moral question from my thoughts. I've got to be confident in my decision and create a plan for success in America. "John, let's stop up at Patrick's place. His parents will surely take us in for a night or two, and I must speak to them to learn of Ellen's whereabouts. Mrs. Gallivan is a close friend of Mrs. Malloy, and they will know where her family is settling in Massachusetts." John doesn't respond.

"John, did you hear me?" I turn and give him a cuff on his shoulder. He winces and glares at me as if I rudely woke him from a deep trance. His thin face looks strained and his jaw tightens, but his eyes are bright and I catch a familiar glint in them. "Did you hear my plan for this evening?" I repeat. John nods, but keeps his face to the ground while we continue to walk in silence. Just as we reach the center of Ballinhassig Village, he stops for a moment, bending down to retie his boot. I pause as well and offer to carry his sack for the remainder of the journey. Finally, John straightens and focuses his eyes on something in the distance as he speaks, "Florence, I think you should go on to your mate's house. I too want to say a few good-byes, but they are in the other direction. I'll meet you in the morning and we'll sort out our future."

"Are you sure someone will take you in for the night? I'd feel better if we stayed together and you can call on your mates tomorrow. It's late already and this has been a grueling day for us. We need to rest and devise a sensible plan."

"I'll be all right. I'm certain of it. Go ahead, go see your dear friend's folks and say a proper good-bye. I'll be just up the roadway. Will you take the sack, you may want to change your slippers," John teases and looks at me with a playful grin. Before I can stop him, John hurries off, whistling an Irish pub song.

"Meet me at the Post at eight tomorrow morning!" I holler after him. He looks back and shakes his head in disagreement. "No," I hear him say faintly, "Meet me at Cobh. Bring the sack; tomorrow we sail." John pivots and sprints into the darkness. I raise my hands in utter frustration, but he is gone. We are not leaving tomorrow, he is daft. I begin walking down the narrow path to Patrick's but unable to shake this odd feeling, like an itch I can't quite scratch. I suddenly realize John is heading in the direction towards Cork City-away from his mates living here on the outskirts of town. But why?

I continue on to Patrick's house and enjoy a restful and comforting evening with his family. Patrick's family is stunned to hear of my father's reaction and expulsion. Mrs. Gallivan is visibly distressed as I tell her all that occurred at our last meal together, and my mother's obvious struggle with her loyalties to my father and her sons. She blames my folk's volatile behavior on the miserable times, and the heightened anxiety of people left in the village. Mrs. Gallivan shows me a letter penned by Patrick after his rough passage to Canada. He survived the journey, but many did not, and now he waits in quarantine. His mother chokes back tears as she speaks fondly about her only son, my best friend. I only wish my folks had sent me off with their blessing and love.

Before retiring for the night, I obtain Ellen's new address in Massachusetts, and stow it safely in my trouser pocket. Mrs. Gallivan bursts into tears again when I tell her that I plan to find her and ask her hand in marriage. If she'll still have me.

In the morning, after a modest breakfast, there are hugs and farewell wishes. Mr. Gallivan offers to lend a few quid for our tickets, but I do not accept the money. I know he has little to spare and what coin he has should be sent to help Patrick. I depart with a satisfied belly, a towel filled with two warm corn biscuits and two apples, and a sack of our belongings. As I wave farewell I feel a slight lightness in my heart, as if the last knot has been untied and thrown into the ocean, releasing us from the anchor that holds us here.

The foggy mist gives the early morning hour an ominous, heavy feeling. Although I can hardly make out the sea in the near distance, I can hear the waves crashing and I can smell the pungent, familiar scent of ripe, salty fish. It is noisy here on the dock and I've seen wagons of cargo and food being transported to the ships. Workmen, crewmembers and fishermen are milling about loading, washing, setting sail, and collecting lures, nets and bait. A large ship called the *Americanna* is docked in front. It looks alive with sailors and crewmembers scurrying around the decks, readying it for the long voyage across the Atlantic. Solemn families, their trunks in tow, collect their tickets and queue in different lines.

I shift the sack from my left to right shoulder and search for John. I am annoyed at my brother's insistence on meeting here by the chilly docks; it's gusty, foggy and crowded. I hope he's not still entertaining the idea of becoming stowaways. I will not be a part of that reckless plan. Where is he? I left Patrick's house thirty minutes ago leaving ample time to walk slowly and arrive here by eight o'clock.

I fret as I wait, hoping John will turn up soon, rested and in sound mind. I don't know what he was up to last night, but I don't feel good about it.

"Is that you, John?" I say out loud, squinting my eyes to peer through the thick fog. I see a tall, skinny lad queuing in line and jumping up and down trying to get my attention. I notice this lad's hair is flying wildly in the air, and his thin face is contorting as he hollers unheard words into the gusty air. This is indeed my younger brother, and I sling the sack over my shoulder and dash to his side.

"Good morning, big brother!" John says grinning from ear to ear. He looks exhausted and disheveled, but his cheeks are flushed with pink stripes and his eyes are beaming. "Nice day for a sail, aye?" John's smile remains foolishly on his face.

"Why are you in this queue? Stop playing, John," I say hotly. You can tell me how you spent your evening while we inquire about work here at the docks."

"Wait, Florence, I've some news. I purchased our one-way tickets to New York on the *Americanna*. See, I have them right here! This is our queue, the boat leaves at half past nine. We are sailing in one hour's time!" John grabs my arms and squeezes tightly. He can hardly contain his enthusiasm. "What?" I wail. "Where did you get the money to buy these tickets?" I stare into John's eyes and give them a thorough read. The rims of his eyes are red, swollen, and glassy, and he has dark circles under his eyes which are droopy with fatigue. His eyes are shifting furiously as he begins explaining the good fortune he's discovered.

"Well, Florence, last night was a wild one. I think sometimes when you are down on your luck, you really can pray and God will answer you. It happened to me! By chance, would you have a bite to eat? One thing I forgot to ask the Almighty Father for was food." John suppresses a smile and strokes his shallow belly.

"John, I demand that you tell me how this money came into your hands. Here, take a biscuit and an apple. Start talking while you eat." I hand over the towel of food from the sack and wait for him to chew and swallow. While he's devouring the corn biscuit, I take my first look around. There are folks in front of us and now there are five or six older gentlemen joining the queue behind us. As I look them over I can't help but notice their fine travelling clothes, bright parasols, fancy hats and shoes, and large, shiny, new trunks. Their mood is jovial, and many of them are talking quietly with one another.

I stand on tiptoes to look over the heads of those in our queue and to see the folks waiting where I stood earlier. They are wearing drab wool clothes and caps without any of the pretty colors, embellishments or fine lace I notice on these passengers. They are huddled together, many with ragged looking children, and they have paler, thinner physiques. A few are standing beside their trunks, but most carry sacks similar to ours. The few trunks are worn and patched.

My head is spinning from this obvious disparity, and I am confused. "John, how did you manage this? Are we even in the correct queue? I don't like this, something smells rotten. We'll probably be arrested before we reach New York." John looks anxiously at me at says, "Florence, you want to get to Ellen, to America, right?" He whispers near my ear, "Well, I found a way to get the money, I meant what I said, I prayed for it. I went to Cork and visited St. Michael's Cathedral to say my good-byes to

Ireland and to pray for good fortune, and then, what do you know, it found me!"

John leans forward and points his finger in the direction of an official checking tickets. He places the uneaten apple to his mouth, covering his lips, and mutters, "If you want to get out of here before we starve then now is our chance. I have an idea as well of how to make more money while we sail, and we should be all right for a bit when we get to New York." He reaches into his jacket and withdraws a small sack of gold coins. "You see this? It is our ticket to freedom; the ticket to set me up in New York, and the ticket to get you to Massachusetts. You have always been so practical Florence. For once, take a risk and trust me." My eyes widen at the sight of the ornate coin sack. I reach out and try to snatch it out of John's hand but he retracts his arm swiftly and buries it inside the pocket of his overcoat.

"John, did I see a cross on the sack?" My heart pounds harder, faster. My minds races. Did John steal that money? Would he take money from the very church where he and I were baptized? Perhaps he's borrowed it or it's been "donated"? John clears his throat and darts his eyes over my shoulder. I can sense the Emigration Master behind me, and see his shadow in a nearby puddle. I hold my breath and pray that we are not arrested.

It turns out we are admitted on board without much trouble. John does the talking, choosing his words carefully, and using his best highbrow tongue. When the Emigration Master inquires about lack of guardianship and our lack of baggage, John explains that our folks sailed off earlier with our trunks and they sent us money once they were properly settled. The Master eyes John's muddy boots and trousers and my torn overcoat and pathetic sack, but seems satisfied with the story. He punches a hole in our tickets and hands us our cabin assignment.

I wipe my moist brow when I see the official continue on down the queue to check in other passengers. I cannot believe this is happening, the feeling of excitement and anticipation gradually rises in my chest, and I manage to suppress the desire to uncover the truth. I want so badly to shake John and make him tell me where the money came from, but I do not press him after we board. I know John has questionable morals sometimes, but he is a good man, and by God, he managed a way to get us to America. I will struggle with this decision in the future, I know. But for now, I am not going to unlock the truth. Instead, I will appreciate peaceful ignorance.

John and I are issued a clean, cozy cabin and enjoy ample meals and beer during the journey. We don't spend much time in our room though, there's only space for two beds and a small desk and chair. Instead, we walk about the ship or meet in the dining area. In mild weather, we pass the day on deck chatting, reading, or listening to the music of the ship's fiddler. I notice, with veiled guilt, that the disadvantaged passengers I saw at the dock are not anywhere in sight on deck. I did not have to ask because I know where they are, crammed together somewhere in the bowels of this grand ship. I suppress the anxiety that rises to my chest each time I think about them.

John, on the other hand, has taken full advantage of our well-to-do travel companions. Immediately he engages them in conversation, inquires about their journey, discovers their background stories and their plans for the future. John listens to others with rapt attention often cocking his head to the side and nodding as they speak. He is charismatic and naturally curious about folks, and soon becomes a popular figure among the Irish passengers and American crewmen. I was hoping John was busy making new acquaintances and connections to help us along in America, but not surprisingly, John has another motive. He and a dubious lad named Collin Walsh set about organizing nightly card games in a stateroom in the officers' quarters. John and Collin carefully select the participants, most of them elderly and of course, moneyed. They spend all hours of the night playing cards, drinking beer and exchanging coins and bills. Most of the loot ends up in John and Collin's pockets, with the remaining paid to the hosting officer.

I shake my head in disapproval when John enters the cabin in the wee hours of the morning, smelling of tobacco and beer. His bloodshot eyes still sparkle in the beam of the light from our tiny lantern. I can barely make out his whole face, but I see him smile as he dumps his coins into the ever-growing sack. As John extinguishes the lantern and bids me good night, I feel something like envy washing over me. How could it be? John is charming and smooth, yes, but he is also dishonest and corrupt. How can he sleep so soundly knowing he's taken advantage of folks, elderly folks at that. Has he no conscious for his impenitent activities? The part that is most troubling to me is that these trusting passengers seem to be in great spirits; they enjoy the lively conversation, the nightly entertainment, and the attention that John provides. They don't even realize that they are being robbed. I both admire and loathe my brother.

As the days continue, I begin to worry about the influence that Collin Walsh has over John. Aside from their gambling ring, which has expanded to placing wages on everything from the day's weather to the night's meals and even days till dockage, Collin and John are discussing their futures in New York. He is a squirrely little man with small, feral eyes. He is short, and thin, but he has a broad face and a bulbous, crooked nose which is most unappealing. He is outspoken and brash, and the mustache that covers his upper lip bobs up and down when he speaks. Collin's pressing John to stay in New York and join him in establishing a political newspaper.

Collin claims that he has money to get this business started as well as good connections through cousins who already live in New York. I bet they are a dodgy bunch as well.

Back in Ireland Collin wrote political articles for the *Cork Examiner*, and he says his dream is to manage his own newspaper. It has been rumored from passengers who lived in his village that he was a controversial writer, and that he has been forced to flee to America because of threats from the British police. He adamantly denies these stories, and says he left because he no longer felt British because the government blatantly abandoned Ireland and stood by and watched as it became obliterated by famine and disease. He asserts that he left Ireland on his own free will after his parents became ill with rheumatic fever, but I am not buying it.

John has indeed formed a bond with Collin based on similar beliefs and mutual paths for their future. I worry John is too captivated by this loud, strong-willed bloke, and is getting indoctrinated into Collin's passionate, rebellious idealism. I want to chat with him and tell him of my concerns, but he is continually with Collin and his mates, and when he is in our cabin, he is always asleep. I will wait until the last night of our journey, and then I will hope to talk sense into him.

However, my talk that evening does not go well. John is defensive and becomes angry when I tell him how I feel about Collin and his unlikely idea of starting a political newspaper straightaway. I remind John that although he has always had a special liking for politics, he has neither the schooling nor professional training it takes to be successful in that arena. I plead with him to follow me to Massachusetts and tend farm. I finish by thanking him for getting us to America, and beg him to make appropriate choices going forward so he will be safe there, wherever he ends up. I pause as John removes his shirt and kicks his feet up onto his small bed. He lays his head on the pillow and breathes a deep sigh.

"Thank you, Florence, for your brotherly concern, but I have not made up my mind yet where I will live and find work. Your dream is to find Ellen and own land in this country, but I'm not convinced this is my fate as well. I left Ireland to find a better future and perhaps New York is the place. Collin's idea of finding investors and opening a print shop is interesting to me, and I feel confident that I can find a way to do it." John turns onto his side and holds his head in his hand as he waits for my reaction.

"But, John, you don't have family in New York. Please don't be foolish and get coaxed into starting a life and business there. Not by an outspoken, unruly man who doesn't have the money to put behind his business. Just consider all I've said, and I'll respect your final decision. You are my brother, and I only want the best for you."

John promises to deliberate, but seems anxious and restless. He rises and says he can't sleep, and that he'd like to consider his future in private. After he dresses for the top deck, he places our sack at the end of his bed and departs the cabin, leaving me alone with my thoughts.

I know I must attempt to get some rest before dockage tomorrow. However, I find myself seasick on the last night of the voyage. We hit a stormy passage off the coast of Nova Scotia and I lay in bed with nausea and fear. Hour after hour I toss and turn, my mind churning and my body refusing to relax. I worry I will not find Ellen or, worse still, I will find her but she'll no longer hold affection for me. Finding sleep elusive, I rise. I attempt to compose a list of requirements that I'll need to hasten my journey to West Springfield, where Mrs. Gallivan quietly confided Ellen and her parents would be. I've read this list several times, but now I suspect I'll be travelling alone, without my brother, and it weighs on my heart. I sit down at the end of my bed, head in hands, wondering what tomorrow will bring.

I slowly steer my thoughts away from my unpredictable future and into the final hours aboard the *Americanna*. I lie back on my bed and feel myself drifting off to sleep. What seems like moments later my eyes dart open at the sound of heavy steps walking past my door. I am unsure of the time; it must be nearly daybreak. I hastily dress and place my tattered slippers into our worn sack. I sling my coat over my shoulder, and stroll to the deck to await my first glimpse of the new land. I wonder where John has gone, but my hunch is that he is with Collin Walsh and others, soaking in the experiences of the last night's journey, and planning their next move in New York. I scale two flights of stairs and am surprised to discover it is brightening as I ascend the final steps. I pass an American crewman and ask,

"Good morning, do you have the time?" He looks at me and places his gloved hand into his heavy coat. He removes his pocket watch, examines it, and says, "Young man, it's 7:30 in the morning, and we've but a few hours until dockage in New York. After six and a half weeks at sea, I hope you're prepared to step foot on land, your new home." I nod and thank the crewmember with a tip of my cap.

As I reach the deck, I notice that indeed daylight is imminent, and it looks as if the weather will be clear as well. I peer over the railing and can just make out a shadow of land in the far distance. I find a place to sit which will block me from the rough, cold breeze, but where I can still see as we sail closer to this new land.

A half hour later I am looking at the outline of land on the starboard side of the ship. We're nearly here! I rise swiftly and make my way to the bow and notice several other folks collecting to have a first look at New York. I strain my eyes to focus in the distance. I observe that the land is remarkably green, like Ireland, but the trees look a different shape and height. They are more pointed and their trunks appear thick and long. I see yellow sparks of light coming from one point of land and I notice our ship is headed straight for it. This must be Staten Island! I can feel my heart race. I stay on the deck until I can clearly make out the rugged land before me. My first impression of New York is its grand size, its great variety of buildings, and the different materials they are made from. These residences are nothing like the cottages back home. This place is new and brilliant, and strikingly distinctive.

When we finally dock at Staten Island I am filled with trepidation. I cannot believe we have arrived. I gaze over the bow one last time and say a silent prayer. When the whistle blows I hurry to find John and collect my bag. He tells me he's arranged our first night's stay in Five Points, where many Irish immigrants settle. When I press him for details, he admits Collin has invited us to stay at his cousin's place, assuring us we will be welcome if we don't mind close quarters and raucous neighbors. I am not too keen with this arrangement but reluctantly agree because it means not having to use our precious coin, and perhaps Collin's cousins can help me find transportation to Massachusetts.

We wait patiently as we queue for the official documentation and then for our immigration photos. John and Collin chat softly, sharing observations of the new land, debating the advantages and disadvantages of city life, and expressing their joy at finally arriving in America. I too feel optimistic as a spasm of excitement runs through me. When the documentation process is finally complete, John and I follow Collin to another queue where we wait to board a small ferry.

John's face falls, "Another boat, god-damn, I'd rather swim."

"That would be worth watching. Why don't you give it a go?" I nudge John, trying to keep his mood light.

We make our way onto the ferry and climb the metal stairs to the upper deck. The scene is entirely different now as the horizon of New York expands before me revealing a land that looks entirely built by man, not the Almighty Father. I imagined what New York would be like, but seeing it now before me, well, it nearly takes my breath away. The city is alive--we can hear the crowds and feel the energy.

When we dock and disembark a short time later, I see Irish looking folks waiting for their loved ones to arrive; other folks are working at the docks or selling their goods here. Still others are walking to and fro and looking quite sure of themselves and their destination. John and I are wide-eyed at this eclectic and densely crowded new city. With Collin in the lead, we hustle through a narrow gate, and then suddenly a large opening appears at the end. We see folks coming and going at a fast rate on buggies, fine carriages, and carts and many hustling about on foot. We observe children playing on the edge of streets and dogs chasing buggies filled with workers. We have made it to New York City! I am thankful and temporarily so dazed by this realization that I am nearly taken down by a group of fishermen transporting their catch on a massive cart.

John has a laugh at my near calamity, then looks at the crowded street and notices five elegant women talking quietly in a circle. He nods to them but receives no reaction. He looks at their fine dresses, their expensive hats, and their white gloved hands. He hollers over the crowd of fellow immigrants passing by, "Good day, ladies. How do you do?" The women appear stunned at first, and then turn away and continue their conversation, ignoring John's spontaneous outburst. "John, please! Let's try to make a good impression here, not that of low class Irish boys," I admonish, but Collin grins and offers John an encouraging nod.

We continue on, weaving our way through the overly crowded streets. I feel a slight panic rising in my chest as I follow Collin and John, and become jostled by passing folks moving in all directions around me. I have never experienced city life like this, and the sea of odd-looking faces in colored garb, as well as the unfamiliar stale, putrid odor of the city, produces a nauseating feeling in my belly. To make matters worse, as we make our way from the dock and through the posh city, I begin to notice the brilliant, new buildings we pass are not in the same condition as the buildings and roads surrounding us now. These are worn-down and some of the roads are covered in dirt piles and human waste, making them nearly impassable.

The folks are different too; those we see now walking about appear ragged, and many ill-mannered. I trot ahead to keep time with Collin and inquire as to what part of the city we are travelling in. Collin's short legs are pumping at a quickened pace, and he is panting from the strain.

"I believe we passed through an area of Manhattan that is obviously a place of great prosperity for many Americans and some fortunate foreigners. We're now heading through the Lower East Side of Manhattan, also known as Five Points. My cousin sent me this map, and I'm trying to decipher his directions and follow the rare signs. Five Points is the intersection of five streets, so if we continue on this road I should think we will stumble upon our destination. Collin scans the dirty roads for clues to our position, and John and I try to keep our ears open for familiar accents. Collin warns us to keep our hands over our coin sacks because his cousins tell him this can be a dangerous place.

As I look around I become more discouraged and increasingly anxious. I am tired and hungry, and long to stop and eat a piece of bread to quiet my upset belly. I am thirsty as well and think that the ship, for all its terrible rocking and crashing, at least supplied us with food and water, as well as a safe, warm cabin. I repeat Ellen's name in my head and remember she is the reason I am here.

John is wide-eyed as we travel through dirty streets passing crumbling homes. He observes the poverty and lists the shortages in this section of town, as if he's storing information he will eventually write about in Collin's political newspaper. We walk a few more paces and then suddenly we are jolted by a loud scream. We whirl around in time to witness a very young, half-dressed woman running out of a tall building with a bar occupying the ground floor. Right behind her in pursuit is a large man wielding his belt and gaining speed on the frightened, filthy lass. Collin pauses and shakes his head.

"That must be one of the brothels my cousin mentioned in his letters. I told you this is a rough place boys. Prepare yourselves for city life and the many evils that exist here."

John blanches and then straight away his ears redden. He turns to Collin and asks, "What do you hear of the police presence, Collin? Are there rules enforced here in Five Points, or is it every man for himself?" Collin shrugs his shoulders as we continue walking.

"I can't answer that, John. I believe most Irish folks are civil and carry on all right here. It is just that the Irish come here just as we have, with little money and without proper skills. Therefore, they struggle as best they can, but it is not always honest I hear. Especially the whoring girls take up for money, or the smuggling and thieving, but what choice do they have?" Collin hesitates near an empty whiskey barrel, resting his elbows on it as he draws open his map. I notice John is distracted by something to his right and the next thing I see is my brother tearing down an alleyway chasing the man who has overtaken the partially naked girl.

"John, no, come back!" I demand. But John is gone and only his sack remains by my side. I turn to Collin who is craning his neck to see where John has run off to. He looks utterly stunned and helpless. "Wait here with our sack!" I sprint down a crowded alleyway filled with women and children gathered in the filthy street. I don't know which way they've run, and I am terrified my brother is going to end up dead on these mean streets. I realize I have gone the wrong way, so I turn back and try to find my way to the corner where Collin Walsh is waiting. Just then I hear some rustling and crashing, and I look to see John beating the drunken man with a hard object. I call to John, but by the time I near his side, he has knocked the stranger clean out. The man is lying face down, and his head is resting in a pool of blood, which is beginning to create a thin stream along the alleyway. I notice the man's pants are halfway down his backside, and it sickens me, forcing me to look away and set my troubled eyes on my brother.

"John, what in the hell are you doing? Look what you've done! We've got to get out of here before someone reports you to the police." I am breathing heavily and cocking my head in every direction listening for a whistle or footsteps. I look around and see no one in the small alley, and then I force myself to look down on the ground and I notice that the injured man is breathing slow, laborious breaths. Thank God for that. I turn to John and grab his arms. He winces and I notice his face is slashed and blood is pouring from his wound. He looks pale and his eyes are widened in shock.

"John, are you all right? Let's go back and find Collin before he leaves us here. We must find a piece of cloth to dress your wound." John does not move, but as I turn to walk he grabs me by my scarf and yells into my face. "Where's the girl?" he pleads, squinting so he can see down the long, murky alleyway.

"I don't know, John. I didn't see her." He releases my scarf and lowers his head. His face is a dark shade of red, and I am not sure if the deep color is from the wound, or because he is angry that he can't find the victim. John looks up and down the streets as we make our way back to the corner where Collin waits.

Collin is eyeing his timepiece but raises his head to us as we draw near to him. Immediately he reaches into his trouser pocket and offers John his own handkerchief. "Well, John, that's the type of passion I'm looking for in a mate and associate. Are you all right? What went on there? Come, we should be off, before more trouble is stirred."

Collin marches ahead, and turns at yet another narrow roadway. His eyes dance from right and left as if he's certain more misfortune is waiting for us. John follows Collin and I take the rear feeling particularly protective of my injured, senseless brother. I have our sack tossed over my shoulder and I see that John has one hand held to his face to stop the bleeding, and in the other hand he has a small white satchel. I lean towards him and whisper, "Did you beat the man with the sack of coins? John, I think you have gone mad. That money is all we have and it could have been taken from us not to mention you could have been killed. To save a wicked prostitute?"

John's ears redden, matching his crimson face. His face twists and he looks disgusted as he snarls, "No man has the right to lay hands on a girl who's not offering herself. I watched that sick man grasp her neck, press her roughly against the building, and whip her backside with his belt. He was hollering at her to stay still, and he was using his knees to wrench her legs apart. She was begging him to stop, but he was not having it. I told him to release her as she was clearly not willing to service him but he swung his belt at me and said she bloody well better because she was new and he wanted to be the first to have her. I had to act on her behalf."

Collin interjects, "Did she take his money and run? I hear some whores try and do just that."

"Nay, Collin, he hadn't paid her. I know because she ran away without her clothes, and I have his money in my pocket." John turns to me and withdraws the small wad of American dollars.

"John, you didn't! Two crimes in one day and we have only just arrived in New York." I take the bills from John and open them, surprised to find there is nearly 75 dollars here. "You better hope he doesn't regain his strength and break your skull or report you to the police for thieving. This man is obviously moneyed and may have influence with the law here."

"I think your act of valor deserves a reward. Well played." Collin pats John on the back, and gives him a conspiring grin.

"Listen to me, John. You can't come here and try to mend all the problems and evils that exist in New York. When you've managed to keep yourself supported for some time then you may begin to look after those around you. As for that young prostitute, save your pity and concern, for she may be far more trouble than even you can handle."

John's eyes widen as he defends the lass, "She's not meant for whoring, Florence, understand that. Her father forced her into it. Now she can't go home or he'll beat her. We shared but a few words before she ran off, but she made it clear that this was not her doing. I'm not sure of what to do now, but I do know, Florence I've decided to remain here in New York for a time. I will not be fulfilled with a rake or shovel in my hand. No, I want to remain here and support our struggling Irish brothers and sisters in Five Points."

"Good man, John. Let's continue travelling to my cousins' and see if they can find you temporary lodging." Collin throws his arm over John's shoulder and guides him down the dim and menacing streets.

I am alone now, God help me.

Chapter 6

Ellen Burke
December 20th, 1848
North Hampton, Massachusetts

I draw the thin curtains aside so that I may take in the full view of the brilliant snowstorm. The flakes are almost as I had envisioned them-- white, fluffy crystals that float and flit through the air, riding on the wind that carries them. I'm fascinated watching the snowflakes make their final landing, forming delicate, intricate shapes, pointed and star-like, impressively original. They appear improbably light and joyful, like they've been blessed from above.

I've been here in Massachusetts for nearly eight weeks time, but everything still feels odd and new. Now I am witnessing my first snowstorm, brilliant and mesmerizing, and it allows me to pause and reflect on the changes I have experienced since leaving Ireland.

The absence of Mother has been the hardest trial to bear. We planned to greet America together and to reunite with my sister Mary and her new husband. However, death's call hindered our best efforts. Now we are finally here in our new country, but there is a palpable emptiness filling the air.

I saw the reflection of my pain in my sister Mary's eyes the moment she realized Mother was not among us. Her mouth widened with shock, and her cheerful, hopeful face twisted and fell into an anguished grimace. She was carrying her two-year-old daughter

Emma in her arms, dressed in a fancy fur-lined coat and matching shiny boots. I'm certain Mary dressed her up in anticipation of a lovely introduction to the family, never expecting that my mother would be missing from the reunion. I met Mary's husband James that day through misty, clouded eyes. James is a stocky, sturdy man, with a pleasant smile and kind eyes. He is nearly bald save for a sideways tuft of hair atop his head, and traces of fuzz at the back. James has been a gracious host, and he's been respectful and patient as we invade his home, carrying our heartbreak with us. Mary's bereavement has opened the fresh wounds of my sorrow, and we have spent the last few weeks mourning together and sharing stories from our childhood.

We settle into Mary's house, and I pass the first week unpacking our trunk and washing our soiled travel clothing. We are staying here temporarily so I must unpack only those items we will need in the short term and leave the rest for our permanent lodging. Mary's house is a small, modest home with a sturdy frame. It is quite pretty from the outside with a painted fence in the front and a vegetable garden in the back. It has two floors, the upstairs holding two shallow bedrooms, and the downstairs containing a large main room and kitchen.

I have been given my own space, a tiny room where Emma will sleep when she is older. It accommodates a full bed and a little square side table, just the size for the lamp resting atop it. I protest this arrangement because I know the room was reserved for Father and Mother, and I don't feel worthy or comfortable sleeping in privacy here while Father rests on mats in the main room with my brothers. However, Father insists I remain in the bedroom and speaks cheerfully of the satisfying slumber he enjoys away from the rocking, confined space of steerage and the foul-smelling, ill-tempered companions. I cherish the solitude, but I can't help feeling a sense of loneliness here, as I lie awake thinking of Mother. And of course, as the days pass and I witness James' gentleness with my sister, I think again of Florence in Ireland, and how he let me go.

Straightaway I perform the duties of the household, much as I had done the last few months in Ireland, except everything is unfamiliar. Some things are easier. Mary has milk delivered in glass bottles, and her fireplace has a cook stove for baking. Now I need not keep watch over the baking or fret about burning the edges of breads and biscuits. Many tasks are just as they were in Ireland, collecting water from the well, mixing disinfectants to clean, and washing clothes and drying them on racks near the fire. Mary has acquainted me with the various shops in town, and I enjoy the hike to buy foodstuff and necessities for the house. I am thankful to be here and I feel obliged to make the most of the simple ingredients for preparing meals and keeping her house in order. I've offered to look after little Emma while Mary and James work the long hours at the dress shop, but James's grandmother watches her in a back room at the shop. Mary says she loves to see Emma during breaks and mealtimes. I suppose I have my hands full with my little brothers.

Mary and I have stolen our moments together and it surprises me how effortlessly we ease back into sisterhood. Mary found me weeping into Mum's handkerchief one evening and she sat on the edge of my bed, holding my hands and wiping my tears. She understood that it was for more than Mother that I grieved, and eventually I shared the gloomy story of my departure from Florence after our two-year courtship. A new reservoir of tears seemed to be tapped, as rivers fell from my eyes. Mary dabbed them away and offered her guidance. She advised that I should carry on here with this new life and believe that happiness will again find me. After our intimate chat I felt hope rising in my chest, for Mary renewed my faith in love. Perhaps the door is not closed on our future.

Three weeks after we arrive, Father has found work with a well-to-do businessman named Keith Greene. Actually, it was Mr. Greene's wife Susan who first met Father as he delivered a dress to her house. Mrs. Greene is a frequent customer at the dress shop, and James asked Father if he would mind delivering it to their large estate near the center of town. Father impressed Mrs. Greene with his manners and neat appearance, and she asked if he was employed. After several meetings Father was hired as a workman on the estate, his experience with tools and farming persuading the Greene's of his worth.

About a week after his hire, Father sent word to me that Mrs. Greene was looking to find a maidservant to work in her private home. She learned that Father had an older daughter and she inquired as to whether I possessed the abilities and maturity necessary to fill the position. Father spoke of my fine cooking skills, cleaning abilities and even temperament. Mrs. Greene was especially convinced when she learned that I had two young brothers to mind, and that I cared for them with a loving heart. For my duties of maidservant are not isolated to cleaning responsibilities. I am also responsible for tending to her three children, Isabelle, Thomas and Christopher.

Even though this new work means dreadfully early mornings, long, solitary marches from my sister's home to the Greene Estate, and arduous duties, I have found contentment here. In the first few days my hands were blistered and raw, and I slumped into bed the very moment I finished dinner. Now I have become used to the long days and hard work, smiling with pride when I receive my wages.

My brothers have been enrolled into a small public school and thankfully Mary and James escort them to the center of town where their school is located. Little Emma loves to be carried by her young, fun-loving uncles. Mary says the journey to town is her favorite part of the day. After school, Phillip and Daniel walk to the dress shop and tidy up the workspace or complete their lessons until Mary, James and Emma walk home with them. As the weeks move on, my brothers have improved in school as they've become accustomed to American accents.

We have all settled into this new country quite well, and despite the crowded living conditions and long, challenging days, we are getting on fine and enjoying this special time together.

Now as I watch the snowflakes fall from the comfort of my dim, narrow room, I fill my mind with thoughts of gratitude for what I now have and suppress the uprising of sorrow and grief for those that I have lost. It has been two months since Mother's death and as I look out my window and clasp her handkerchief in my hand, I feel her close to me, as near as if she could reach out her arms to me. I wonder why this blissful feeling has occurred just now? I know I should be laying my head to rest at this late hour, but I have been excited by the snowstorm and I cannot quiet my mind. I reach under my bed and find my nightcap and salve. I rub the soothing cream across my ankles and toes, saving a small portion for the blisters on my palms. There now, I must sleep for dawn will be calling in a few hours' time and I must be rested and alert.

"Ellen, come quick!" I am jolted from my slumber and I sit up wondering if I am dreaming. Was that the voice of James? I look to the window and the sky is dark and the snow continues to fall, glowing in the light of the moon. "Ellen, hurry down here!" That was surely Father's voice. Oh, dear, I start to panic. What is the trouble?

I remove my heavy blanket and suddenly the door flies open and I see Mary there, with a reddened face and twinkling eyes. She is carrying an elegant, light blue cloak in one hand and a small lantern in the other. She places the lantern on the table beside my unlit one, and she urges me to rise and don the new cloak. I am quite baffled, and wonder what in God's name is going on? I ask what time it is and why everyone is awake at this hour.

Mary's face tenses as if she is suppressing a secret. She purses her lips and all at once her hands rip my cap off and her fingers weave through my loose, matted hair.

"Mary, for God's sake, what are you doing?" Have you been drinking this evening?" I pull away from her and draw the blanket to my face. Mary smiles a knowing smile but does not answer. Instead she pulls the covers from my hands and yanks me to my feet. She wraps me in the cloak and leads me down the stairs. I can hear men's voices as I approach but the sound fades, then silences when I enter the main room and see Father and James standing in front of a tall man veiled in snow. Father immediately comes to me and offers a warm kiss on my cheek. I look for understanding in his eyes, but I am further baffled by the tears I see swimming in them. I look past Father to James who gives a nod to the stranger and takes Mary's hand and leads her off to the kitchen. Mary's face is flushed to a violet shade, and she has her right hand firmly sealed against her heart. Father releases me and closes the embrace with a tight squeeze to my hand. The one clutching Mother's handkerchief.

I am left alone with this man who somehow doesn't seem so strange to me anymore. I slowly make my way to him and a feeling of joy floods my body.

I notice his cap is still coated with fluffy snowflakes, and his eyebrows, eyelashes, nose and beard are sprinkled as well, allowing his sky-blue eyes alone to sear through the white mask. I gasp as he smiles, the recognition of those radiant eyes coming to me. "Florence...?" I take a step back and stumble, feeling light headed and dumbstruck. "Florence, you've come?" I shake my head hoping that this is not a dream. The beam of his grin seems to have melted the last of the snow off his face and his full countenance comes into view.

"Ellen… it is me. I've found you." I lean forward, hands smacking my cheeks in shock. Florence comes to me, gently straightens my bent back, and laces his fingers through mine. He arches his back just slightly so that he can lock eyes with me and attain my full attention. "Ellen, I'd many rehearsed speeches planned for this moment, but they've all gone adrift. I…," he fades, seemingly in disbelief himself. He regains his composure moments later and continues, "I have journeyed here to find you, and now I see you are as beautiful as the day I last saw you in Ireland." My arms are beginning to shudder as Florence draws me to his chest so he could whisper in my ear. I feel his wet clothing against my body, but somehow I do not feel cold, just warmth emanating from his thin frame.

"My love," he continues, "after you departed it became clear to me that I cannot think of a future without you. I promise, if you will have me, I will never let you go again. I love you, Ellen Malloy." I feel the tears flowing down my cheeks and I long to sweep them away so I may see Florence clearly. He, too, is shivering, and not from the cold but from the energy pulsing between us. It's as if our union has ignited the light within our souls and now it shines brightly, an explosion of happiness. I release my right hand and bring it to Florence's red, chapped cheek. His eyes are soft and pooling with tears, but his mouth is shaped into a most brilliant smile.

"I have prayed you would not forget me and…" I find my handkerchief and wipe my tears and then dab Florence's dewy face. The snow is melting and he is dripping, tears mingling with cold precipitation. "You truly are here." I look into his cheery face and take a step back. Then, without thinking, I leap into his wet arms!

"Oh, wait Ellen, there's more." Florence releases me and then right before my eyes he bends down on one knee and fumbles for something in his coat pocket. I gaze down, in shock. Florence's entire face is flushed a handsome crimson. His eyes are sparkling, the tear droplets catch the lantern's ray, looking as if tiny diamonds are dancing in them. He opens a small sack and takes out a thin, golden band. I lean close to Florence as he says the words I have dreamed of these past few months.

"Marry me, Ellen?" Those simple words are the undoing of a raging flood within my heart. I nod wildly, not being able to answer, and I bend to the ground and fall into his arms. I am not certain how long we hold this embrace, but soon I feel my family's stare as they enter the room. I know they were trying to give us this moment, but they long to share in it. I jump up taking Florence's scarf with me and holler at the top of my voice, "Yes, Yes, Yes!"

The last memory I have of this day is hearing my little brothers' voices, awakened by my elation. They too were in a state of excitement, but not for my news, but for the sight of their first snowstorm! Only baby Emma slept undisturbed that evening. The rest of us celebrated into the wee hours of the morning.

Part Two

Draft Law of the Civil War

"The U.S. Congress passes a conscription act that produces the first wartime draft of U.S. citizens in American history. The act called for registration of all males 20-45, including aliens with the intention to welcome citizens. Exemptions from the draft law could be bought for $300 or by finding a substitute draftee."

History.com 2010

Chapter 7

16 years later…

Ellen Burke
January 4th, 1864
West Springfield, Massachusetts

"What's keeping your father?" My words surrender to the overpowering sounds of the plough and horses I'm following. I look to the sky for an indication of the time of day. The dense, dark-gray clouds conceal the sun's position, but the dropping temperature, the change in precipitation from soft, cool rain to solid, icy flurries, and the painted streaks on the horizon indicate that it is nearly sundown.

I signal to Jerry to stop and unhitch the exhausted horses for the night. Jerry's pale- blue eyes are barely visible under his thick wool cap and unruly locks. He is trudging alongside the horse with a crop in one mitted hand, and the leather reins in the other. Jerry nods to me and halts the horses, tugging on their reins and digging his dirty boots into the earth. His slight frame gives the horses an advantage, but his skill in whispering and waving his crop finally beckons them to a halt. Jerry relaxes his grip and immediately caresses the smooth, shiny coat on Old Henry's muzzle.

"We've made good progress today, I hope Father will be pleased." I smile in agreement and take a moment to regard my eldest son. Jerry is growing fast for sure and it won't be long until he's plowing, fertilizing and planting on his own. He might still have a boyish face, the unruly head of hair like his uncle John's, and a slighter version of his father's muscular build, but he's getting older, nearly in his teenage years, and he's slowly becoming a man. Watching him now, carefully unhitching the horses and praising them with his gentle words, I close my eyes and smile inwardly at the remarkable passage of time.

I finally remove my own weighty harness from around my waist and shoulders, and sigh at the release from the tension. My back is aching, and I bend and twist trying to ease the tightness and cramping that has plagued me these six months past. Oh, my! I suddenly stand erect and gaze across the vast muddy field, searching for Michael. I spot him chasing chickens near the coop, with a sack of feed in his hand. Michael's responsible for feeding and watering the farm animals, but at this time his main duty is to mind Grace as she naps in the warmth of the hay and horse blankets in the barn. He loves his baby sister, but at ten years of age Michael needs reminders to stay on task. I can see his slick hair glistening in the rain as he leaps around the yard, his wellies sinking deeply into the dense mud and his stained barn coat flailing in the wind. Where is his cap and mittens, and how has he forgotten to fasten the buttons on his coat? Oh, that boy is too carefree for his own good. I must get his attention.

I wave my arms in the air and whistle into the wind and rain. By lucky chance, Michael looks in my direction and I point to the barn. "Grace, Grace!" I shout. Michael gives a slight jump in the air as if suddenly he's remembered his sleeping baby sister, and turns and heads quickly in the direction of the barn. I'm certain my precious baby is all right. Though three hours have passed since she's been laid down, somehow she can sense sundown on the farm. It's as if her little spirit awakens to witness the day's closure, her intense eyes calling for attention, and her toothless grin inviting tender cuddles. When the boys are sleeping and Florence is reading the newspaper, I relish the time alone with her, rocking and singing lullabies, caressing her soft skin. I often gaze into her bright blue eyes and try to imagine the girl and eventually the young lady she will become. She commonly responds with a joyous grin, and I can't help but laugh and burrow my face into the silky creases under her chin. I often wonder if the boys were this responsive at six months of age? I can't quite remember now.

Shaking myself back to reality, I'm fatigued and realize I've become stiff from standing still and momentarily daydreaming about my lovely family. I begin to march towards the barn as Jerry follows me with the horses in tow. He comes up alongside me and his pace becomes in step with my own. "What's for dinner, Ma? My belly is rumbling and I feel I'm hungry enough to eat Old Henry here. May I help?" He looks to me with a serious face, aware as well that the day has grown late and awaits my instructions. "Yes, I will need you to lay the fire and collect the large cooking pot from the cellar. Since your father is delayed, we must start the corn stew without him, and I will need your help in lifting the pot onto the iron rail."

"Are you fretting about Da? I'm sure he'll turn up any minute." Jerry gives me a sweet wink and trudges ahead into the horse barn. He's right about my worries over Florence. I am becoming unsettled. Never mind, I am certain he's on his way home. He left late this morning to inquire about the price of fertilizer for the new field, and he was sure he could walk the two miles to town and back before dusk and dinner. But it wasn't raining when he left, and the mud on the town road must be thick as pudding. Dinner-- I must attend to that now so the children will be fed and tucked into their beds before it turns bitterly cold in the tiny farmhouse.

I finally arrive at the horse barn and smile with relief when I see Michael holding Grace tenderly, as she smiles and coos in his face. "She's soiled, but she doesn't seem to mind." Michael dramatically holds her out to me with a scrunched nose and a tight grin. I take Grace from him and kiss her warm cheek, as Michael fans his small hand in front of his nose, then backs away toward the horses.

"Well, Michael, since you prefer the odor of the horses, would you please feed and water them and remove the manure with the wheelbarrow? Jerry and I will go to the house and start the evening preparations. Hurry please, for it's getting late." Jerry turns toward me as one of his eyebrows arch. He's finished removing the last of the harness and places the horses into their stalls. I know he would love to tend to the horses himself. He latches the gate and approaches his younger brother.

"All right, Michael. It's getting dim in here so you'd better hurry with the horses. They've worked hard today so be sure to give them extra water. Old Henry here needs a quick brush because his mane looks ratty, and…"

Michael is half listening as he eagerly grasps the pails and sprints towards the door. "Mind yourself, don't be bossy Jerry. I know how to look after the horses." Michael turns his back against the large barn door and gives a shove. To his disappointment the doors do not budge and his face reddens and twists. He quickly drops the pails and turns facing the doors. He hesitates for just a moment before taking two steps back and then springs forward smashing his right shoulder into the door as it gives way under the hardy force. Michael quickly returns for the pails, gives his shoulder a quick rub, and with a grimace that rapidly transforms into a wide grin, trudges his way out the door towards the well. Jerry and I exchange a glance, he sighs and rolls his eyes, and I suppress a laugh.

I peer through the narrowly opened barn door and see that the day's greyness has turned to dusk, and I can hardly make out the farmhouse in the near distance. Evening has crept surreptitiously into our farm, and now we must hurry before the last of the day's light is gone. I swiftly gather the blankets around Grace's body, all warm and limp, and pull her close to me bracing for the biting wind and ice-cold rain. I look behind me and regard Jerry offering Old Henry a final pat over the wooden stall.

Jerry loves those horses so, and ever since the boys have been pulled from the schoolhouse to help prepare the land, he has become obsessed with them. I know he misses the companionship of children his own age, and the horses seem to offer him comfort at this time. At least he has his brother Michael and they get on quite well despite their differing personalities. Michael often cajoles Jerry into playful, imaginative games both inside and outside of the house, keeping Jerry entertained and allowing him to savor the last of his childhood. Jerry in turn helps Michael with his letters, practicing with Florence's ink pen, making up stories and printing them on scraps of paper or thin bark. They're good boys put to work too young. But I mustn't fret over that now. Besides, most of the Irish in West Springfield have their children home readying the land at this time.

As I enter the chilly, dim house with Grace in my arms, I pause as I always do, and say a prayer to the Almighty Father. I pray Florence is coming home soon; I pray the children will remain healthy, and I pray we'll always have a roof above us. I thank God for keeping the boys safe today, for making Grace the easy baby she is, and above all for keeping us together, especially during wartime.

I slide my hand into my dirty barn coat, and I run my fingers over the embroidery of my special Irish handkerchief. My mother gifted it to me, and it reminds me of Ireland and of the happy childhood I experienced there. I miss the sweet salty air and ripe ocean scent. The handkerchief will always be a reminder of the past, sweet memories of laughter, loving parents and carefree childhood experiences. If only it ended there and everything were as green and enticing as Ireland itself.

Oh, I've been reminiscing and it's time to get dinner prepared! The children are hungry and I must light the lanterns before this house becomes veiled in darkness. Grace's soiled, and needs to be changed, and Jerry's going to need help attaching the cooking pot and kettle to the rod. There is much to do, so I stow away my handkerchief and close the door behind me.

Chapter 8

Florence Burke
January 4th, 1864
West Springfield, Massachusetts

My mind is still reeling and my stomach in knots as I try to absorb and justify my actions this morning. My intentions in travelling to town this morning were twofold: one to purchase fertilizer and arrange a delivery to the Jenkins farm, and the other to finalize the conscription trade with Mr. Day. I leave for home without an order for the fertilizer delivery. I never made it to the Mercantile; instead, I possess papers that enlist me as a volunteer in the Union Army. To make it worse, I'm not going in place of Day himself. I'm taking the conscription of his spoiled, indolent son! I am sweating miserably now despite the frigid temperature. Can this be real? How did this come to pass so swiftly and silently? I lower my head and press my thumb and fingers against my aching temples and contemplate just how this came about.

I had walked to the West Springfield Town Hall three year's past on a bright, spring morning. The air was light and hopeful, the flowers along the town green were beginning to shape the landscape and decorate it with its many vibrant colors. I had come to the Town Hall with the intent of securing a loan. I held a letter of recommendation from my present landlord, Mrs. Jenkins, hoping this would assure the loan officer that I was experienced with managing a flourishing and profitable farm. We've lived on

Mrs. Jenkins' farm for over a decade, but our position here is no better off than it was in Ireland. We are still tenant farmers. We're given a tiny farmhouse and a trifling percentage of the harvest, but it's not enough to sell and get ahead. My family's needs are growing each year, and because of that, our profits are minimal. I need this loan to help my family subsist here.

When Mr. Day strolled into the crowed loan office as I completed my application, I caught just a glimpse of his abundant backside as he passed by me to his private office. I waited over an hour to see him, and when my name was finally called, I gathered my papers and strode into his office with all the confidence of a man of good fortune. With his back turned to me, Mr. Day directed me to take a seat and to state my business promptly.

I waited uncomfortably until he finally turned around to face me, then I swiftly rose to hand him my papers. I paused in front of him, noticing that his head barely reached my chest. I took one step backwards so that he would not have to crane his neck as I addressed him. "Thank you for your time, Mr. Day. I've brought you a reference here from Mrs. Jenkins, I work her land and she's been increasing yields and profits ever since I set foot on her farm more than ten years ago. I am now prepared to manage my own land…" Mr. Day looked at them quickly before tossing them across his desk.

"Your loan is denied. I am unwilling to take a risk on yet another Irish immigrant with very little money and no assets to secure the loan. Good day," he said concluding our meeting and ushering me out the door. I felt the heat of anger rising through my chest to my face as I regarded the closed door before me. I need this loan! I must do this for my children… before I could suppress the impulse, my hand was on the doorknob and I poked my crimson face into his office.

"Mr. Day, excuse me again. I want you to know I will do anything to own land. I'm desperate. I would make a deal with the devil if it would buy me land. Won't you reconsider helping me?" Mr. Day looked up from his desk, his eyes now wide with shock and confusion. A moment later his eyebrows slanted and his eyes narrowed as he calmly pointed to the door and spat, "Go back to the fields, and if your situation improves then surely we will reconsider your loan application. Please close the door behind you Mr. ah," his eyes scanned the sheaf of papers on his desk.

"Burke, Florence Burke," I added, lunging forward to hand him my discarded paperwork. Without another word I exited his office and sped to the Jenkins's farm in low spirits.

It wasn't until two years after the war broke out that Mr. Day made contact with me again. I was knee deep in manure when Mrs. Jenkins came running towards me waving her hands in the air, looking troubled. When she caught her breath, she explained that a gentleman from town named Julius Day was here to speak to me. I was stunned when I heard his name, Mr. Day the loan officer? He's sought me out, after all this time? But why? I removed my work gloves and wiped my brow, then made my way to see him.

When I finally met Mr. Day in the warmth of the horse barn, he was pacing and his round face was scrunched up, not used to the pungent odors that were assaulting him. He was dressed in a finely tailored dark suit, and his polished shoes were crunching on the hay as he carefully made his way around the mud and manure.

He looked up as I entered and his face relaxed and unexpectedly his frown turned up at the edges. He raised his stubby hand to me and somehow managed a wide, buoyant smile.

"Hello, Mr. Burke. Florence, may I call you Florence? Hmm?" I extended my hand to his and gave him a simple nod of assent. He was acting oddly for sure.

"Good, good. Well, I had hoped that your money circumstances would have improved and I'd have seen you back at the bank sooner, but that doesn't seem the case. Anyway, I have not forgotten about you, and I'm here to propose a plan that could very likely benefit you and your family." I lean forward, forearms resting atop the stall's gate, baffled. Why would Mr. Day want to help my family now? I tighten my jaw and lower my eyes. "Go on."

"Ah yes. As you know, this is wartime and hundreds of our brave men have gone off to fight because of the conscription or because they have volunteered on their own. It seems you and I have been fortunate so far as our names have not been called to serve, and we can remain at home to perform our regular duties." I nod and scratch my chin, still in the dark. Mr. Day takes a careful step towards me and places his thick hand on my shoulder. "Florence, I think I just may have a way for you to get your land and also do me a favor. I know you do not have the money to buy a farm, but I have a plot of land that has a small farmhouse and could accommodate your family."

"What? Are you saying..."

"Let me finish outlining the plan Florence. What I am proposing is for you to take my son Samuel's place if he is conscripted before you. In return, I will offer a portion of my land, deed and all. My son is nineteen, he's just starting out in life. He's meek and bookish, not meant for fighting. He wouldn't benefit our military; he's built like me, short and how should I put it, ah, well fed. He's never worked outside, and he wouldn't know the right end of a rifle if it were pointed at his head. His constitution is better suited for work at the town office, he is after all, the son of a banker! But you on the other hand, Florence, you are built for battle, just look at the size of you. The Irish are a tough lot, good, clever fighters, just the kind Lincoln needs to defeat the Johnny Rebs. What do you say, will you give it some thought?"

I sigh and look to the sky for answers. Shite, I've been in fear of the draft ever since the war began, and with his plan I would have an additional chance at going to war. My head is aching and I am feeling a wave of nausea rising from the surface of my belly. The shock of his proposal has left me unable to speak.

"I like to think of it as a gamble, Florence. Are you a gambling man?" he says. "You see the Draft Law permits folks to pay a commutation of 300 dollars to find a replacement in the event that a man of means and importance is conscripted. If you get lucky and my son Samuel is drafted in the near future, then I am willing to give you fertile land with a finished barn, a well, and a cozy, comfortable farmhouse. That, Florence Burke, is worth far more than 300 dollars. I would even throw in a roadway to the house as it now sits on the top of a rise with only a rough path leading to the main road to town. This would be quite an opportunity for you and the future of your children. You would be a landowner straight away and owe nothing save for taxes, which would be easily afforded by the checks you would receive from the United States Government." Mr. Day went on selling me his idea. He told me I would receive a $100 Bounty, a bonus for signing on to volunteer. He also said Ellen and the children would be granted State Aid whilst I was away. I finally had heard enough and knew what my decision would be.

"Mr. Day, I must get back to work, but hold that parcel of land for me and if your son is conscripted, I will take his place in the Union Army. I have tried all other means, and this does not seem to be my last hope, but it is perhaps my best hope in acquiring land of my own." With a reluctant, surrendering heart, I extended my large hand toward Mr. Day and we shook on a deal that was to lay dormant for just two months.

The evening before I was summoned and now the day to formalize our arrangement is here. When I enter the bank, a receptionist named Mrs. Wall gestures for me to go directly to Day's private office. Mr. Day wears a wide, toothy grin as he puts down the paper he is reading, "Ah, Florence, you indeed have the luck of the Irish, my son's conscription arrived." From the satisfied expression on his face, I knew he was contemplating his good fortune and applauding his own clever plan. I am slowly collapsing on the inside, but I stand erect and nod as Day gives me the instructions on how to move forward with our agreement.

"I will have a formal deed drawn up, but in the mean time you must take this contract to Mr. Parsons office to have it authorized and submitted. He will give you further instructions on your enlistment. If you wish to hire a lawyer, you may do so." Mr. Day rises and hands me the contract. My hand is shaking as I take it from him. I pause for a moment, stalled in time. Perhaps I was waiting for a handshake or a thank you from Mr. Day, but that congeniality was not offered to me. I feel my knees crumble as I rise and make my way out of Day's office and down the hall toward Mr. Parson's workplace. I fumble desperately for the tiny cross around my neck, the one I had received from Ellen and the children last month in celebration of my birthday. I bow my head and say a prayer before turning the knob on the final door that will seal my fate.

Now, as I walk along the uneven cobblestones of downtown West Springfield, I soak in the crisp air and the afternoon sprinkle dancing off the roofs of the modest buildings. I have come to feel a keen respect for this town and for its impressive architecture and its simple features. I admire the grey, brick buildings, the massive pillars and stone staircase on the old Town Hall, and the cobblestone streets lined with lovely lanterns. It'll never compare to the landscape or village feel of Ballinhassig, but for sixteen years, it has been a comfortable home to Ellen and me, and a good place to raise our children.

I suddenly think of the new farm property and pray to God that this gamble pays off. I finally own a piece of America but wonder if it will it cost me my life? Will I die a terrible death and leave my family to work this land on their own?

But death is not the worst of my fears now. My immediate worry is telling Ellen. How shall I break my news to her? She's been a devoted wife, working hard, never complaining of our shortcomings, making the best of what we have. I know our family is sacred to her, and here I am fragmenting it. I rub my eyes as tears cloud my vision. Will she understand that I am doing it for our children? Will Ellen forgive me?

Chapter 9

Ellen Burke
January 4th, 1864
West Springfield, Massachusetts

Half past nine. Where in God's name is he? I sense something is wrong and I'm aware of an ominous rhythm in my heart. Some force is shifting my world, but what is it? I glance at the clock once again and notice that only five minutes have passed since my last check. I see the candle on the mantle is nearly down to its nub, and the flame is flickering in the draft. Shall I continue to tend the fire and brew strong tea? I've become stiff from sitting in the rocker and waiting; the house is uncommonly silent, numbingly cold, absolutely still. I hold my mother's handkerchief tightly in my hands and lean in towards the warmth of the small fire.

At last steam billows from the kettle, and it forces me to rise and make my final cup of tea. I grasp a thick cloth and remove the kettle from the rod over the fire. I pour the boiling water into my cup and watch as the tea stains the clear water. As I wait for it to steep, I take a lantern from the mantle and shine it around the small house. I shall tuck the house in for the night but leave the outdoor lamp lit for Florence. The fire will dwindle eventually, though, in case they are needed, I leave candles and matches on the table near the front door. There, the house is readied and now I will take my tea to bed before I catch a chill. I see my breath in the air as I walk about to take a final peek into the boys' room and to offer Grace a soft kiss on her warm cheek.

I place the lamp on the side table and don my sleeping cap for warmth. The sheets are cold and stiff, and I'm shivering as I reach for my cup of hot tea. I know there's no use in fretting all evening, for Florence will turn up eventually. Perhaps he's delayed because he's had to queue for fertilizer or take care of some business for Mrs. Jenkins. Although, I suppose the Town Hall has been closed now for hours. Has he been sidetracked by an unexpected acquaintance?

The few times Florence has been delayed in the past, poor weather was involved, and I'm certain that must be the case this evening. I draw the curtain aside and peer through a single pane of glass, seeing tiny flakes of snow whip against my window. I draw my blanket close to me as I watch the flakes scurry in all directions. There, it's probably impossible to find the road home, and he's staying the night in town. Perhaps he's with Nathan, the owner of Porter's Tavern. Florence used his spare bed last winter when a storm blew in, returning home two full days later! While he waited for the weather to clear, Florence helped Nathan build a sleek new bar and he carved a wooden sign to hang over the entrance. Oh, my husband is clever and useful all right, I just wish he'd walk through the door and tell me of his errands in town.

For now, I shall wait for Florence as long as I can stay awake. I take a soothing sip of tea, replace the cup to the side table, and close my eyes. I must rest my fretful mind, and relax. At least the children are comfortable, well-fed and sleeping peacefully. It was a pleasant evening with them, I reminisce, distracting myself from Florence. The boys ate a hearty meal of barley and corn stew and two apples each for dessert. Grace took her milk with fervor and slurped nearly a quarter canister of applesauce. I'm blessed. After dinner, the boys completed their chores and then dressed in their long evening gowns and stockings. I sat at the edge of their bed with a thick Irish blanket draped around the drowsy baby and me and read several verses from the Bible. Afterward, I told the boys a quick tale of two princes ruling over their land in Ireland. They listened carefully, asking for details and changing the story to add more adventures and battles. At the end, they had no more will to complain about wanting to wait for their father's return.

Finally, I directed them to bow their heads and say their prayers, for it was too chilly in the room to kneel on the cold, drafty floor. I overheard Jerry praying to God that his father would return safely with the fertilizer, and I watched, momentarily bemused, as Michael scrunched his face, slammed his eyes shut, and prayed to God that his father would remember to bring him a sweet treat from the Mercantile.

After hugs and kisses all around, I rose stiffly to make baby Grace ready for bed. Thank goodness I have my darling baby to keep me busy. I gaze into her blue eyes and hold her little heels in the palms of my hands after she is changed. When I gather her, she feels safe and warm in my arms, and I hum a soft lullaby to keep the dark thoughts at bay.

Oh, I must have drifted for a moment! I open my eyes and notice it is nearly eleven o'clock. I rise and carry the lantern to the main room, hoping to see Florence there, but it is cold and empty so I stir the red ashes and place the screen in front of the fireplace. It's a freezing January evening, the wind is howling in the shaft of the fireplace, and there is still no sign of my husband at this late hour. The weather, it must be the reason for his absence.

I return to my chilly bed, grasp my handkerchief, and bow my head. Please God, keep Florence safe tonight, wherever he may be. Suddenly my heart starts beating faster as I lie back in my bed-- there's that fretting again. But why? I pray that I am overreacting and that this will be resolved in the morning.

Chapter 10

Florence Burke
January 4th, 1864
West Springfield, Massachusetts

My head is pounding as I slowly trudge through the outskirts of town past the Mercantile and West Springfield Post Office. It's sundown and I should be moving swiftly to reach home before it becomes pitch black and the day's rain turns the roadway to a solid sheet of ice. It's bitterly cold, but that is not the reason for the numbness in my body. I am still in shock, petrified to disclose the news to Ellen and my children.

I take three laborious steps forward, and then suddenly I hear my name being called and I automatically turn in the direction of the caller. There, across the road and in the doorway of Porter's Tavern, I see my friend Daniel Sheehan waving his hands wildly in the air, his round eyes wide with excitement and his red hair flailing in the gusty wind.

I press my lips together. Oh, not now Daniel. I decide to continue on. I raise my right hand to my cap, offering a nod, hoping he will see that I am hastening home. Instead, Daniel hesitates a moment as a carriage noisily passes between us, and then turns to his left and right before tearing across the street towards me. He must have seen me through a window at the tavern because he isn't wearing a coat or cap, and his hands are dug deeply into the front pockets of his overalls.

"Florence," he delights, "what brings you to town this late in the day?" He releases his hand from his pocket and shoves it toward me. His hands are even bigger than mine and as rough as old leather. He begins to shiver, and he plunges his hand back into his pocket and raises his broad shoulders to his reddening ears. I stare at him without answering. Daniel's my best friend, my closest neighbor, and I have kept this vital secret from him too.

"Florence, what is it? What's happened?" Daniel regards me while he shifts from one foot to the other to stay warm. His broad grin fades in confusion.

My voice returns, though the words are a lie, "Daniel, I'm all right, just surprised to see you. I am here getting a price for fertilizer and it has delayed me longer than I anticipated. I am rushing to get home before dark; you know Ellen will be fretting if I'm too late. Now go on back to the tavern before you get frozen, good to see you." I point across the street. Daniel hesitates a moment, lowering his eyebrows as he thinks. His face is red with cold, but his eyes still regard me warily.

"Yes, I must get inside, I'm freezing," Daniel says; he is shaking slightly and his mouth releases cold, visible breath. "Mate, why don't you come in for a quick pint, I've got Mr. Gorrie's wagon here. I can give you a lift home and you'll arrive sooner than you would on foot. What do you say?"

I know I shouldn't accept, but I can't think clearly and honestly, a glass would fortify me for the discussion ahead. "Alright Daniel. I'll join you for one quick pint; it may be my last for some time." Daniel's eyebrows arch but I elbow his forearm and leap off the curb before he can question me. "Come Daniel, before I change my mind and before you catch your death."

We enter the dark, smoky pub together, and I have to rub my eyes because they are tearing from the cold. Daniel is blowing warm air into his hands and walking to the back of the room where we take our seats at a small oak table. Daniel retrieves his coat, throwing it over the front of his large chest. He quickly uncovers his hand and finds his half drunken beer. My eyes shift around the shadowy room, and I am thankful that the place is nearly empty save for a few locals at the bar's end. The only light is cast from the tiny candles on each table, and a few across the long, mahogany bar. I rub my temples trying to ease the tension in my throbbing head.

"I can see something is troubling you, Florence. What did you mean by saying that this may be your last drink?" Daniel leans forwards, his broad face bathed in the candlelight. I draw in a deep breath, but before I can speak, Nathan takes his place in front of our table. "This must be a special occasion to have you out on a Thursday night, Florence? I hope you're not needing my spare bed, mate, because my old man is up there snoozing. He tasted my new shipment of whiskey this afternoon, and it got the better of him." Nathan says, his thin, angular face easing into a smile. He's wearing a neat white apron and drying his hands on a crisp cloth.

"Nay, Nathan, I'm only here for one drink. Bring me a large pint of your house lager, would you?" My throat feels bone dry. Daniel signals with two enormous fingers, but does not utter a word. He hasn't moved from his position, but his large eyes have narrowed as he waits for me to speak.

When our lagers come, Daniel raises his glass and waits for me to disclose my news. He continues to remain still as I drain half my beer and then loudly slam the glass on the table. I draw in a deep breath and with my left hand, I fumble around in my coat pocket until I grasp the paperwork. It feels light and delicate in my hand, as if it is as fragile as life itself. I take one look at it before tossing it on the wooden table.

"I was not straight with you outside. I've got some troubling news, Daniel. I am joining the Union Army tomorrow, here are my official papers." Daniel's eyes widen with fear.

"Shite, you've been drafted?" he says in a low voice, his eyes shifting around the room. "When did your conscription come mate?"

I shift in my seat and feel my jaw tightening. "The government hasn't drafted me. I made a trade with Mr. Day, the banker. You know that bastard I spoke to about a loan?" Daniel looks shocked, but nods his head. "I promised Day that I would take his son's conscription and he in turn is giving me a parcel of farm land-with a house for Ellen and the children. This is the signed deal with Mr. Parson's authorization. I am awaiting the deed from the lawyers, but it is done. I am a landowner, Daniel," I finish with a weak smile. I sit back in my chair and I'm surprised that I feel a release of the tension in my back. My face seems to soften as well.

"Why did you make this deal?" Daniel asks, his eyes crease as the lines on his forehead multiply and deepen.

I let out a loud breath of air and then begin, "Hear me out, I was desperate to secure a farm of my own. I could work a lifetime twice over and never raise enough money. With this deal I am guaranteed land in my name."

Daniel shakes his head in disbelief. "Going to war for another man? A wealthy banker's son no less? I can't believe you would do this. For God's sake, Florence!" Daniel's voice raises and his face flushes.

I am beginning to feel the tingle of anxiety creep back into my spine and I try one last time to make Daniel understand my decision. "Daniel, you are my best friend and I am sorry I kept my plan secret. Is the gamble a good one? I don't know." I lower my eyes. "Here

I am in this land now sixteen years and I am still just a farmhand, and my family remains in poverty. I need this land Daniel and I need this trade. I can't imagine any other way of owning property and giving my family a name here in West Springfield."

We sit in silence for the next few minutes, and then Daniel raises his glass to me.

"Well, Florence, if you are leaving for war tomorrow, you ought to have a proper farewell. Nathan, two more beers and a shot of whiskey for us," Daniel declares. "We are celebrating a hero here tonight!" Daniel clinks glasses with me then raises his glass to the folks who have gathered at the bar.

The next few hours pass in a clamor of drink and glory. The Tavern has become a crowded, boisterous scene, and its energy has lifted my spirits. In the far corner of my mind I know that I should leave and get home to my family, but I am stalled in the moment. Daniel and I have long abandoned our table, and we are mingling with familiar and many unfamiliar faces in the crowed, noisy pub. With the courage of the drink, I talk openly about my conscription and receive loud, enthusiastic wishes from our townspeople. Folks are paying for my beers, sharing stories of their loved ones fighting now, and patting me on the back for support. Glasses are raised, and cheers and songs break out as the rowdy evening wears on. At one point I am lifted in the air and asked to give some parting words. Thank goodness the river of beers has caused me to lose my inhibition; I address them confidently and give the revelers an inspirational speech. By the end of the night, I am feeling like a local hero, and I promise to make West Springfield proud, to lick the sons of bitches in the South, and to return with the other brave boys from our small town. I leave Porters a patriotic soldier.

"It'll be warmer in Virginia I think," Daniel says as we sit on the wagon, faces covered with our scarves, tiny snowflakes whipping at our foreheads. The road is dark and the sky is starless. I pull my cap down low, nodding in agreement. We remain silent for the rest of the journey. I am lost in my own thoughts. Images of Ellen and the children whirl around my head. They sleep now innocently, trusting in my return, assuming tomorrow we'll be together. I have been a coward, remaining at the Tavern, blatantly putting off my news. How have I allowed the whole night to slide by? I've sliced the time remaining with my family by too many hours. The cold blasts of night air make me rigid with panic. How can I do this to them? I pull my scarf up and over my eyes. Daniel probably thinks I am ducking from the wind, but I'm really attempting to conceal the shame and regret that is devouring me.

When Daniel finally pulls on the reins, I adjust my clothes and leap off the wagon. Still wobbly, I fall forward, landing hard in the thin snow. I rise, brushing snow from my coat, and try to conceal the fear in my voice.

"Thank you for the ride, Daniel. Carry on safely home."

"Florence, I will be by tomorrow with Lara and young Dan to bid you a final farewell. Lara's nearly to term but she will help Ellen along while you're gone. Please tell her we're here for help and support. She's a brave woman to allow you to do this."

"Aye Daniel," I respond weakly. My face tenses as I turn toward my house and whisper into thin air, "only I haven't told her I'm leaving."

As Daniel rides off, I feel a biting blast of air on my face. I wonder whether Ellen is awake at this hour. I enter the house as silently as I can manage. I notice my breath is visible inside so the fire must have died several hours ago. There is no sign of my wife, no stirring or lamp lighting. I carefully remove a match from my trousers and light a lamp left out for me by the doorway. I wonder what time Ellen finally abandoned her hopes of seeing me? I wonder what she was thinking.

I stumble to the fireplace to see if there are embers remaining that I can stoke for warmth and heat for tea. I'm famished but realize preparing a bite at this late hour may wake my family, and that is not a risk I want to take. Not in my present state. I'm very cold, and my hands are turning white and feel numb. I blow air from my mouth into them and get a whiff of the drink I enjoyed at the tavern. Maybe a nice glass of whiskey would help settle my nerves so I can sleep. I take an unsteady step to the wooden cupboard and seize the best bottle of Irish whiskey we have. I grasp a small Waterford glass gifted to me from my friend Patrick. A smile comes to my face as I recall our boyhood friendship. The famine over, Patrick returned from Canada as promised and lives with his mother in Cork.

I take a seat in my rocker and sip my whiskey in the chilly, silent house. The lantern sheds light only onto a tiny portion of our living space, and I feel fortunate for it. I can't bear to look upon visible signs of my family. I can't even check upon Ellen and the children because I fear breaking down at the sight of them. I must collect myself first, and then I shall be all right. But first, one last drink. As the whiskey draws warmly over my throat and continues its calming effect, I suddenly think about my brother John. I must write to him with the news that I am going to war. He will be shocked, but I know he'll understand my reasons. He knows I will never be at peace until I own land and prove to my father that I have succeeded here, that his miserable forecast of gloom is challenged. I will show him. With that thought, I sink into my chair and pour myself another drink.

Chapter 11

Ellen Burke
January 5th, 1864
West Springfield, Massachusetts

I wake suddenly and feel our house trembling. I hear a loud whistle blowing outside the unsteady walls, and inside the draft shifts my bedroom curtains angrily. The temperature has dropped and the precipitation has changed overnight from light snow to sleet. I look out the window, but I can't see the night as the panes are covered in a thin coat of silvery-white frost. The bitter combination of the howling din outside and the chill in the house sends shivers straight through my frail body, jolting me to awareness.

I remember that Florence wasn't with me when I went to bed, and I know he's not here now. We have always complained that our shared bed was spare and especially scant for such a tall, long-limbed man such as my husband. However, I would give anything to have Florence here beside me, his lengthy, comforting arms wrapped around me, his legs bent at the knees to align with mine, and his broad chest radiating a most lovely heat.

What's the time? I swiftly find a match and light the candle on my side table. I reach into the single drawer and find my father's old pocket watch; half three in the morning! I take the candle in hand and survey my room, adjusting my sleeping cap while trying to locate my slippers and night coat. I creep into the main room quietly, so not to wake baby Grace who is breathing softly in her makeshift crib. I shine the candle in front of me as Grace's gentle exhales become overpowered by noisier, deeper ones ahead. My heart quickens as I recognize the familiar low rumble, and I shine the candle in front of me bringing him into view at last. What's this? Florence is sleeping in his damp clothes and overcoat. He's even wearing his muddy boots, and he's tread dirt and water throughout the house. That's not like him, not at all. He's always tidy and careful, even surprising me with a bin he built for boots on the front porch.

As I draw the candle from the boots to his lap, to his face, I am shocked to see an empty bottle of Irish whiskey overturned on the floor beneath his chair. I rush over and examine it, trying to recall how much of its contents were remaining before Florence drank from it. I move the candle toward the fireplace and see sparkling fragments of crystal at the base of the stone hearth. I instinctively find my broom and dustpan and begin tidying the sharp slivers, recognizing the force that must have caused this glass to fracture so.

I begin to shiver and am torn between waking my intoxicated husband to discover his troubles, or allowing him to sleep his drink away and speak with him in the morning. I decide I shall remove his wet clothing and boots and perhaps he will waken in the process. His muddy boots are covered to the laces, and my freezing hands are hardly nimble enough to plow through the dried mud and untie the wet knots. After a few moments of frustration I rise and decide Florence can sleep the night in his boots. I suppose I should lay a new fire and dry his overcoat so he can make use of it tomorrow. I take the candle to the fireplace and find a newspaper to fold and kindling to top over the paper. At last the flame rises and I add small pieces of wood until the fire is abundant enough for two large logs. Thank heavens the boys remembered to fill the log bin before bedtime.

I could have remained near the fire for hours, so comforting is the warmth that spreads through my body. However, I know I have to tend to Florence, and make him comfortable and warm so he won't fall ill from sleeping in his cold, soggy clothes.

I remove the Irish blanket Florence has carelessly tossed over his lap, and begin to detach the overcoat from his body. His snoring pattern interrupts when I pitch his body forward to remove the backside of his overcoat, but he restores his rhythmic breathing when I rest his heavy body back against the chair. I bend to replace the warm blanket around Florence and as I stand and move around him, papers fall to the floor from his coat pocket. I hang his coat on a wooden peg near the fireplace, and seize the candle in order to gather the loose papers from the floor. I flinch and feel faint because I suddenly understand that these official looking documents must be the reason my husband has come home in such a miserable state. I take a deep breath and begin to read. I look up from the papers for a moment and shine the candle onto Florence's sleeping face, and cry out much too loudly, "Florence, what in hell have you done?"

I suddenly need to sit as I am becoming stiff, even though my legs and hands are shaking. I take deep breaths and remind myself that we've been through many trials here in America but we've had no troubles that we couldn't manage with love and patience. Even as I struggle to control my fears, my whole body begins shivering and I pause a moment to gaze around the dim room and watch my beloved sleep beside the warm fire. I love him so much, the handsome man who left Ireland to find me here in America, married me, and gave me three beautiful children. I drop to my knees, clutch my handkerchief, and slowly unfold the documents.

Chapter 12

Florence Burke
January 5th, 1864
West Springfield, Massachusetts

Trying to bring the room into focus, I rub my eyes with my thumb and forefinger, but this movement causes a sudden jolt of pain to my forehead. I lean my head against the stiff backing of my rocking chair and try to remain as still as possible. It feels as if a bayonet has found its mark in my skull. My throat is bone dry and raw, my stomach is churning with bilious contractions.

While waiting for the pain to subside, I have a sudden realization that I've been sleeping in the rocking chair, and that my clothes are damp. My eyes dart open. I ignore the white flashes of light floating in front of my eyes. I blink them away and try to orient myself here in the cold, dim main room. I place my feet beneath me to stand, puzzled by the weight of them. I lower my eyes and spy my muddy boots; then a flood of memories assault me so swiftly that I feel light-headed and nauseated all over again. I lean forward, head in hands, and squeeze my eyes shut. I am leaving for war today.

Trying to overlook the turbulence coursing through my body I rise, removing the warm blanket from my chest. I tap my hands upon my damp jumper searching for my timepiece. A steel-like sensation fills my mouth as I realize my overcoat is missing, even though I was certain I wore it home from Porter's. Surely Daniel would not have let me ride home without it. I turn around and collect a single candle and match set on a small table by the doorway. Ellen must have left these out for my return. I sigh and light the candle. The small room suddenly visible, I dart my eyes from the fireplace, to the entryway, and then back to the fireplace, spotting my coat hanging on a peg. A long breath draws slowly from my mouth. I run my hand through my thick, wayward hair and remain still for a moment, trying to recall the late night events. I amble over to the fireplace, grasp my coat, hoping to find two items: my pocket watch and my enlistment papers. I sigh with relief when I find the conscription exchange and my watch. I hesitate for a moment and wonder if my arrival woke Ellen or the children, but it seems that I have made little disturbance here, which comforts me.

I click open my timepiece and my eyes widen as I realize I have but ten hours until I depart for Boston. I replace the watch into my coat pocket. In the still of the morning I hear baby Grace's slight movements and soft babbles. My family will soon be alight. With that sudden thought my stomach lurches forward and I taste putrid bile in the back of my throat. I choke it down, trying to suppress the burning sensation in my throat and chest. I take a few steps to the fire and fall to my knees. I will lay a small fire so that Ellen can make tea and prepare our final meals together. After the fire is ablaze, I replace the screen, grab my coat and make my way through the dark to the privy.

A hundred thoughts dash through my mind, and once again I feel unwell. In addition to making arrangements for Ellen and the children to move and informing Mrs. Jenkins' of my departure, I need to prepare a list of items to bring to Boston. Oh, mercy. Without warning, the contents of my stomach, mostly liquid, come heaving up and I bend over the small hole to deposit it with the other repulsive waste. Thankful that it is here that I am sick and not at home in front of the children, I feel slightly better now and head straight for the well. I swallow greedily but cautiously because I know my stomach is still queasy. I wipe my mouth and refill the bucket for the animals. I will hurry and complete the early morning chores so that our family can gather together round the table where I shall deliver my news and prepare for my conscription. Cold sweat breaks across my forehead and I dab it away with my sleeve.

As if denying the impending events, the morning feels common. The sun has yet to fill the barn so I must light lanterns and keep the barn doors wide open. My breath is visible in the dim light and I pause a moment before beginning the morning work. I inhale deeply and savor the familiar scent of wet hay, earthy must, and gamey hides. I gaze up to the rafters, noting the intricate cobwebs and the tiny particles of hay and dust floating down towards me, dancing in the beams of the lantern light.

I finally set about feeding and watering Old Henry and the other horses, the pigs, the goats and the chickens. I bend down to check the coop for eggs when I hear the faint sounds of crunching straw behind me. I whirl around to see Jerry standing in the faint light of the open doorway. He's dressed in his work clothes and cap, his blond curly hair flailing in the wind, wreathing his small face. One of his cheeks is redder than the other, with a fresh line indented upon it, undoubtedly from the sewing hem on his pillow. Jerry's eyebrows draw down, "You've made it back. Are you all right?" Those words seem to hit me like a wave off the Irish Sea. Inside my head, words are forming that I do not utter. No, I'm not all right; I'm in the most miserable state of my life. I'm a shattered man, and perhaps a foolish and selfish one at that.

I lay down the empty egg basket and walk slowly towards Jerry. His worried eyes follow me and I motion for him to sit down on one of the large hay bails. I sit beside him and clasp my hands in my lap. I'm hoping to find the right way to say a farewell to my elder son.

"Jerry, I've got some news that I have yet to share with anyone." Immediately Jerry's eyebrows raise and his pale complexion flushes at the cheekbones. He shifts uncomfortably, but his eyes remain fixed on mine. "Today I am leaving to join the Union Army." Jerry lets out a loud gasp, his face now completely enveloped in crimson. "No!" I turn and place my hands on Jerry's small shoulders. I can feel his shock beneath my grip.

"Jerry, hear me out. I will not be gone long as the war is nearly over. The newspapers are reporting that the Confederates are caving. I'll probably arrive in time to see the white flags and the backsides of the Rebels." Jerry juts his chin at me, "But you could be killed; Jim Halpin's father was killed last month, shot by a picket guard, and Little Dan's uncle was captured trying to cross a river in Virginia! Please don't go, I don't want you to die, Da." Jerry is tugging at my arm and finally rests his head against my chest and wraps his thin arms around my waist. I lean my face down and kiss the side of his cheek, his curly hair tickling my skin. Tears spring to my eyes but I collect myself, holding in the thoughts of fear and rage. I hold Jerry tight, and let him weep into my arms. A few moments later I pull back and lift my son's tear-stained face towards mine. His eyes are downcast as involuntary teardrops begin to flow.

"Listen here, Jerry. I want you to know something before I leave. I made this plan to join the war effort alone. Your mother does not even know about it yet." Jerry's eyebrows arch and his eyes become the size of saucers, but he doesn't speak. "I've made a deal with a gentleman in town to take his son's enlistment and he in turn is giving me a parcel of his land with a farmhouse for our family. Jerry, do you understand, we now own our own farm? I have the legal papers right here; it's done. We are true Americans and we can build a better life here."

Jerry's eyebrows lower as he looks off to the distance, but he remains very still. I lean closer to him and wrap one arm around his neck, drawing his crumpled face next to mine. "I have one last thing to say to you, Jerry. I want you to know that I would never have dared to make this exchange if I did not have you at home helping to manage the farm and aiding your mother with the household duties. You've grown into a fine young man, and I know you can step up and take my place for a spell. You've made me a proud father. I love you, son."

Jerry flings his arms around my neck and begins to plead, telling me that getting a farm is not worth the risk of dying, that he wants us to stay on this farm, Mrs. Jenkins farm, even if it is not our own. He gasps as he speaks, the words coming out of him so fast they're barely comprehensible. Jerry spills out memories from our past; picnics by the pond, card games with neighbors, long jumps into hay bales, and songs and prayers by the fire. His eyes are wild with panic as he desperately continues.

"Do you remember my first ride on Old Henry here? Remember you lifted me into the saddle, handed me the reins and guided the horse around the farm?" I nod feeling my heart in my throat.

"What about the time Michael caught a bullfrog and frightened Mother causing her to spill the entire pail of milk? And… and… what about baby Grace? She loves the way you toss her in the air. You can't leave us, we're a family!" His eyes are filled with tears as he grips my face and pleads with me to stay home. He begs me to tear up the papers and to rescind the offer because he fears I will die in war. Loud wails and protests fill the barn and echo in my ears. I feel my own wet tears on the side of my cheek as I whisper into Jerry's ear that I remember all these wonderful memories and more, and that I will carry them with me on my journey to Virginia. I tell him I will be careful and leave the fighting to the experienced Irish Rifle men. Finally I ask Jerry to be strong for his little brother and sister and especially for his mother. We remain in an embrace until our eyes have dried and there are no more words to exchange.

We rise and finish the morning chores in silence. I wince when I hear his lingering heaves, but I know that I must carry on for I still need to inform the rest of my family, and I will need all my strength and courage to do just that.

The shadowy barn is cast in lantern light, but the animals have become lively. It is just another day for them, as it should be for my family. However, I am shifting their world, without warning, and my heart is ripping in my chest. Though the thought of dying in the war is tucked deep inside the recesses of my mind, my greatest fear at present as I turn toward the house is this one thought: I am leaving Ellen for a second time, perhaps a final time.

Chapter 13

Ellen Burke
January 5th, 1864
West Springfield, Massachusetts

Silence has fallen upon our breakfast table like a heavy fog, stagnant and menacing. Florence's news has washed over us like a powerful tidal wave, pounding and bruising our hearts. Now the tension is palpable. We sit in cold silence, too hurt to make even the slightest small-talk.

Michael alone has not been informed of Florence's enlistment. He sits, unaware of the ominous atmosphere, preoccupied with the lavish meal, devouring the smoked sausage and diving into the eggs and boiled potatoes. The sounds of his fork scraping the plate and his mouth chewing on his food are the only sounds audible in the room.

My mind drifts to Grace, sleeping soundly in her little crib. Will she wake and remember my state of shaking, tensing and wailing as Florence and I discuss his departure? Having seen the documents the night before still did not prepare me for the pain I would suffer hearing it from Florence himself, especially learning that he must leave this very day. Florence came to me while Jerry and Michael were finishing the morning chores and I was feeding baby Grace. Poor Grace, I soaked her with my tears, frightened her with my gasps and moans. Finally, she refused to drink, refusing to latch on to my breast, so I rocked her, in silence, Florence kneeling beside my chair, caressing the thin wisps of her baby hair. She drifted into a fitful sleep, and she remains in her small crib while we try to deal with the consequences of my husband's desperate enlistment.

Several minutes have passed, yet all remains the same at our table. The uncomfortable silence still looms, the food untouched (save for Michael's), words left unspoken float in the air whirling despondently around us. Michael finally places his fork down for a moment. He has a satisfied look on his face, but after flitting his eyes among the three of us, his pleasant countenance fades. He senses that something is terribly wrong as he observes our full plates, our steaming cups of tea, our untouched silverware upon the table and of course, our troubled faces.

I witness Michael's suspicion and watch his face whiten with dread, yet I cannot move to comfort him, I cannot even speak to him as I have been paralyzed by my own emotions. The silence in the air has taken on a new character; it is filled with childlike fear.

Jerry is the first to speak as he also senses Michael's distress. His voice wavers but does not crack as he addresses us, "May I be excused, I'd like to brush down Old Henry and the other horses. They need fixing. Michael can help since he's done." Michael's eyes crinkle and I see a look of terrified confusion cross his youthful face. He longs to uncover the troubles that surround our breakfast table, but he looks too frightened to ask for an explanation. Instead, he stalls.

"But I'm not finished yet, I was going to eat more. And you haven't touched your food. Are you ill? May I eat yours?" Jerry suddenly rises from the table and yanks Michael's arm.

"Michael, let's go now, I'll let you sit on Old Henry while we brush his mane. Come with me, I'll collect your coat." Michael reluctantly follows Jerry, but his worried eyes never leave mine as he dons his barn jacket. I try to mask my sorrow and convey a sympathetic smile, but I feel my mouth begin to twitch so I swiftly place my napkin to my lips and offer him a hopeful gaze. Jerry turns away and grasps Michael by the elbow, leading him out of the house. Florence and I are finally alone, and the silence shifts from uncomfortable to unbearable.

I lower my eyes, knowing I should speak my mind to Florence for I'm infuriated by the pain he is causing our family. I long to chase after the boys and comfort them, cry with them and console them. But I suppose there will be plenty of time for that in the coming days. For now, I must confront Florence and try to come to an understanding of why he would enlist without informing me.

Florence seems to read my mind. He leans forward, places his sweaty hand on top of mine, clears his throat and beseeches, "Don't you see, Ellen, I couldn't tell you because you wouldn't have allowed it, you wouldn't let me endanger myself for the improvement of our lives--" I feel heat rising in my chest for I've reached my boiling point with his heart-wrenching news and I finally feel uninhibited and prepared to voice my opinion. I slam my open hand on the table and stand, pressing my face into Florence's.

"You're damn right I wouldn't have allowed it! Why would I want you to join the bloody war when we read about the casualties piling up like logs in the forest? The newspapers are quite descriptive about the Union casualties, and I do not know how you think you will be the fortunate survivor to return to us!" I pause and take a deep breath, but my mind has been reeling over this information, and I can't stop my ranting, "Do you expect me to remain here wondering if a bayonet has skewered you, or a rifle bullet has put a hole through your thick Irish skull, or you've contracted some awful disease? Florence, you know don't you that it's the Irish soldiers who are thrown onto the front lines, who die from even minor scrapes because they are the last to receive medical care. I don't want you getting killed or rotting to death in this American war! This is a silly feud, based on greed and pride, and you've no right participating in it. It's their war, not ours! For God sake's Florence, you're a father of three children. Does your family mean nothing to you?"

I fix my intense gaze on my husband long enough to see that my words have stung his heart. His face is crimson, heat blazes from his ears across his entire countenance. The dam has broken in my eyes, and floods of tears fall down my cheeks and onto the table. Now that I have released my anger toward him, all I feel is sorrow and grief.

I know my final reference to family hurts Florence because he's torn when it comes to kinfolk relations. He was severely injured by his father's expulsion and his mother's acceptance of it, but I do not understand how that lingering campaign can cause him to put our lives in jeopardy for the price of land. Is this senseless act avenging his father's spiteful departing words? Is it worth it? I had no idea the gravity of Florence's deep-seeded feelings, finally causing him to make this ill-conceived trade.

Why can't our little house, our work here on this profitable farm, and our loving family be enough to satisfy him and make him believe he has attained success here, that success is measured by more than coin or land-owning? Why can't he see that his greatest accomplishment is finding us a safe home and working and raising three darling children? And loving me? If only he believed as I do.

I raise my head toward him, our eyes filled with tears. I whisper my final words toward him, "Florence, what pains me most is that you've broken your promise to never leave me, and I've always drawn comfort in believing those words. Now I feel abandoned. You are betraying the family that loves you, and I can't bear it." I lower my head in my arms and sob. Florence rises and covers me with his lengthy body, wrapping me in his strong arms, trying to shield me from this pain. He presses his soft, warm lips to my ears. "I know, Ellen. I'm sorry for hurting you, for doing this to our family. I will return to you. I love you, Ellen. I will come back."

It is too late now for last minute hopes of a payout or contract breach, and I must try to find the strength to temporarily discard my anger to see my husband off to war. I shift under his weight and he releases me, but once erect I crumble into his arms and soak his whiskey-stained coat with fresh tears.

The boys clamor through the door. Michael's jaw drops upon seeing me; he takes a step back, lowering the pails of water he carries to the floor. "What is it, Mother?"

I take my sleeve and wipe my face clean. Although I can feel my eyes have swollen and my throat is stone dry, I walk to Michael, kneel before him and gaze into his freckled face. "Michael, today your father is joining the Union Army, he's to be a hero. A real hero! I am sobbing because I am so proud of him as you should be too! Come, let's all join together and celebrate with him."

We embrace and remain huddled together for several minutes, all the while the breakfast meal remains on our plates, the tea has turned cool, and my beautiful baby sleeps innocently in her crib. Florence looks over the heads of the children and mouths a silent, "Thank you, my love." I nod, and pledge that I will not waste these final hours with resentment; I will give him a hero's farewell. Later I will think about all that has occurred today, and I will try and sort out my feelings.

Part Three

"The Art of war is simple enough.

Find out where your enemy is.

Get him as soon as you can.

Strike him as hard as you can, and keep moving on."

Ulysses S. Grant

Chapter 14

Ellen Burke
January 1864
West Springfield, Massachusetts

"Do you think Father's wearing a Union Army uniform yet?" Michael asks, his face shadowed but his eyes twinkling in the flicker of the lamplight. He turns, resting his arm under his raised head and peers at me over Jerry's prone body. The boys are tucked in bed, wool blankets and a patchwork quilt pulled firmly to their chins. The house feels raw tonight on this chilly January evening, and as I sit on the edge of their low, oak-framed bed, I shiver and gather my shawl around me.

The new farmhouse is still and barren. It's not for our lack of furniture or personal items still tucked away in crates, but because Florence is gone and his void is terribly hard to fill. The loft where the boys sleep is just wide enough for their simple bed and tiny lamp table. Our dear friend Daniel Sheehan built the bed out of a mat and spare barn boards. It makes a cozy resting place for the boys, but reading to them is difficult because I must hunch forward to avoid hitting my head on the wide beams of the roofline. Even climbing the six rungs to the loft is arduous because of the nagging pain in my lower back.

Once we are able to afford furnishings for the main living area, I will read to the children downstairs, in front of the warm fire.

For now, I want the boys to settle down swiftly so they may be rested for tomorrow's workday. I know the best way to calm their energetic minds is to lay them in bed and read a passage from the Bible or tell a story.

"What's that Michael?" I vaguely hear his small voice in my head. I'm worn-out, preoccupied by my own considerations, and desperate to crawl into bed beside my soft baby girl. She is sleeping soundly, and warm as a bread loaf from the oven. If only her blissful sleep would last the night through. The past few nights Grace hasn't been sleeping well and I've been woken several times in the night, frightened by her cries. I fear she's fallen ill and I instinctively check her head for fever. These sleep disturbances have taken a toll on my daytime state, and I often find myself weary and short-tempered. My thoughts are interrupted once again.

"I said, do you think Father has a uniform and, um, a rifle yet?" Michael repeats. He has folded his arms behind his head and although his eyes are bright with curiosity, his body is still, recovering from the day's hard work. Before I can respond to him, Jerry turns on his side and adds his thoughts.

"Of course he has a uniform, Michael, a rifle and bayonet too. He's in Boston learning how to use it now." Michael suddenly lurches forward, his eyes filled with fear.

"The war hasn't reached Boston has it?"

I nod "no" in response and place a hand on Michael's chest, easing him back down against his feather pillow. Jerry straightens; narrowly clearing the ceiling beams, and lets out an annoyed sigh.

"How many times do I have to tell him that Father is in Boston training to be a soldier? He's not in the real battlefront yet, the fighting is down south. He's daft, Mother."

Michael makes a sour face. "I bet he's eager to fight. I would be." Jerry and I exchange anxious glances. I attempt to change the subject.

"Boys, have you said your prayers?"

"Yes," Jerry replies first. "While you were putting Grace to sleep. I prayed for Da and for Uncle James. Michael's prayers were very short, because he said he was freezing." Michael's mouth flies open.

"I was freezing, but I talked to God and asked him to help Father become a hero. Ma, Jerry is getting cross with me all the time and tonight he hit me," Michael adds.

"Please, boys!" my voice rises unexpectedly. I feel tears springing to my eyes. I take a moment to place my hand over my face and collect myself.

"I'm sorry, Mother," Jerry says immediately. He places his hand on his brother's shoulder. "Sorry Michael." Michael nods and draws the blanket to his face.

I don't mean to lash out at Michael and Jerry. I know they are trying to be good, but they are still young boys. I need to get some sleep, then I'll have my patience back. Michael turns his tired eyes to me.

"Mother, will you still tell a story before you leave? I love the story of Father and Uncle John's first day in America, will you tell it to us? Please?" He yawns and rubs the blanket against his cheek. How can I refuse him? I shift my body onto the very edge of the mat; the three of us are pressed together like dried fish in a salting box. I close my eyes, trying to recount the story Florence has told the children and me many times before. In my softest voice I begin.

"Your Father and Uncle John had just arrived from Ireland, with only a single sack of clothes between them. They were young, skinny lads with little money, but oh, did they have big dreams! Well, just as they were making their way through New York City, taking in the new sights and sounds, Uncle John saw a young girl being chased by a ruthless man. He could see that the girl was terrified and taking her to be an Irish lass in distress, he ran after her and clobbered the man with his satchel of British coins. Once the man was knocked out cold, John rose to speak with the girl, but she ran away in fear. Father arrived to help, but it was too late. As you know, the girl, your Aunt Bridget, had run off without a trace. Uncle John vowed to remain in New York City to find her and that is just what he did. He told us later that he must have been shot by cupid's arrow that day because he couldn't remove Bridget's lovely image from his thoughts. He couldn't concentrate, he had to find her, it seemed his destiny."

I pause, moving my back to the right, trying to get more comfortable. Jerry signals with his eyes that Michael has drifted off. Jerry, however, seems eager to hear the whole story so I continue.

"Your father on the other hand, was eager to find me in Massachusetts so he left New York City the very next day and ... well you know this bit, he surprised me and proposed." I suddenly feel a lump in my throat, but I clear it away, determined to finish this bedtime story. "We didn't hear from your Uncle for a long spell. When a letter finally arrived, in six month's time, John wrote that he had found Bridget begging on the streets, burning with fever and half starved. He carried her to a nearby charity hospital and remained by her side until she was well enough to speak. Although it took time for Bridget to trust your Uncle, she finally realized that it was he who had saved her, and she slowly let herself fall in love. Once her wounds were healed and her strength was improved, Bridget was released from the hospital and John hired her to clean ink stains at the print shop. So, years passed, and their love grew stronger. Five years after they met, John asked for Bridget's hand in marriage and they have lived happily in New York City ever since. The end!" I crane my neck to look at my boys as I rise from their bed. Michael is breathing rhythmically, and Jerry turns on his side and whispers goodnight. I move slowly, wincing at the pain in my neck and back and realize one of my feet hanging over the side of the bed has fallen asleep. As I wait for the sensation of needles to arrive, I hear Jerry stir and his face is scrunched, like he's been thinking.

"Do you think Uncle John will join the war?" Jerry's voice is hoarse and he sounds drained. I turn and lean down, placing a kiss on his warm cheek.

"Jerry, I don't think your Uncle will become a Union soldier. He fights in a different way at Tammany Hall; he fights to get better conditions and rights for immigrants coming to live in America. He tries to convince folks in politics, ones with more power, that rights should be allowed for all, not just for the privileged few." Jerry's face slackens, then one of his eyebrows rises.

"Yes, but didn't he get wounded in the draft riots a while back? I remember Father talking to me about that," Jerry says with a yawn. My eyes widen, and I suddenly feel a jolt of fire through my veins. I take in a breath and choose my words carefully.

"Ah, yes, Jerry, but he was not a true soldier, he was just a civilian. The rioters in New York City were fighting because they wanted a law changed that Abraham Lincoln had signed. Nothing more, just politics." I change the subject. "Some day, after the war, we will pay a proper visit to New York City and you can see where your uncle works. It's a shame that we live so far away from them. Your father and your uncle John were close, but now work, money and distance keep us from seeing each other. I think the last time they came here was just after Michael was born; you were only two years old so you probably don't remember. They're lovely folks, and we haven't even met their little girls, your cousins, Sarah and Denise. Some day we will, I am sure of it. "

Jerry closes his eyes and leans his head deeper into his pillow. "Yes, Mum, I'd like that." It seems my son is played out so I whisper a "good night" and pull the blanket to his chin. His face fades in the darkness as I carefully make my way down the ladder with the lantern in my hand. I am relieved that I was able to satisfy Jerry's question without having to explain the irony that his father used the very law that his Uncle John rioted against! The draft law, allowing wealthy folk to sell their draft to a poor immigrant. What bollox! Ah, I do not have the energy to agonize over this now. I'm too weary even to make a final cup of tea though I am shivering here before the dwindling fire.

I am grateful that our new farmhouse is sparse and there isn't much to tidy up at the end of the day. We've only four plates and utensils to use and no furnishings save for the beds and a rocking chair. Thankfully the kitchen has adequate cooking tools, kettles and pots. At the Jenkins' place our little cottage was furnished when we arrived, but this farmhouse is quite bare, it seems no one had lived here for some time. Who would choose to live in this remote place?

I have a look round the small house searching for any familiar sight that would remind me of our old home--the one I shared with Florence. The chill is the same, the fireplace is larger but older, and we finally have a small cook stove for baking. I look upon the only chair we possess, the one Florence slept in just a week ago. I begged Mrs. Jenkins for the chair and she playfully allowed me to take it to this new house. "You want that old rocker?" she teased. "Go ahead then, but mind your back because it is the hardest chair we ever owned." Mrs. Jenkins shook her head, her long grey hair swishing back and forth, and gathered kitchen items in a basket for us to take. She was a wonderful Landlord and a dear friend, and I miss her daily company.

Hearing the eerie sounds of the wind howling outside, and feeling the wooden walls creak and shift against the gusts, I pull my shawl close to me and quickly close the house for the night. My lamp is flickering as I move about. I must find paper and pen, and get into bed before I freeze in this drafty house. I promised Florence I would write and tell John and Bridget of his parting. I can only imagine John's reaction to the news. Do I dare mention the draft law, or should I simply write that he's enlisted? John is a clever man, he will want to know the truth, but I must be true to my husband. I will write a brief, direct note that is all. Florence has put me in a terribly difficult position. I also long to reach out to my brother and sister-in-law, to commiserate with them and to share my grief and displeasure with Florence's decision, but I won't. I will not betray my beloved. We must stand as a united front for the sake of our children and our marriage.

But Florence, how could you leave me? My mind plays his departure over and over again, like a bad dream that I can't wake from and turn off. I see him standing in front of me, his sack of clothes and supplies slung over his sturdy shoulder. Florence looked so handsome in his fine travelling clothes, his blue eyes piercing through the wisps of his wavy black hair. When he came to me for a final embrace I felt the same passion I experienced that day he turned up in America.

I never expected Florence to whisper in my ear and beg me to write to his brother and parents. I must have given him a bewildered look, because he repeated his request and gave me a slight wink. His face that commonly strains at the mere mention of his parents looked slackened and slightly amused. Florence seemed pleased and relieved to be moving forward with his plan. I suppose it should be of some comfort knowing that he feels this course is the right one, but I still haven't forgiven him for making this move without my consent.

My cheeks burn as I pull the crisp, cool quilt over my body, and draw nearer to the warmth emanating from baby Grace. I feel warm tears forming in the corner of my eyes and I close them, willing them to stop. I am fatigued and shall write these short notes only after I get some sleep.

Florence Burke
January 14th, 1864
Camp Long Island

My Dear wife,

I now take my pencil in hand to let you know that I am well, and that my journey to Boston was a safe one. I am writing to you from my tent at Camp Long Island. The chilly wind blows outside and all I can hear now is the rustling of the flaps on the outer portion of the tents surrounding me. I'm comfortable though as I've been issued a heavy blanket and mat, and tomorrow we muster to receive our uniforms and battle equipment. I have six tent mates, one of which you will recognize as Edward Begley, Jr., our dear neighbor's son. He said he's late in joining the war effort because he's been concerned about the welfare of his aging parents and hasn't dared leave them. Speaking of age, I am the oldest volunteer in this tent; so many fresh-faced boys here that it reminds me of a schoolyard.

The train ride was long and tiring because I stood, grasping my satchel close to me, packed together with recruits from New York and Connecticut. Our train stop in Springfield was the last, and as I stood on the crowded platform, I wondered where the fifty of us would fit on the already-congested train cars. When we arrived in Boston, some young recruits opened the doors of our car and sat, dangling their feet over the sides, waving to the cheering folks. My spirits lifted with the fresh air, freezing as it was, and I waved along with them.

As we entered Boston the sun was setting and light snow was falling. From the moving train it looked like the snowflakes were afire and chasing the train. For some reason this particular spectacle reminded me of you and the children, perhaps dancing around the barn yard last year at sundown. Anyway, it made me think of cheerful times and I hope these memories comfort me until I find my way safely home to you.

I hope you're doing all right Ellen, I hope you're not working yourself too hard. I'm looking to send enough money back in time so you can hire farmhands to perform the bulk of the work and hopefully the boys may return to school.

I have been paid today the 14th of January which I have sent to the town Treasury of West Springfield in care of Mr. Parsons. I want you to collect the money as soon as you can and pay off the taxes for this deal and keep the rest for future taxes and for your own expenses. Please also take a lawyer or Matthew Rooney with you to get the official Deed to our land as it should have been prepared by Julius Day by now. Go without fail so that I can be sure that this land is secure and we won't get cheated. My love, I am sorry that I am not there to take care of this business, but I know you will do right by this, especially with a lawyer on our side. I am, however, uneasy until I know we have the Deed so please do not delay with this matter.

I will end this letter by sending my love to the children and especially to you. Please tell the boys I think of them each time I unfold the razor and brush they gifted me last year for my birthday. I will treasure it and bring it back for them to use as they grow to be men. I will write again when I have a spare moment. Ellen, so many words we still need to exchange, but for now I am sending you my most adoring love.

Yours Faithfully,

Husband F. Burke

Chapter 15

Ellen Burke
January 1864
West Springfield, Massachusetts

"We're home at last!" Jerry turns to me, the expression of relief stretching across his face. His cheeks are flushed with crimson smudges, and tiny dots of perspiration twinkle just under his wool cap. Jerry's carrying two heavy baskets of foodstuff in his arms, and he's having to bob and weave through the thick bush. It's no wonder he's perspiring so. I'm struggling along slowly, Grace heavy in my arms, my legs and lower back aching from the steep climb. Unlike Jerry, I'm shivering even with baby girl in my arms. My hands, face and feet are numb from the cold. Michael is panting heavily next to me; his exposed face is red and raw from the bite of the violent wind. We press forward, upward, our heads tucked against our chins.

This is our first trip to town since moving, and it is trying to say the least. Without a clear roadway connecting to the main road we've had to make our own passageway. Removing tree limbs, beating back thick bushes and stomping on dangerous roots, we've each taken a few scrapes and bumps today. To make matters worse, our farmhouse is situated on a steep knoll, with a rolling, thick landscape surrounding it. As treacherous as the climb down was today, it is even more arduous scaling the overgrown, unsteady hill with a baby and baskets of supplies in our arms. I don't know why this farmhouse and barn were built way up here in the first place. There must have been some pathway cleared years ago, but it has been unattended and nature has prevailed, allowing the weeds and thick grass to overtake the man-made path.

I feel a burning in my ears when I stop to think that Florence made this deal without seeing the land, and without considering the consequences for us. Today's journey was difficult and it was merely uncomfortably cold, tangled and steep, but when the worst of winter hits and snow accumulates, how will we manage to get to town? It's January, and winter is at our doorstep. I feel a cold shiver down my back as I look around at the vast, abandoned field, tall grass swaying with the stony wind. How will we turn this land into a fertile, vibrant garden for vegetable crops? My eyes scan the vacant barn, the well, and finally settle on our modest farmhouse. The children and I are on our own here, and until Florence sends money to establish the farm, we must manage with what little we have. I feel the hairs on my neck stand to attention as I think about all that has happened today.

The children and I set out to town early this morning. We rose before sunrise and sped about completing the morning's chores: collecting firewood, filling buckets of water from the well, laying a fire, brewing tea, heating milk, and boiling the water for clothes washing. The house was filled with the lovely smells of yeast and cinnamon. Early in the morning I baked a tray of biscuits to offset the price of chicken parts at the butcher, and I warmed the scones gifted to us from Mrs. Jenkins. When the house was readied for our late afternoon return, we dressed in our warmest clothing, donning hats, scarves, mittens and boots, and I wrapped Grace so tightly that only her bright eyes could peer through a small opening in the thick blanket. Michael carried the savory biscuits in a hamper, raising them to his nose regularly as his face brightened with a dreamy glow. Jerry held baby girl in his arms, and I toted a basket filled with her necessities and the papers for the trade.

We planned to meet Matthew Rooney in town to help us settle the matter with Mr. Day. Matthew Rooney is our dear old friend and neighbor. He was a practicing attorney for the town of West Springfield, but he's retired now and works part time at the newly established Town Hall Library. After Matthew's wife Mary Beth died two years past, Florence befriended him, often calling on him after work. They would sit on Matthew's porch, drink lemonade and play cards or smoke pipes. Matthew's been a generous friend and I look forward to seeing him today.

As we slowly made our way to town, the children and I passed acquaintances and neighbors inquiring about Florence and how we are getting on in his absence. It seems Florence's sudden enlistment has caused quite a stir here, and even the most reserved folks have come forward to hear our story. Although I thank them for their inquires, I don't offer details. Florence and I prefer to keep our affairs private. But, honestly, I also fear that I may unleash a torrent of words I can't retract or arrest. Instead, I accept the warm tap of a hand, the odd embrace, the sympathetic eyes that danced from the boys to the baby and back to me. I force a smile when folks lean forward to talk to Michael and Jerry, often touching their pink cheeks, and commenting on how proud they must be of their father. I can see that Jerry is unnerved by this attention, but Michael's face breaks into a wide grin as he nods rapidly, loving the attention.

When we finally reach the Town Hall where the Treasury is located, I search for Matthew. I do not see him amongst the folks coming and going into the grand building, so I hand Jerry and Michael my lists and send them off to attend to our errands. I advise them to inquire on the best price for cornmeal, sugar, cheese, eggs, and other items at the Mercantile, and to make the exchange of biscuits for chicken parts with Liam at the butcher shop. The boys are pleased to be shopping on their own. I watch them as they walk together, Michael already chatting into Jerry's scarf-covered face, taking long strides in order to keep up with his elder brother. Jerry keeps his eyes straight ahead, probably concentrating on the tasks at hand, paying little heed to Michael's endless rambling. I lower my head and snicker into the warmth of Grace's blanket, and she responds with a slight wiggle.

"Good Day, fine lady." I whirl around to see Matthew Rooney gliding toward me with a wide, lined grin. I take two steps forward to greet him, my one free arm opening for an embrace.

"Hello there, Matthew! Thank you for meeting me here on this chilly morning. How are you?" I reach my arm around his thin shoulders as he pulls me close to him.

"Matthew, you look as if you're shrinking away! I think Grace here weighs more than you. Are you getting on alright?" I take a long look at my dear friend and notice that he is indeed reedier than last I'd seen him. His face is narrow with high cheekbones, and his bony, pronounced nose balances wire spectacles. The skin around his face and chin is sagged with age, but his eyes still emit a sparkle that could rival the brightest star. A sudden gust of wind struck, and Matthew's thin, wiry hair takes flight. He looks to me and clasps my free arm, leading me up the steps to the main entrance of the Town Hall.

"Yes I'm fine. Have the boys stayed behind to ready the fields?" Matthew inquires as we enter the grand foyer, shaking off the cold. I begin to answer, lowering my voice in the echoing hall. "No, they are here in town buying food and supplies for me. We'll meet them outside after our business is concluded. They're looking forward to seeing you." Grace begins to fuss in my arms, the change in atmosphere perhaps discomforting her. I unfold her blanket and lift her to my left shoulder, gently patting her tiny back. I worry she will require my attention—wanting to be fed, or requiring a fresh nappy… Fortunately she settles down and grants us a sweet smile. I follow Matthew down a formal wooden hall lined with framed portraits of past town officials. Matthew looks confident and chats easily as we walk.

"How are you getting on with the new farm?" Matthew asks.

I draw my scarf down under my chin. "Well, we're making steady progress with clearing, but it hardly looks prepared for tilling and planting. It's a daunting task, and with no proper roadway to the farmhouse, getting tools and supplies up the hill will not be easy, but we'll manage."

Matthew nods in agreement. "I'm happy you have Daniel Sheehan close by to help."

"Yes, so many wonderful neighbors have offered to assist us with the farm. Daniel has been over the last few evenings making a chicken coup in the barn. Little Dan and my boys are helping to build it too…it's coming along. I'm coping the best I can without my husband." I turn my eyes down to the floor. Matthew takes his thin hand and folds it over mine.

"Indeed you are, Ellen. Well, here we are. Welcome to the West Springfield Treasury. I shall inquire about seeing Mr. Parsons. Why don't you have a seat and rest a moment?" I did just that, finding an elegant chair near the window. I sigh for a moment, taking in the formal setting. The dark wooden walls, bookshelves, and desk give the room an intimidating, masculine atmosphere. The candle-lit sconces on the walls hardly shed enough light given the dark interior, leaving the room dim and murky. Traces of cigar smoke, brandy spirit and leather fill the air, and I feel a bilious churning in my belly. I unbutton my heavy coat and unwind my scarf, yearning for some fresh air. I take a good look around realizing I've never stepped foot in this building because Florence has always looked after our banking and other business affairs. Here I am though, in this stark building trying to secure his secret trade and get our deed. Fancy that. The atmosphere suits him more than me; it's probably why I have an unsettled feeling in my bones. I also feel a lingering itch of irritation.

While we wait for Mr. Parsons, Matthew carries Grace around the dim room, gently humming an Irish lullaby. I collect the signed trade and tax money from my coat and hold them tightly in my hands. I am prepared to conduct our business with Mr. Parsons and Mr. Day.

"Mrs. Florence Burke, Mr. Parsons will see you now." The young receptionist suddenly appears in front of me.

"Matthew, it's our turn." I am relieved that Grace has fallen back to sleep, the lullaby and the walk surely comforted her. We enter a large office lined with more bookshelves and sconces. It seemed to be a common theme. As I take a seat, I notice the only decorations on the walls are old town maps and framed college diplomas, licenses of authority and awards received by Mr. Parsons. His large nameplate glares at me as I reached eye level with his massive oak desk. Mr. Parson enters from a door in the back of his office and immediately beams when he sees Matthew.

"Good–day to you, Matthew old boy, what brings you in?" Mr. Parsons greets Matthew with a firm handshake and as he releases his hand he turns toward me and offers a tight-lined grin. Or was that a sneer?

"Hello Edward, good to see you. I'm here with my dear neighbor, Ellen Burke. As you may recall, Ellen's husband Florence used the Draft Law to make a trade with Julius Day and she is here to pay money for the taxes and to acquire the deed." Mr. Parson's leans on the edge of his desk; he crosses his legs and rubs his temples.

"Yes, yes," he begins. "I do remember this deal, Burke took Mr. Day's son Samuel's conscription." Mr. Parson's mind seemed to drift momentarily. "Well, Mrs. Burke, I am sorry to say that Mr. Julius Day is on official town business in Hartford so we cannot inquire about the completion of the new deed. I will, however, note your appearance here today and I'll make certain this matter is settled within the month." He rises and walks around his desk, searching through his papers, and begins penning some notes. His gray, unruly eyebrows dance up and down as he tightens his jaw and concentrates on the documents. I purse my lips and feel blood begin to boil beneath my skin.

"Mr. Parsons, sir." I clear my throat, willing it to sound steady and confident. "My husband signed this trade and was immediately sent to training camp in Boston. He was not given a proper deed outlining the boundary lines of our new property or..." My voice rises as my cheeks flush with anger, "Or a road to the main thoroughfare to town. I have three children to mind and I...,I can't get to the main road though the dense forest. I need a bloody road!" I feel my mouth tremble and I immediately stop and look away before I lose control. Matthew immediately takes the paperwork from me and hands it over to Mr. Parsons.

"Here's the trade agreement and payment for the taxes. As Florence has honored his end of the bargain, bravely taking young Samuel's conscription, it is only right that Mr. Day honors his side by presenting an official deed and keeping his word that a roadway indeed will be made, without fail." Matthew leans toward Mr. Parson's desk and looks the Councilman squarely in the eyes. His voice is lowered. "Edward, please see to this matter immediately, as a personal favor to me. If word gets out that volunteers are not getting their fair wages or land for the trade, there will be trouble here and your required quota of enlistments will surely decline. That would not look good for West Springfield now would it?" Matthew's eyes remain fixed on Mr. Parsons' as his glasses slowly slide down his nose. When he finally sits back and adjusts the frames, I notice Mr. Parsons is frantically scrawling notes on an official-looking ledger. His gray, fluffy hair looks disheveled, and I see a single bead of sweat atop his furrowed brow. He clears his throat, loosens his bowtie, and cracks a forced smile.

"Mrs. Burke, if you wouldn't mind leaving your address, I will send a messenger to your house when the documents are complete. I apologize for the delay and if I can be of any further assistance to you please contact me here." Mr. Parsons rests his back against the leather chair, folds his hands together and raises both eyebrows, hopeful that the meeting is concluded and Matthew is satisfied. We rise silently, and I notice Matthew departs without offering a handshake to Mr. Parsons.

As we leave the Town Hall, Grace, who blissfully slept for that tense exchange, suddenly wakes from the whisk of the cold air. I've forgotten to replace the blanket shielding her little face, and she looks shocked and uncomfortable. I bind her tightly once again and rock her in my arms until I feel her heavy against my chest. Matthew taps me on my shoulder and points his gloved finger ahead. I look past the carriages and see Michael and Jerry walking toward us with heaping baskets in their arms. Matthew waves his hand back and forth signaling to the boys, and they smile when they catch sight of us.

"Hello boys!" Matthew gives them each a solid pat on their backs and upturns Jerry's wayward curls. "Can you see there, Jerry?"

"Yes, enough I suppose." Jerry smiles and his eyes sparkle, making him look like a little boy.

He turns to me, "Did you get Father's business done?"

"No," I reply, my voice still quivering. "But Matthew was helpful and I expect this matter to be concluded soon. Do not worry, Jerry." I pat his arm, trying to conceal my disappointment. Then I turn my attention to Matthew. "I'm sorry to have wasted your time this morning; thank you for your support and for speaking on Florence's behalf." Matthew draws a sharp breath.

"Come now, Ellen. I am pleased to be of service to you and Florence. Why don't we go to Porter's tavern for a quick bowl of stew and have a chat about the little surprise I have for the boys?" I raise my eyebrows. What surprise? Immediately Michael is tugging at my skirt. "Mother, we must join Mr. Rooney for lunch! Please?"

Jerry looks to the sky, possibly trying to predict the afternoon forecast or not wanting to appear too excited about the unexpected surprise. He waits for my decision. I unfold the top of Grace's blanket and see her bright eyes peering at me. I, too, look at the cloudless sky.

"Well, it looks as if the weather will hold, and Grace is doing fine, though I may need to feed her at Porter's. I suppose you children could use some energy to help you with the journey home. Yes, Matthew, we will join you for lunch at Porters. Thank you." I feel my spirits lift knowing that the boys are going to experience the rare treat of taking a meal in a tavern. I don't think they've ever done so. How I wish Florence could see their eager faces. Matthew beams as well.

"It's settled then!" he bellows, "Here, let me carry that little gem. Oh, Jerry, do you think you can lug those baskets to my carriage? It's behind the Town Hall, you know my horse Clover, right?" Jerry nods.

"Yes sir, I do, and I'm certain I can manage." Jerry looks proud of himself as he turns to Michael, "Hand over your basket,

Michael." Jerry extends his hand towards his brother, but Michael resists and holds the basket out of his reach.

"Mother, may I go with Jerry? I can be trusted as well." Michael's face tightens as he tugs at the basket. Before I can scold Michael, Matthew intercepts, somehow knowing just what to say. He gently takes the basket from Michael and passes it off to Jerry.

"Go on Jerry, my boy. You can do this, we'll meet you at Porters." Matthew turns and takes Michael by the arm,

"Michael, I want you to be the first to hear about the special surprise I have for your family. We will talk at the tavern and when Jerry gets back, you can tell him all about it!" I watch Jerry set off pleased to be given this responsibility. Michael jumps in the air, liberated from the release of the heavy basket and excited about our mid-day plans. As we walk to Porters, I notice Michael has grasped Matthew's free hand, and I am touched and grateful to have such a dear friend. I lean into his chiseled face and whisper,

"Matthew, your experience with your own children has served you well. I may require your valued advice on both family and legal business," I nudge his arm gently and relax for the first time today. He smiles and nods in response.

As we walk in silence to the tavern, I suddenly feel hopeful for our future. I think, while we wait for Florence to return, for trades to be secured, for checks to arrive, and for our farm to be prepared for planting, we can still enjoy the simple pleasures that life has to offer. For me, it is lunch in a cozy tavern with a wonderful friend; for Michael, it's the anticipation of a special surprise, and for Jerry, it is feeling a respected gentleman's trust at a time when life is uncertain. I believe Matthew's happiness is found in our companionship. He saunters along cheerfully telling Michael about the surprise: a pig and a pen he's to build at our place! It seems his joy is in helping others and being surrounded by those who love and adore him.

After a delightful meal at Porters, Matthew gives us a lift in his shiny black carriage. The journey from town to our hill is a wee bit over a mile long, and his place is another five miles up the way. Reaching our rough path, the boys jump off the carriage and collect our items as we thank Matthew Rooney for his kindness, and head toward the steep climb.

The wind has begun to whip around us, and it has turned bitterly cold. As we make the difficult ascent, I try not to curse under my breath when I stumble or feel the sting of a branch slicing my frozen cheeks. I am breathless as we exit the worst of the densely-packed woods. However, I'm relieved that we're home and that we have provisions, at least for the time being.

The scattered clouds have clustered and their dark gray color conceals the late afternoon light. Our house is cold and stark, and I realize we have much to do before dinner. Jerry places the baskets to the side, and immediately begins laying a fire. I ask him to place the kettle on the rod so I can make tea. Michael sets about lighting lanterns and empting the baskets. I tend to Grace who is wailing because she's hungry and soiled. My milk seems to be diminishing from my breasts every day, and it is not enough to sustain her for very long. I wonder if it's the stress or the added responsibilities here that is causing my milk production to slow down. I nursed Jerry and Michael well beyond a year, and Grace is half that age. I will have to supplement with cow's milk if I am unable to provide my own. How I wish this farm came with animals, especially a cow. I must look into finding the cost of milk delivery. Will anyone agree to transport milk bottles here? Ah, just another worry.

I holler to Michael to set a basin of water by the fire. I won't give Grace a soaking bath but I will wait until the chill is gone from the water to take a flannel to her little body. My baby girl gazes into my eyes; I know she's willing me to feed her. I pray the milk will come. I offer my finger to suckle while I slowly remove my day dress and the strap from my petticoat.

"Mother!" I hear from the other room; it's Michael I think. "Jerry and I have a surprise as well! We've another letter from Father! The postmaster gave it to us and said that it is postmarked from the very same day as our first letter," Michael proudly announces.

"Oh, that's brilliant, we'll read it just as soon as Grace is settled." I look down at her and see that she has latched on to my breast, and she's sucking intensely. I lower my head, willing the milk to flow and fill her little belly. Grace pauses momentarily to give me a bright, glowing smile. I suddenly recall Florence remarking that Grace's features remind him of his late sister Louisa. I'm pleased that he takes comfort in this, and I wish he could see her now, hungry, soiled, but still grinning ear to ear. However, when I see her eyes sparkle in the glow of the lamplight, I see my mother's radiance bursting through her beautiful face. I reach for my handkerchief and pray for family members who are no longer here with me and for my children who I alone must nurture and protect.

Florence Burke
January 14th 1864
Camp Long Island

Dear Wife and children,

I take the pleasure of writing to you hoping to find you in good health as this leaves me at present thanks to be to the great God for it. Dear wife, I would like to know about yourself and the children. Let me know how Jerry and Michael are getting on and are they being right by you. I have trouble sleeping here and it's not for lack of a warm cot, but because I miss those at home and the simple routines we kept. I have a Bible with me, but its words do not move me the same way they did while reading together as a family. I miss the comfort of hearing the boys' chatter nearby and feeling the warmth of Grace's small forehead when I kiss her. How is baby girl? I hope she's not getting sick in this cold weather.

Let me know how Daniel Sheehan and his family are getting along and if Don Unger got home from Virginia. Please let me know what you hear from my brother and let me know how my neighbors are. Give my love to them all.

Dear wife, it is the warmth of you beside me that I miss most at present. I lie here alone, picturing your beautiful face and long to reach out and find you here so I may stroke your ginger hair and whisper a goodnight to you. I wish you would take very good care of yourself and not get cold or frozen from the winter. Please pray for my return.

Yours Faithfully,

Florence Burke

Chapter 16

Ellen Burke
January 1864
West Springfield, MA

A blast of icy wind blows across our house, rattling the windows and shaking the wooden beams. I hear the sound of tree limbs cracking and splitting nearby and falling to the ground. Inside. The fire wanes as a draft sails through the cracks in the roofline. The light in the house is dim, with only two small lanterns gently glowing.

I curse as I stare at the flames extinguishing before me. I've got to patch these walls-- I can't keep the fire lit! I begin to kneel on the rug, searching for small twigs to add to the dwindling fire. Suddenly I hear a large crash above my head, it startles me, and I drop my sticks. My eyes search the ceiling for cause of the clatter. I hear a high-pitched wail followed by a loud shushing sound, and I rise to my feet and hurry to the loft. I grasp the lantern from the wall and climb three steps, high enough so I can peer into the boys' room. I'm alarmed to see Michael sprawled out, half on the bed and half off the end of the bed. Jerry's trying to help him up, although I see a flash of guilt cross his eyes when he sees me. Michael's face comes into view; it's bright red as he grits his teeth. He doesn't notice me, instead he's glaring at Jerry, his eyes full of contempt.

"Why'd you go and toss me off the bed? I'm only telling you what I heard." Michael continues to lock eyes with Jerry, but

Jerry turns his head toward me, looking fearful, not sure how to proceed. I know he's panicked because one of his eyebrows is raised, entirely hidden under his curly hair. Jerry turns to me and begins,

"Mother, Michael and I were nearly asleep when he starts talking, going on and on about how father is coming home. I told him to stop lying because it wasn't funny, but he wouldn't hush so I pushed him a little..."

"A little, you tossed me clean off the bed, Jerry!" Michael exclaims, his eyes wide and his face flush with anger. I always marvel at his reddening freckles, flaring the moment things get heated. However, I see that his eyes look wounded, so whatever he's saying, I know he believes it to be true. I am not sure of the time, but Grace was put to bed about an hour past, so it must be nearly nine o'clock. I sigh and place both my hands on the floor of the loft. "Michael, tell me what this is about? Why are you saying your Da is coming home when he only left two week's past?" Michael sits up straight and looks across in his brother's direction.

"I was only telling him what I heard Mr. Sheehan saying to Mr. Rooney yesterday when we were building the pig pen!" Michael whines and then flails a thin arm toward Jerry's face. Jerry grabs his wrist and holds it down. Jerry looks like he's restraining a wild dog. I climb the remaining steps, place the lamp on the tiny side table and crouch at the end of their low bed, gesturing the boys to release each other and come towards me. I try to remain calm, but it is late and I'm tired. "I want both of you to stop hurting each other, do you hear? You've got to settle your differences in gentler ways. We can't afford to have one of you injured, now come, get yourself tucked in and say a prayer of forgiveness to the Lord." Jerry places his hands together and lowers his head to pray. He immediately pops his head straight up.

"I'm sorry Mother, but I must ask. It isn't true what Michael says, is it?" Jerry slinks down into his blankets and pulls a section atop his brother. Michael's lowered head is now raised, hopeful that I can corroborate his story. Unfortunately I have heard nothing of Florence coming home, Michael must have misunderstood what the men were talking about. Tomorrow I will speak to him about not listening in on others' conversations. For now, I want to get my sons to rest, for tomorrow is another trying day. I lean on the end of the bed and whisper.

"Michael, Jerry, I have heard no such news. Your father is training in Boston, and it is unlikely that he will be coming home before he is sent off to war in Virginia. We must accept this, although it's difficult." Jerry turns to Michael but does not say a word, Michael, too, is silent. He crosses his arms and lowers his head, pretending to pray.

I know the boys are trying their best to get along and help me manage. They've missed so much of their childhood already working on the farm ten hours a day. They should be going to school and playing games, but instead they're here, helping me establish the farm. I must be fair and remember that they are, after all, just youngsters.

I try to change the subject and send the boys off to sleep with happier feelings. "Tomorrow looks to be clear, and if the wind dies down we should be able to complete our work clearing two more rows in good time. Perhaps there will be time for you boys to do me a small favor?" Jerry's face is turned to me, his wayward curls cover his beautiful blue eyes, but he's listening intently to my words. "Would you walk to the Jenkins farm and deliver the baskets to Mrs. Jenkins? It shouldn't take you but an hour or so to get there, and she'll certainly offer you a ride home with one of the new farmhands."

"I'll go!" Michael says first, his face bursting with joy. "Jerry, we can visit Old Henry and the other animals!" Michael is tugging at Jerry' shoulder, trying to energize his reserved brother. Jerry lays his head back on his pillow, looking dreamily into the tiny cracks of the roofline. I'm sure he's excited, probably imagining himself brushing down his old favored horse. He finally turns to me and says, "Mother, are you sure we won't be needed around here to help you with the washing and the preparations for dinner?"

"Yes, Jerry, as long as we have enough firewood and water, I will be fine here with baby girl. Now I must get you boys settled and be off to bed myself. We must rise with the early birds if we are to complete all the chores and send you off for a visit."

"Mother," Jerry whispers, "thank you for allowing us to go to the Jenkins' farm, I can hardly wait to see Old Henry!" Michael turns and lifts his head off the pillow, "Me too!" I was hoping the boys would be drowsy, but I see that the anticipation of their visit has roused them once again. I gently lay them down and kiss their cheeks one final time. Michael looks to me and I can see he's hoping for a story.

"Ah, let's see now…" I try conjuring up an old tale or a bible passage but I can't recall any at this time. Then I have an idea. I'm not certain why or how this memory comes to me just now, but it seems like a suitable time to share it with my boys.

"Michael, Jerry, when I was young, about your age, I would gather my friends on the edge of a steep cliff overlooking the Irish Sea. We would let our hair blow in the cool breeze, and flap our arms pretending we could soar like the seagulls circling the water below. Some days we would recite songs or silly poems and shout them straight into the wind, imagining that our voices could be carried off over the English Channel. We pictured the British Royalty throwing back their wigs and laughing at our cleverness.

To me, boys, southern Ireland will always be my most beloved place, it's magical, it's where I feel the most free. And I will tell you a little secret. I have a way of getting back to my emerald isle whenever I want to. It lies in the little old handkerchief my mother passed on to me. You see, if I hold it in my hand, close my eyes, and concentrate really hard I can transport myself back to my childhood, to my lovely green isle. These memories are carried in my heart and they can never be taken away. I've only to relax and concentrate to retrieve them. Ah, that is how it is done. Now, off to sleep boys, I love you."

When I finally open my own eyes and glance at my sons, I see Michael is sound asleep, a look of whimsy encircling his freckled face. Jerry is chewing on his bottom lip, and seems troubled. I whisper, "What is it child?"

Jerry answers cautiously. "I was just thinking of what my memories will be. I know they'll include the Jenkins' horses and our new farm, but I worry that they won't include Father." I sigh and lay my finger on Jerry's face, outlining his soft jaw line, coming to a rest on his chin.

"Jerry, don't fret about looking back now, you're only a lad with many wonderful memories to create. Your recollections will always include those you've loved, your father most of all. Now, it's time for bed. The horses will be thrilled to see you tomorrow."

"Yes, good-night, Mother."

Jonathan Burke
January 1864
New York, New York

Dearest Ellen,

I received your unexpected letter and in haste, I am writing back to you for further explanation. I fear that Florence has gotten himself into a fix, because you never mentioned a draft, only that he's enlisted and departed. How did this come about so swiftly, Ellen? Why would Florence volunteer now and leave you and the children? Please write straight away and reply to my questions. I can't make sense of this.

Please tell me how you and the children are getting on in Florence's absence. Do you have an address for the training camp? I must write him and hear in his words what the hell he is doing. I am truly sorry Ellen, I've always believed that I was the rebellious Burke, and that my brother was the saint. I hardly know what to think now. Without a doubt Florence loves his family and farming, so enlisting is peculiar and bloody ludicrous, isn't it? I fear for his life, joining the war. I may have a rough edge, but Florence has always been as gentle as a lamb.

Ellen, I'll try to use any political influences I have to spare Florence from deployment but I worry it is too late, rendering my connections useless. Bridget and I are distraught and confused at the moment. Please give me more information.

Little Denise and Sarah send sweet prayers to their cousins Jerry, Michael and Grace.

Your loving brother-in-law,

Jonathon Burke

Chapter 17

Ellen Burke
January 1864
West Springfield, MA

"Enjoy your afternoon rest, baby girl. You've earned it." As I exit my bedroom I hear the whistle of the wind through the fireplace. Oh, that wind. I raise my hand to my face and feel raw, chapped skin. My lips are dry and cracked as well. Winter is taking its toll on my skin, and I haven't the salve to heal it. I run my finger over my bottom lip and try to remember how I have restored my skin in the past. Ah, yes, last winter Mrs. Jenkins showed me a remedy using milk cream and a touch of rose water, but I don't think I have either of those here.

Thank heavens we do have milk delivered now. It's costly, but it is a necessity now that my breasts have gone dry. I didn't waste any time mourning the end of my nursing experience or question why my body failed me so, I simply walked to Mrs. Jenkins' farm and told her I needed to find a dairy farmer who was willing to deliver to our remote cottage. Mrs. Jenkins immediately spoke to her neighbor, Richard Devaney, pleading with him to assist us here. I'm sure she spared him no details of my desperate situation, but that doesn't bother me. Richard owns a successful dairy farm, and luckily he's a family man who's been fortunate to escape the draft thus far. He tells Mrs. Jenkins that he will always support those who have family in the Union Army. He sends his young, nimble sons Matthew and Thomas up the steep, woody climb to our farmhouse every week, and I don't know how they've managed, but not a single bottle has been broken. Richard says it's just the right thing to do in wartime, but I believe his motivation comes from a deeper place-- his kind and generous heart.

I rub my hands together for warmth and feel a stinging sensation. Oh my, just look at these blisters on my hands! I'm beginning to resemble my late father with his red stained face and rough, calloused hands. I suppose hauling stones and clearing brush with our old tools is the same hard work he endured, and he was twice my age. But now I too am feeling old and craggy with a chapped face, weathered hands and black sacks under my eyes. It's no wonder my milk has gone dry in these conditions. I'm not certain of the state of my neglected hair because its commonly covered with a bonnet, even in the house. I'd probably scare the children if I released it and let free my red mane! Never mind, living and working on this remote farm hardly necessitates good fashion-sense. Oh my, I am stiff and worn out. And it's only mid-day.

I pause near the fireplace and notice the boys have filled the log rack, thank goodness for that. I don't think I'd be able to carry a single log into the house after today's work. I arch my back, attempting to loosen the tightness that's causing the pain. Grace was in the baby carrier most of the morning, and although I love to hear her babble into my ears and feel her warmth, the added weight is a stress on my back. My poor baby wasn't able to nap with all my bending and moving about, but she never wailed or made a fuss. I think she was content enough to watch the boys and I work, snuggling in her winter layers.

With Grace finally at rest and the boys on their way to the Jenkin's farm, I have time to make tea and soak my beans for dinner. Then I will have a rest for a moment. I place the kettle on the rod and empty our dried beans into a large pot filled with water. There, now, I will take my tea and sit in the rocking chair. My mind immediately starts fretting as I consider John's letter and imagine how to make an appropriate response. What shall I say to him? Just then I hear movement outside, the heavy pounding of boots and the rustling of clothing. I feel the hairs on my neck stand to attention as I swiftly place my tea down and rush to bolt the door. As I reach the door I jump back hearing a soft tapping from the other side. Before I can wonder who would be calling at this time, I hear a familiar voice.

"Ellen, are you home?" followed by more gentle knocks. My face immediately slackens and I sigh, realizing it's my dear friend. I open the door and greet him.

"Hello, Matthew!" I say cheerfully, "what brings you out here on this cold afternoon?" I offer Matthew Rooney a warm embrace, feeling his icy cheeks on my face.

"Matthew, you're nearly frozen. How did you manage on the rough path? We've done our best to clear it so late in the season, but it is still quite treacherous isn't it?" I take Matthew's hat and scarf, but he seems eager to leave his coat on, so I don't press him further. Instead, I place the kettle back over the fireplace and turn, searching for a place to offer Matthew a seat. Matthew takes a few steps to the fire and rubs his hands together.

"It's quite cozy in here, Ellen. The path was a wee bit thorny, especially for an old man, but we'll get that sorted out soon." He turns and takes a good look around, noticing the empty loft and small bedroom in the back. "Where are the children? I didn't see them outdoors."

"They've gone to visit Old Henry and the other horses at Mrs. Jenkin's farm. I expect them back in a few hours. Grace is napping so you chose a grand time to pay a visit. I'm sorry we've so few seats in this house, would you please sit in our rocking chair. It was Florence's favorite chair, I mean it is his favorite chair." I feel my face redden at my clumsy words. The kettle makes its boiling sounds and I make myself busy readying Matthew's tea. If only I had some scones or biscuits to offer him. Matthew remains standing as he turns to me.

"No worries Ellen, I can only visit for a few minutes, then I am off to the library. I have a delivery of almanacs arriving and I must be there to find a good spot for them. I'm here to convey some news to you, I only wish it were better news…" Matthew pauses, folding his arms, his face looking solemn and his eyes search the ceiling for guidance.

"Yesterday I worked at the Town Hall and Mr. Bagg, one of the West Springfield selectmen, approached me. He said he had received a letter from Florence Burke asking permission for a furlough. Mr. Parsons had seen it too and denied it at once. Mr. Bagg was more sympathetic, but said he doesn't have the sole authority to grant permission for a volunteer soldier to leave training camp. Mr. Bagg learned that I was a close friend of yours, and he gave me the letter so I may pass it on to you. He sends his regrets and hopes it gives you comfort knowing that Florence was indeed hoping to fix a way to get home." I place my hands to my face feeling heat rise from my neck. Oh, dear, Michael was telling the truth when he said his Da was trying to come home. Florence wanted to see his land and say a proper farewell to us. Tears form in the corners of my eyes, but I blink them away.

"You have the letter, may I see it Matthew?" I ask, my throat suddenly dry and shaky. I take the letter and automatically hold it close to my heart. What I feel next is a quickening of my heartbeat and a cold chill running down my spine. I raise my eyes and look to Matthew; he's standing in front of me, arms folded.

"Matthew, do you think Mr. Parsons denied this furlough and saw to it that other selectmen go along with him because he doesn't want to upset or trouble the prominent Mr. Day? Florence should be able to see what he is risking his life for…" I turn away from Matthew, ashamed of my display of outrage and emotion, and try to calm myself by pouring Matthew's tea. He stands motionless for a moment, I sense his eyes boring into my back, but I don't dare turn toward him yet. I know it's not Matthew's fault, but he works with these selectmen, and he must share some loyalties with them. I take a deep sigh and turn to offer Matthew his tea.

"Sorry, I didn't mean to take my frustration out on you. I've not fully accepted my fate of managing this farm alone, and having Florence home for even a day or two would be truly valuable. I have so many questions on how to proceed here, and he would know just what to do. I wish he could see his trade, his farmhouse, his land. Above all, I wish he could see his children one last time." Matthew places his cup down immediately and comes toward me for an embrace. His face is lined and his eyebrows are narrowed. He folds his thin arms around my back and I suddenly crumble within them. Matthew too, is feeling my grief. He places his head on my shoulder and remains still until I stop shuddering. He finally breaks free and tucks his withered hand under my chin.

"Ellen, you're right to be vexed, but I'm certain Mr. Parsons is not protecting Mr. Day. He just doesn't have any authority over an officer of the Union Army. I'm not saying he's a good man by any means, but in this case none of us have the power to get Florence a furlough, even for business needs. I will make you a promise though; I will have this deed worked out with Mr. Day and Mr. Parsons. I've already showed them an article I've written about the unfair deals immigrants are getting here in West Springfield, and Mr. Parsons said he'll have an immediate meeting with Day and his lawyers to be sure the deed is drawn up and granted to you forthwith. He does not want my article to go to print, so he'll be swift in completing this with you. I know it's not much, but it's all I can do for you and for dear Florence."

Matthew's wrinkled mouth turns up slightly, even though his eyes remain despondent. I take Matthew's tea from the hearth and hand it to him, and at the same time I place my letter in my apron and pat it gently. I refill my tea with warm water and we sit on the braided rug in front of the fire.

While we sip, Matthew offers his own wise advice on the farmland. He says we're off to a good start, but we should continue clearing so Daniel Sheehan will have an easier time tilling with the horses come spring. He also advises me to have the manure ready for planting. Finally, as he rises to leave, Matthew mentions his pig Josephine. He wants to come by at the end of the week and help finish the pigpen. When I see Matthew to the door, I embrace him again, thanking him for delivering the news and letter personally, and warn him to mind his way on that dreadful road. I secure the scarf around his small face and open the door, as tiny specs of snow sail into the house.

As I heave the door shut, my apron and dress flutter in the wind. The letter peeking out from my pocket launches in the air, floats to the chimney and finally lands on the floor in front of the fire. I retrieve it and decide to read the contents before the boys come home. I will spare them this great disappointment; instead, when they return I will tell them about Mr. Rooney's visit, our shared cup of tea, and the delivery of the pig. This news will surely end their day with joy and excitement.

I turn to the fire, stirring the embers, stoking it with two more logs. I listen intently for sounds of Grace stirring in the next room. I walk over to Florence's rocking chair and drag it close to the fire. I have the letter in my hand, and I trace my finger over the top and down the edge, picturing Florence in his tent, writing this letter to the officials. I'm certain he was hopeful, sitting proudly, imagining the train ride back to West Springfield.

A single tear falls down my cheek and onto my letter. I wipe it away with my apron. My heart is full of pity for my husband, my children and mostly for me. I couldn't even muster the courage to ask Matthew about the road Mr. Day is to make for us or for the current news from Virginia. I simply could not get the words out probably fearing Matthew's response.

Nonetheless, I am trying to live day by day and see to it that each day is filled with some kind of hope and joy. I will write to Florence tomorrow and reserve room for the boys to tell about their day at the Jenkins' farm, and news about their new pig. We will comfort Florence in words and show him that we are managing. Hopefully our letters will ease his mind as he waits for the deed and works to become an accomplished soldier. I gently rip the top fold of the letter.

Florence Burke
January 29th, 1864
Camp Long Island, Boston Harbor

The honorable Selectmen of West Springfield, I am here in camp getting on finely at the request of General Devens. I have joined the 13th Battery and in consequence I shall be detained here some time and I would beg a favor of you. It is to intercede to get a furlough for five days. I have yet to receive a deed on my new place, and I'd like to have it drawn and signed before I leave if possible. I have not tried to get a furlough as I am not acquainted with any of the officials. If you will do me the favor to release me no doubt I can get my wife to lodge the amount of my Bounty in your hands to ensure my return.

Yours Respectfully, Florence Burke

Ps. Please direct your recommendation to me and I will take it to General Devens

Chapter 18

Ellen Burke
February 1864
West Springfield, MA

"We're nearly out of food in the icebox, Mother," Jerry whispers, pointing to the depleted bin. It's been snowing incessantly since last night and now it is mid-day and there's no sign the storm is waning. We hear a constant, eerie sound of wind howling outside, and our house is raw and cold. We've tried to fill the gaps in the walls with extra stockings and bits of material, but the farmhouse is old and has far too many little cracks. I'm frightened and feel exposed to the elements. If only we'd been warned of the storm. We hadn't made our journey to town this week and that's where folks converse about the weather, especially approaching snowstorms.

Today Jerry was meant to ride with Daniel Sheehan to the Mercantile, but I'm certain it is far too dangerous to travel, especially with the wild gusts of wind tearing at tree limbs. We haven't heard from Daniel or any of our neighbors; they must be hunkering down until the storm passes. If only I'd known we'd be kept up in this house I would have sent the boys to collect more firewood and top the jugs of water. I also would have ordered twice the amount of milk from Mr. Devaney.

I turn to the modest fire and then to the half-filled wood rack. I'm afraid to send the boys outside, but we must bring in some logs to dry out so we can stoke this fire for cooking. I wish we had proper clothing for severe weather like this, but what we possess must do for now.

"We'll be all right, Jerry. I'm sure this storm will end shortly and then we shall collect the necessary items in town. We've enough cheese and applesauce, and I'll use the remaining flour, eggs and yeast to make a fresh loaf of bread. Will you check on the water reserve?" I foolishly used buckets of water for warm baths yesterday not knowing the weather would turn so quickly. The cold is running through my bones and I can't seem to find warmth even as I stand straight in front of the fireplace. I can see Michael's breath as he sits on the rug next to me, shivering. I don't dare make more tea or hot milk because I want to spare these staples. We will just have to heat the odd bricks and place them close to us for heat.

If only the well wasn't so far away. I simply must remember to fill all three large jugs with water each day and find a new place for reserve since the water in the porch basin is frozen through. The barn? No, it's 200 hundred yards from the farmhouse and the snow is too deep now, leaving no traversable pathway. Where's our shovel? I fear it's in the barn, it's useless then, too. I must plan and make a list of necessities and supplies needed to survive this harsh winter. For now, I'll need to ration the water. I'll use just a cup or so for the bread and a few teaspoons to dilute Grace's milk, and three large cups for tea to keep from freezing tonight. I suppose we can always resort to collecting snow and melting it over the fire. There is plenty of that outside! I can use the large cooking pot, and although it will take mounds of snow to fill one teapot, at least we'll have water until we can reach the well.

"My whole body has goose bumps, Mother." Michael complains and blows hot air into his mittens. Although he's wearing his barn jacket and hat and mittens, he's chilled, as our small fire is not supplying enough heat.

"Michael," I say, "why don't you find your Father's warm dress coat, the one he wears to Sunday Mass? It's made of wool and it's very warm." Michael speeds off to find the coat. Any item from his father is special and he's overjoyed that I am allowing him to wear it in the house.

I walk to the back of the house and find baby girl sleeping in her snug, confined space. She's been napping fitfully for the last quarter hour, and I must check to be sure she's not tossed her blankets away. I've made her a cozy crib in the small closet off the inward facing wall of my bedroom. The heat from the fireplace warms this area, keeping her insulated and clear from drafts. Her bed is made of a padded shelf, and I've wrapped her with my warmest Irish blanket. At night she still sleeps with me, but during the day my full bed does not provide enough heat so I've fashioned this little hidey-hole for her.

"Look at the snow Mother, it's nearly to the window pane," Michael says as he points to the ever growing mounds outside. He stands before me proudly displaying the fine coat he's wearing.

"Michael, you do look dashing in your Da's dress coat. I'm pleased to see the snow covering our house; it'll insulate it, and we'll be nice and snug this evening. We must keep a watchful eye on the chimney to be sure it doesn't become clogged with bits of branches from the strong winds. Boys, we must get a better method for drying wood, or we won't have any for this evening. I've been thinking, why don't we take the remainder of the wood from the woodpile outside and we'll make furniture for our house. The large, wide logs would make lovely stools, and smaller logs could shape a table by stacking the pieces in a staggered formation and covering it with a tablecloth. It will make fine temporary furnishings, and the wood will be dry and ready when we need it." The boys' eyes become bright and I see them each imagining how they will build the log furniture. "And as the weather clears we must find and chop more wood to reload our supply on the porch. February looks to be harsh so we must stay ahead and prepare for these great storms. For now, let's make log furniture for this house, and let's collect a load of snow to melt in our pot."

Jerry nods and begins preparing for the journey outside. He dons his high wellies, overcoat and hat and mittens. He offers a prompt salute as he and Michael heave the door open and trudge through the piles of snow on the porch. Oh, heavens, it is freezing when the door opens even for a moment. The fire wanes in the cold breeze and threatens to lose its flame, but I'm near and I stoke the embers and add bits of bark. As I watch the fire begin to reignite, I add the remaining two logs and begin to think about the darkness closing in. Fortunately we've enough oil for the lanterns thanks to Jerry who reminded me to add it to our list the last time we went to town. I've replaced our candlesticks with lanterns because this house is so drafty they keep extinguishing. We'll reserve the candles for fair weather and special dinners.

My thoughts are interrupted by the return of Michael and Jerry struggling with large stumps to use as chairs for our log table. The occasional opening and closing of the heavy door, along with the freezing blasts of cold air and snow that follow it, finally wake Grace and I lift her and draw her into my chest for warmth. She seems warm enough except for one little hand that has escaped her cozy blanket. I tuck it back in and take a deep breath into her belly. Oh, my, her nappy is soiled and with the door opening and shutting this is not a good time. I carry Grace to the main room and begin to heat a small amount of water in the kettle and warm her milk in a tiny pan over the fire.

"You'll have your milk, but it must be watered down so it will last, little one," I whisper, offering her a kiss on her soft cheek. She smiles a great toothless smile and tries to free her hand from under the blanket again. Poor baby is always swaddled and held tight for warmth, I hope she'll develop and thrive as an infant should. She seems to be getting on all right, despite her restless sleep. She's coughing less and doesn't show signs of fever-- thank heavens for that. If we can muddle through this winter, then I'm sure she'll endure and become a lively child in time.

The boys deliver the last of the logs from outside, and Jerry journeys out a final time to collect snow in our pot. Michael and I fill the wood rack by the fire and pile the others in a neat row.

"I've never seen such a storm!" Michael says. "I'm half frozen and we were only out for a short bit. May I have some warm milk with cinnamon?" Jerry's just entered the house with the snow, and he flicks his hand onto Michael's shoulder as he passes him. "Mother's carefully rationing our milk Michael, you'll have to have tea or nothing." Michael's face grows a shade redder and I can tell he's going to lose control if I don't intercede.

"Boys, warm yourselves for a moment and then put on your dressing gowns and caps. While the wood is drying you may wrestle on my bed for a bit." I am also thinking it will expel some of their energy. "Afterwards, you must assemble our new furniture and tend to Grace while I prepare dinner. I'll make a thin stock for soup, and I'll make warm bread and melt cheese on it." I try to muster a reassuring smile. Michael's red nose twitches and his eyebrows disappear under his long bangs.

"Mother, you are allowing Jerry and I to tussle?" Michael's shoulders are raised and he looks baffled. He's right, I'm not normally one to promote fighting.

"I have lightened up on certain rules now that your Father has departed. You boys have been good and helpful the last few weeks and I think you merit a little fun. Just mind the picture frames and move the lantern so it won't get broken. Place the pillows on the ground to break your fall and be wary not to harm one another.

Jerry, you're older and stronger, and you must be sure not to harm Michael."

If Florence were here to see that I've allowed a friendly clash, he's be stunned. I hope he's getting on all right in Boston, it must be bitterly cold there as well. I've written to him with news of our neighbors and progress on the farm. I'm keeping my news light hoping Florence won't sense my worry and concern. I will support you, Florence my love, whilst you are away fighting, but right now my allegiance is to the children as we try to survive this winter without you. I'm putting my best effort forth to keep the children safe and finding strength, one day at a time, as I succeed. I take a moment to grasp my beloved handkerchief. I lower my head and ask my mother to watch over us. I realize that she was the strongest woman I've ever known and that I must--I will-- follow her example. No more tears. No time for weakness now, I think, as I rise and light the lanterns and prepare the cook stove for dinner.

Florence Burke
February 12th, 1864
Brandy Station, Virginia

*My Dear wife, I take pleasure in informing you of my safe arrival
here hoping this letter will find you well and healthy as it leaves me at
present. I'm sure you are quite surprised to see my new address here in
Virginia. It was rumored that we'd be training for some time in Boston,
but it must have been incorrect information for here I am on the very
soil where I will eventually encounter the Rebs. I'm not prepared for
battle but I am pleased to have left that unfavorable training camp. We
Irish volunteers are not respected even here. We were given the most
demanding corporal duties and the simplest, most tedious tasks. A
few of us spent an entire night cleaning Union Army issued rifles and
washing uniforms and boots. It seems the Colonels see us as hardy,
senseless men who cannot think but who can fight. I hope views will
change on the battlefield as we band together--all of us hoping to survive
and return home.*

*Hours and minutes pass by so swiftly these days, Ellen, probably
because I know that my life is in jeopardy. I long to be home passing my
day in the fields, and enjoying endless evenings with you and the children.
But my place is not there now, it's here.*

*I'm sorry you were informed of my attempt at a furlough. I hoped
to surprise you and the children, but that failed miserably and now here
I am in the south. My dear wife, I would have given one hundred dollars to
come home for a little while so I could see you before I left. You must keep
a good heart and not fret.*

*What a miserable time we had getting to Virginia! The boat that I
came on broke her engine so we had to go back to Boston and get another
boat for Alexandria. We motored all night and came by Fort Monroe. Some
of the boys got drunk and had a fight on the boat so the Colonels tied*

them up. The cook was tied up for selling liquor to the soldiers for one dollar a glass. The cook and the soldiers were tied up to the rigging by their hands so that their feet did not touch the deck, a pitiful sight. One man spent three quarters of an hour hollering to be let down, but he was soon knocked in the head, and he remained eerily still, dangling, for the rest of the boat ride. I have not tasted any liquor since I left and I don't intend to till I come home and share a glass with you. My back pains me since I spent the night in a chair on the deck of the boat. I cannot sleep with the bodies of men clustered around me but I paid the price opting to rest on the stiff wood.

I am sorry I did not get your letter till I came out here. You didn't mention if you wrote to John or my parents. Let me know what you hear from them if you do. Let me know how the boys are getting along and if they obey you. Tell Jerry and Mike to be good boys and I will send them something next payday. Last night I dreamt of baby Grace. She was in a golden crib but her face was covered with a white cloth. I woke disturbed thinking my memory was fading so soon, but as I roused the image of her came clear in my mind, just as if she was sleeping in the same room. I wish you'd get a portrait taken of the children and yourself. I'd like to carry it with me in my haversack, reminding me of what I'm fighting for.

I'm sorry I was forced to leave West Springfield so swiftly, and in the dead of winter. I would not have accepted this deal if I knew I only had one day before departure. I'm hoping the neighbors will look after you until I arrive home. Anything you need, you get it Ellen. Let me know how Daniel Sheehan is and if their new baby is well. Give my best to Mrs. Jenkins and thank Richard Devaney and Matthew Rooney for lending us a hand whilst I am at war.

I am now in a company with James here at Brandy Station and he is well. Give my love to all my friends and write soon.

I love you, Ellen. You and the children are my greatest happiness though you're miles away from me now.

When you write, direct it to Florence Burke Company A. 37th Regiment Volunteers Washington DC.

No more at present, this from your affectionate husband, Florence Burke

Chapter 19

Ellen Burke
February 1864
West Springfield, Massachusetts

"Is the storm finally ending?" Michael asks as he stares out the frosted window and wipes his runny nose with his hand. These have been the hardest days we've endured, and I fear we've been abandoned here in our freezing house, and we may not survive. Today is our fifth day of isolation. Suddenly I hear a tree limb crash on our roof and slide down the large beams, landing in silence in the deep snow. Another one. I suppose I should be pleased that we will have loads of firewood to collect when it's safe to journey outdoors.

As we sit before the small fire, I turn to my boys and observe their faces fading and flickering in the orange light. I know they're hungry and anxious, but I see a glint of hope in their eyes. They've been taking turns looking out the window and they both agree that the flakes are larger and diminishing somewhat. But oh, that cruel wind still thrashes, shaking our house and sailing through our cracked walls.

I'm exhausted and my back is cramped and throbbing, making it hard to do the simplest duties here at home. I cannot imagine all we've been through these past few days. Not only has this storm hit us without warning, I don't think I have ever experienced weather of this severity and length. It's surprising and unprecedented. Or, is it more harrowing because I am alone with my children and I have no husband here to help me? I don't know. I'm trying to remain strong and positive, but this is turning into a desperate situation. We're shaking from the cold, we're running low on food, and our milk supply is nearly depleted. How shall I feed Grace? Our firewood supply has been my main worry because we must keep this cottage as warm as possible, and we must have fire to heat water and broth. As the storm continues day after day, I am running out of comforting words for the children. Please God, have mercy on us. Let us be rescued.

I sigh and take a moment to consider our existence these last few days.

After the third day of incessant snowfall, loud winds and freezing temperatures, I recognize that we are simply trapped here. I know we have no choice but to set out into the storm and collect our staples or we'll end up frozen. I instruct Michael to stay indoors and mind Grace. I also tell him to keep the fire burning and stoke the embers if strong gusts threaten to snuff the flames. As expected, Michael protests, begging to leave the house and join his brother. I patiently explain to Michael that it is far too dangerous for him to brave the elements at the moment. To emphasize my point I take his small hand and place it on the icy windowpane. He immediately removes his fingers, shakes off the cold and smiles at the handprint he's made. With Michael's attention diverted, Jerry and I dress in our heaviest winter clothing and prepare to journey into the white squall.

The first few steps on the porch are bearable but then we quickly descend into deep, compacted snow. The drifts are so great at some points that Jerry and I have to grasp onto tree branches in order to pull our legs out of the hip-high mounds. It is nearly impossible to see even a few feet away; dense flurries propelled by massive wind gusts assault us from every side. Jerry and I plough our way to the barn, our heads tucked to our chins. We are searching for a small opening on the side of the barn that Daniel Sheehan made. It is meant for the chickens, a small hatch so they could come and go as they please. Daniel hadn't finished placing the flap on the door so Jerry and I hope it would be our entry into the barn. We know we'll never be able to open the heavy doors with snow piled three feet in front of them. Using only our woolen mittens to dig through the snow, we scoop and claw until we finally find the opening! I don't know how he managed it, but Jerry wiggles his thin body through the teeny door and retrieves our shovel and ax.

The next step is to find the well, but with the ground covered in white snow and the mass of silvery snowflakes flailing through the air, we've no sense of direction. I look around, my eyes blinking from the constant assault of icy precipitation. Everything is covered in a great, white veil. Jerry points his snow-covered mitten in the opposite direction of the smoke just visible above our concealed house. I follow Jerry through the drifts and snow banks until we come to a stop in front of a gray-white mound that looks like a grand statue. He's found the well! It takes Jerry and I about a quarter hour to dig to the lid and chisel away the thick ice in order to lift it off. Our hands are nearly frozen through before we finished the job. However, I know my heart will rest easier once we have fresh water in our house. I signal to Jerry to return to the house and retrieve the buckets and check on Michael and Grace. To remain as warm as I can, I shovel heaps of snow around the well, and start on a path to the house. When Jerry finally comes bounding through the snow piles, my back is burning with pain and my hands and feet are numb. I wonder how we'll manage to get the water buckets to the house without spilling them, but we use the same path that has been trodden upon several times. Even though snow has accumulated in our fresh boot holes, we arrive home with most of the dear water. Thank goodness. Melting snow is laborious and inefficient; we just can't make enough water from pails and pails of solid snow and ice.

Jerry and I immediately set our wet boots and winter coats to dry before the fire as we make tea, adding a pinch of sugar to mask its bitterness. Michael is attending to Grace in my room, attempting to change her nappy on my bed. I can hear her wails of protest, so I relieve him and gather her close to me for warmth and comfort. She's hungry and we've so little milk left. I will water it down and it will be thin, but I need to make it last.

After a noontime meal of warm goat cheese, toast and turnips, we rest in front of the fire and sip more tea. The boys prefer heated milk with cinnamon, but they do not complain about the tea because it takes the chill off their slender, cold bodies. When Jerry finishes sipping, he places his cup in the wash bin and goes toward the fireplace to check on the state of our coats, boots and mittens. Unfortunately, they are still damp. Jerry points to the three remaining log stools and notes that although they are thick, they may not last us the entire night, especially with the bitterly cold wind seeping through the house.

Michael is chasing a stray feather floating in the air. It probably came from a pillow in the loft and the draft from the many unsealed cracks is sending it flying through the house. At least this amuses Grace, her full face alive, her laughter filling our ears. Michael stops for a moment as he realizes Jerry is planning another trip outdoors. He turns to me but before he can utter a word I hold up my hand and tell him that after Jerry and I find a proper tree to cut, he may then go out and collect the wood. Michael realizes it would be useless to press me further, so he begins pursuing the elusive feather, his baby sister overjoyed once again.

Reluctantly, Jerry and I return out into the storm in our semi-dry clothing. It doesn't take long for our damp items to freeze and harden, making our task all the more miserable and dangerous. Luckily Jerry is quite skillful with an ax, and he finds a thin tree to chop. That is the simple part of this effort; the difficult part is clearing and shoveling a spot for Jerry to cut additional pieces. My back seizes again, each scoop of snow sending shots of pain up my spine to my neck. We are shivering now with our frozen mittens and uncovered faces. We didn't wear scarves because they hinder our vision so, but now our cheeks are red and exposed to the full assault of the snow and wind. I try to encourage Jerry along so we can hurry and get back into our sheltered farmhouse, but it is no easy task chopping wood in deep snow.

While Jerry chops, I begin digging a path to the privy. When I finally reach the loo, the door won't open because of a heaping snowdrift, so it takes loads of painful shovels to clear a spot big enough to open the door. I manage to make the loo accessible, jarring the door a bit, and widening it so the children and I can slip through. Thank heavens! The chamber pots at home are at their capacity, nearly spilling over the tops. We've placed them in the cellar since we hadn't ventured outside or reserved water enough to wash them. As a result, the tiny cellar is becoming contaminated and foul-smelling. The use of the loo is vital even though the boys and I will nearly freeze getting to it. Also, for me, the pungent odor evokes the horrid memories of my six weeks journey from Ireland, and I desperately want to remove them, or I fear I'll lose heart.

When I make my way back to Jerry, I am pleased that he has chopped over a dozen logs, and I call to him but my words aren't received because of the deafening, violent winds. I know I should check on Michael and Grace, so I collect four logs and enter the dim house. I place the logs in the carrier near the fire to dry and tell Michael he can dress warmly and assist his brother in collecting the wood. Michael is more than pleased to finally leave the confines of our house, but I know his tolerance for cold weather is short-lived.

I warn him to set straight to work, for he'll have many days ahead to play in the white playground. I once again tear off my freezing layers and lay them in front of the fire to dry. I find my last day dress and tuck my hair under a dry bonnet. At last I collect my tired and hungry baby from the rug. I shall heat her some thin milk and place her down for her nap.

What a long, hard day it's been, and it's not nearly over yet. I know darkness is already closing in upon us, and as I light the lamps surrounding the main room I shake my head and try to keep my spirits from drooping. My muscles are aching but I am proud of our achievements here today. For the time being we have well water, firewood and a narrow path to the loo. The children remain healthy and we have enough milk and food to last us a day or so longer. I bow my head and thank God for giving me strength today. The children and I will have an early bedtime tonight and things will surely look up in the morning.

But when I wake the next morning, stiff and sore, I look through the window and am sickened by the sight of more snow and high winds that froze icicles all round our roofline. I hear Grace shift and moan, and I know she will wake hungry for milk again. I can't remember what day of the week it is, a Tuesday I think? I doubt that Mr. Devaney can deliver our milk even if it is our fixed day. I fear the main roads are no better off than here on our white mount. I wonder if we could manage to find our way to the main road if we dare venture out in this gale. Jerry wants to try, but I worry he'll become disoriented, lost, and overcome by the freezing temperatures. I don't dare accompany him and leave Michael and Grace alone in the house. We could be gone for hours and Michael is still too young to tend to Grace and the fire at ten year's of age.

I start to panic and I can feel my chest becoming constricted and tight. I am trying not to allow the feelings of frustration to overpower my strong will, but these days it is getting more and more difficult. My emotions sway like a see-saw-- although I make every effort to keep them level. Florence, I think to myself, why aren't you here protecting your family? How could you leave us in a house you've never seen, with its many cracks and thin walls? Did you truly see this isolated farmland as an advantage or were you just trying to prove to your father that you're invincible enough to survive your tour of duty and return a landowner? What if none of us survive? I am bloody pissed and heave my face into my pillow and sob. I will not upset the children for I cry silent tears, but I need to release my feelings before the children wake and I must wear a false countenance. I realize I am shaking with anger and from cold. I must continue trying to suppress resentful feelings toward Florence and concentrate on surviving without him.

How I wish my father was alive to help; he was a clever man who could overcome any trial, and like Mother, keep positive through it. After he died two summer's past, my younger brothers journeyed west to California in hopes of steering clear of the draft and finding better work. I've only received one or two letters since they departed and in them they describe California as a rough place where criminals and prostitutes dwell. However, they find the climate pleasant and they've both found solid work building railroads.

My sister Mary is my only remaining relation here; she lives half a day's carriage ride in North Hampton. Mary and her daughter Emma are managing the dress shop while James is fighting in Virginia with Florence. They've taken in a boarder, and I believe the young woman also works at the dress shop. I wonder… is my niece Emma old enough to mind the store in her mum's absence? Emma's grown up in the business, spending her days there since she was an infant. I remember she learned to sew at a very young age, and I know James taught her how to keep the books. She'd have company in her house with the female boarder. Let me think, how old is dear Emma now? The last time I saw her we celebrated her sixteenth birthday, and that was nearly two years' past. Oh, my, I believe she is eighteen years of age! Perhaps Mary could slip away, at least until the worst of winter is over? I must write and plead with her. I feel my spirits rise as I consider the possibility of a companion. I limp out of bed, lay the fire and heat water for tea. While I wait for the water to boil I grasp onto my handkerchief and plead to my mother to continue watching over us.

I must check on our food and milk supply. In the icebox we have one egg, a small bit of cheese, two canisters of applesauce, and one half cup of milk. In the cupboard we have half a bag of sugar, dried peaches, crusty bread, various spices and two crates of tea. Thank goodness Patrick gifted us tea for Christmas! I will cook the egg for the boys and divide it over a slice of bread. For Grace, I will add water to her milk, and soak tiny pieces of bread in the applesauce. I wish I had one potato remaining to mush for her, but we ate the last a few days ago. Why are potato shortages such a common worry for us? This thought makes me smile, I'm not sure why; the irony and my exhausted state has me out of sorts. The more I think of it though, it is kind of silly that a bloody potato, a root vegetable, has been the culprit in determining our survival. I start to laugh and for a moment I feel I might be going mad, but then I hear baby girl crying and I collect myself. Suddenly I'm aware that levity might be my way to cope today. Perhaps my mother in heaven is urging me to smile and cherish this day with my family, even with its shortcomings. I will try to remain in high spirits until the storm abates. As I walk to my bedroom I find Michael playing with Grace underneath the bed covers. He'd made a tent with pillows and blankets, and she is delighted by his game of peek- a-boo. I smile and give them both a warm greeting realizing that my mother's "inspiration" has been received by more than just me.

This new day of scarcity and isolation is mercifully filled with joy, prayer and thankfulness. The boys are lovely, offering to fill buckets of water, bringing in fallen branches for our fire, and even changing baby girl when her nappy is soiled. We make a list of items we'll need at the Mercantile, and Jerry vows that tomorrow he'll find his way to our closest neighbors, the Ungers, if we can't get to town. He'll at least ask to borrow milk for Grace, and yeast and eggs too, if possible.

After we discuss the items we will need immediately, we then create a list of necessities we must purchase in order to make our home livable through the long winter. These include materials to patch up the cracks in the walls and expand our cellar for food storage. We will also order wood to be delivered, and most importantly, double our order of milk until we can afford to buy a cow. Florence said in his letter that I should get what we need, and though a cow is dear, we need it to survive here on this isolated hill. I must also make a visit to Mr. Day's office and collect our deed and demand a proper, clear roadway.

The boys are eager to participate in the planning. They take turns sharing ideas and describing their elaborate designs for the barn and cellar. Together, we write to Florence and answer his inquires concerning the deed and farm. Michael wants to know about his father's weapons and gear, and Jerry wants to tell his father that he's chopped a whole tree by himself. Our words are encouraging, for we do not want Florence to worry about us. By nightfall, the children become restless so we dance to a beat created when Michael hits two small sticks together. I hold Grace in my arms and we twirl and sway until my back can bear no more. We laugh at ourselves, falling to the ground in a heap, cuddling on the rug in front of the fire. With dinner, we drink tea with sugar that helps us to choke down the stale bread and cheese. We finish with a dollop of applesauce. Grace sips the last drop of the remaining milk, and goes to bed without a fuss. I gather the boys and we pray for the storm to clear, as we have done for the past four days.

Today I wake early, light a small fire, and heat water for baby girl. I feel anxious knowing that I have no milk to satisfy her. I know that when she arises she will want real sustenance. I'm certain the warm water and sugar mixture isn't going to appease her empty belly.

The children have woken and are sitting before the fire. Grace is waiting patiently for her bottle on Michael's lap. He looks to the window and then to me.

"Will the storm ever end?" he asks.

"Yes, darling. It looks brighter outside, and I hope Jerry will be able to walk to Mr. Unger's or Mr. Jenkins's house to borrow milk. For now, I'm preparing tea and heating water for baby girl." Just as the kettle begins its low rumble, a knock comes at the door and I jump with surprise. My eyes widen and fill with hope as I look to the children. Without hesitating, I run to the door and unbolt the lock as swiftly as I can, for no thief would be caught out in a storm like this! I whip open the door and there is Daniel Sheehan, covered in snow up to his waist, carrying a sack of items over his shoulder. I can't contain myself and I step back and begin to weep into my handkerchief. Michael and Jerry come to greet our visitor and take his wet and snowy clothes. I'm ashamed for my tears and retreat to my bedroom for a moment to collect myself and to comfort Grace, as I frightened her with my outburst. I return to the main room and notice Daniel and Jerry have placed a pan of milk over the fire to heat.

I step over to Daniel and say with a laugh, "Thank you for saving us, dear friend. I think I expended all my strength and wit these past days, and now I'm a right old mess." I give a quick laugh and leap into his arms to give him a hug. As I do so Daniel steps back, surprised at my impulsive show of gratitude, and both of us nearly topple to the ground. Grace, who's watching from the safety of Michael's arms bursts out in tears once again, frightened by the commotion. I'm certain it is my elation at being safe at last, because I can't control my laughter. I prance over to Grace, take her from Michael, and sway her back and forth until she settles. Then I turn my eyes to Daniel. "How is Lara faring? And the new baby? Are they in good health?"

"And Little Dan? How's my mate?" Jerry inquires immediately. Daniel steps to the fire to check on the milk and removes the kettle from the rod. He takes a moment to respond and I think I saw a flash of concern cross his face, but perhaps I am just very tired.

"Everyone is in good health, and relieved that this storm has passed. Lara's not slept enough as you can imagine, and she seems a bit out of sorts, but that's probably because of the baby's nighttime feedings. Little Dan is at home now minding the baby so Lara can get some rest." Daniel tests the milk temperature and begins filling the two bottles I have on the hearth. He's a seasoned father for sure.

"I was concerned for the animals in the barn." He continues, "The temperature was bitterly cold and their water kept freezing, but Little Dan and I covered them with blankets and we took an axe to the icy bucket." Jerry is listening intently to the conversation and wants to pose questions of his own.

"Mr. Sheehan, how are the conditions on the main road, is it cleared?" I know Jerry is eager to get us to the Mercantile.

"The main road was cleared enough for my single horse, but I had to leave Tessa at the bottom of the hill because the snow was too deep for her. It was almost too deep for me as well, Jerry. I was wading up to my waist and had to use these two ice picks to keep from falling back down the slippery path. I brought these tools to help dig out your well, but it seems you have done this for yourself--and chopped wood? Jerry my boy, your father would be pleased." Jerry's smile grows and his face reddens.

"Thank you sir, we did what we had to do here. Mother worked beside me the whole time."

"And me, Mr. Sheehan, I helped too. I carried in the cold logs!" Michael exclaims, not wanting to be left out.

"Good show boys! Now let's get some tea made and feed your baby sister. Ellen, Lara's been fretting about Grace, how long has she been without milk?" Daniel asks.

"I've been watering her milk for the past three days, and offering her applesauce and even soggy bread. I'm nearly out of food, and this morning I was fixing to give her sugar and water. I must feed her small amounts, for she's not had full milk for some time. I'm so thankful to you, Daniel." I tip the bottle to Grace's mouth and she reaches for it with both hands. She hungrily gulps half the bottle in seconds. I prop her on my lap and remove the bottle from her tight-pursed mouth. She lets out a protesting wail and I turn her about and over my shoulder to try and render a release of gas. She complies, then searches for the bottle herself by reaching over my back.

"She's a strong little one, that's good to see, Ellen," Daniel says cheerfully. Daniel takes a step towards the door and spies the sack. "Oh boys, Ellen, I've sweet potatoes, tomatoes, corn and even good sausage we made from our old pig, Gertrude. Would you like to get your pot and make a stew?" Daniel asks as he begins to unload the food and lay it on the cupboard.

"Hurray! No more stale bread and applesauce! Thank you Mr. Sheehan," Michael hollers and offers Daniel a grateful embrace. Daniel straightens and turns to my other son.

"Jerry, would you like to help little Dan and me hitch the horses to the sleigh so we can journey to town to buy food, if the butcher and Mercantile have any left? I'm sure their deliveries have been halted due to this storm. Michael, you may come along too if your mother can spare you for the afternoon." Michael's eyes light up and he immediately begins tugging on my skirt, begging me to let him join the others. I couldn't possibly deny my high-spirited child this trip. But I give the boys strict instructions on what chores we need done before they leave for the day. They dash about collecting their warm clothes so they can fill water pails and collect fallen branches. I set about preparing a quick morning meal, sausage with onions, and soon the house iss filled with the most delightful smells. Even baby girl, who is full and content to rest in my arms, tilts her little nose and inhales deeply. Daniel retrieves our large pot from the cellar and places it on the iron rod. I will make a fantastic soup with these lovely ingredients! Daniel fills the pot with water and turns to me,

"Ellen I forgot to mention that Don Unger has returned from his duty in Virginia, and now he and his father Jacob are starting a wood delivery service to folks in West Springfield and Springfield. He has loads stacked at his place. When I see him I will ask him to make a delivery."

"Thank you, I only hope they can get through the woods with the logs." Grace is squirming in my arms. I place her down on the wool rug so she can play with her two favorite rag dolls. Daniel smiles down at her and turns to me,

"Don't worry, Ellen. Jacob has horses and a log carrier; he'll pull the load to deliver it here, and Don can surely carry a few bundles up the hill. He's a strong young man, and he'll certainly make the effort knowing Florence is away fighting." I wince-- somehow the mention of my husband at war still feels raw and painful.

After the boys and Daniel take their meal and depart for town, I close the door gently and breathe a deep sigh of relief. We've made it! I watch Grace contently playing on the rug, and bend down to kiss her soft cheek! Oh, Grace, I'll cook a nice broth, and serve the heartiest stew in town. I turn to look at the pot heating over the fire and begin preparing the stew with the leftover sausage and vegetables. My stomach growls and I realize I've eaten very little these past few days. I must make tea and tide myself over until the stew is prepared, then I will fill my empty belly. I'm eager for our icebox and cupboard to be replenished with food again and I hope most of our items will be available in town. Now, to add spice and flavor to my stew... thank heavens Mrs. Jenkins brought dried herbs on her last visit. They hang from my ceiling, and will add tremendous flavor to our meal.

When the stew is readied and baby girl settled for a nap, I finally find a bowl and eat my first satisfying meal in days. I'm feeling cheerful as I go about washing up, washing the children's clothing and Grace's nappies, and hanging them to dry on the line by the fire. Soon, though I become tired, probably from the night wakings and the stress of the past week. I think I will rest with Grace for a spell. The boys will return soon, so I must lay down while I have a moment. Later, I'll bake biscuits if yeast and eggs are found, for we deserve a celebration, and I want to thank the Sheehans. For now, though, I'm played out and need to sleep. I'm placing my head to the pillow, in drowsy relief, filled with a sense of tranquility and security. We'll survive this winter yet.

Then: "Mother, wake up, we've a letter from Father!" Michael joyfully declares as he walks toward me for a kiss. The boys have returned from town and they've bought most of our necessary foods. Thank goodness for that.

"Yes, oh my, what time is it? Has the fire died out, it feels quite cold in here. You boys must be frozen, come let's get you warmed up and heat the stew for your supper. How was the journey to town?" I feel groggy but I rise to greet my children and assist them with their load of supplies. We chat softly while Grace enjoys another hour of peaceful sleep. She slumbers contently, as if she too knows the worst is over.

Florence Burke
February 17th, 1864
Camp near Brandy Station VA

My dear wife and children,

The next day after my arrival here from Boston I wrote you a letter but have received no answer. I shall patiently await the arrival of today's mail hoping to get a few lines from the dear ones at home and hope on the receipt of this it will find you as it leaves me, in the enjoyment of good health through the mercies of God.

We marched a short distance yesterday and made camp last night in an open, muddy field. I sit before the cook fire now; smoke stinging my eyes, hands numb from the cold. We're on the outskirts of the battlefield, but I can hear the eerie sounds of marching men, galloping horses and moving cannons. We remain here in training, and await the arrival of other regiments.

Today is awfully cold and last night we had about as much as we could attend to, to keep from freezing and it bids fair to be no better tonight. There are three of us tented together in a little shanty built of small logs about six by ten feet and plastered on the outside with Virginia mud, then covered with thin cotton cloth. This is made to serve as a house, or tent, but I awake and find myself on a pine stick like a chicken at roost which makes me wish this cruel war was over.

You might ask what kind of country is Virginia, so far my experience goes as this, mules; mud and cold weather; and for not the sight of a woman, black or white, have I seen since I have got here. As I look around now I see endless rolling hills and gray, cloudy skies above them. What makes this place foreboding though is the lack of green contrasting the trees and occasional wooden house. The thick brown mud dominates the landscape making it look dark and drab even in the daylight hours. It's not a place of beauty — perhaps it will cheer up come spring .

Enclosed you will find a certificate to enable you to get your war time service State Aid which will be entitled to you on presenting it to the selectmen, if you have not already received it.

The request I asked of you right before I left home, to write to my parents and brother, still remains unknown. Have you had time to inform them, and have you received word from them? John will surely be displeased but it is my father's response that seems to weigh the most heavy on my heart. Please let me know in your next.

I wish you would get your photograph taken and send it in a letter to me. Take the boys on one card and yourself and the baby on the other. I want to see the faces of the family that I love so dearly, my fair wife and lovely children. Last night I stared up at the star-filled sky and imagined our new farmland with you and the children tucked together in the little house. I hope you're warm and safe enough, and that this land will flourish come spring.

I hope I receive a letter from you tomorrow for they are all I shall have to cheer my lonesome hours. That is all for now.

Please send and receive my love to you and the children.

Yours Faithfully,

Florence Burke

Chapter 20

Ellen Burke Late
February 1864
West Springfield, Massachusetts

"Father's not receiving our letters." Jerry states, placing Florence's letter carefully on my side table. "What happened to them, Mother?" Jerry's come down from the loft, obviously troubled by his father's recent letter. The lamp behind him casts light on the curls surrounding his nightcap. He looks like an angel adorned with a bright halo. I shake my head and blink, for I am overtired and my mind is playing tricks on me. I take Jerry's cold hand in mine and look into his blue-grey eyes.

"Jerry, your concern is well-taken. But your father will receive our letters in good time. He keeps moving and the letters have to chase after him is all. They'll probably end up arriving on the same day and he'll be overwhelmed by all our news! Now get yourself back to bed, we've got to trek to town tomorrow and you'll need your strength. We have more letters to mail to your Da, and if we're lucky, we may receive a letter from him saying he's smiling over our loving words.

"All right, Mother. Good night," Jerry whispers and offers me a quick kiss on the cheek.

After Jerry returns to bed, I turn down the lamp and close my eyes. My head is spinning, filled with worries over mercantile lists, farm supplies, household duties and children's needs. Oh, and now I'm fretting over Florence because our letters have not found him. I must check at the post tomorrow and inquire about why they are taking so long to reach him. Fortunately my sister received our correspondence in good time and she wrote back immediately with encouraging news. Mary's just hired an experienced seamstress and Emma is certain she can manage the shop for a spell. She and her boarder, Dana, will mind the house. Mary just needs some time to work out the details and to get her business in order. I pray it all works out and she joins us at this barren farm. I desperately need her.

Oh, the state of the farm. It's nearly March and we haven't finished clearing the land. Will it be prepared for tilling when the ground finally thaws? We've received some money from Florence and one check from State Aid, but its not enough to hire farm hands yet. We must manage by ourselves and with help from our dear friends and neighbors. My mind suddenly drifts to the joyful outpouring of gifts following last month's crippling storm. After Daniel Sheehan's life-saving donation of milk and food, we were astounded by the number of kind folks who journeyed through the snow and up our steep hill to deliver assistances.

Our neighbor to the west, Mrs. Begley managed to traverse the climb assisted by her husband Edward Sr. The Begleys arrived with a Virginia newspaper and a lovely basket of baby clothes sewn for Grace. After taking their coats and asking if they'd like tea, Jerry inquired straightaway about Ed Jr., their son who enlisted and left West Springfield the same day Florence departed. Mrs. Begley wore a look of concern but answered Jerry in a pleasant tone.

"We've received word from him, Jerry, and he seems to be getting on just fine. He says your Da's become a splendid cook, making meals for the boys in camp. Imagine that Ellen! The latest I've heard is that they're still training, marching and camping. Ed mailed us a newspaper and it seems the fighting has stalled a bit in Virginia. Brandy Station is being used as their winter retreat, so they'll remain there and join forces with other Union regiments." Mrs. Begley looks at the innocent faces of my boys and points to the newspaper. "Look here Jerry, Michael, here's a photograph of soldiers sitting around the camp fire, writing letters and smoking tobacco."

"But when will Da get to fight, Ma?" Michael says, looking at the photo with disappointment. I take a deep breath and lean down to my son.

"When they are properly trained and when the weather turns fair. Michael, can you please check on Grace?" I am ashamed that I have not had the courage to speak to Michael about the realities of war, that men die, that war's not a game. I have been trying to protect him but now it is apparent that he believes his father's invincible and that battle is thrilling and something soldiers desire. I clear my throat and redirect my attention to the new clothes Mrs. Begley has sewn for Grace. I hold each dress up high to admire them. They are beautifully crafted with soft silks and in baby pink colors. I tell the Begleys that I shall have Grace wear them when our portraits are taken.

Mrs. Begley smiles and unfolds some old cloths she's brought for Grace's nappies. They're gratefully received because our present cloths are worn out, stained and frayed. After a cup of tea and warm biscuits, the Begleys make their way home and we set about doing our daily chores and preparing for a trip to town.

Just as we finish our mid-day meal, we hear rustling outdoors and Michael runs to the window and spies Jacob and Don Unger hauling bundles of logs in their arms. They've come! I haven't seen Jacob since… oh goodness, since December. That's when the weather turned too cold to take the children to Sunday Mass. When the boys were very young, the Ungers would give us a lift to church in their covered wagon. Now Don is fully-grown and has already completed a tour of duty with the Union Army in the same Virginia Regiment that Florence and James have joined. I am so pleased that he's returned unharmed, perhaps he will share some insight into the Union's present position. I ask the boys to clear the dishes and mind Grace while I pay for the delivery.

I open the door and see Don stacking logs in careful rows on the side of the house. He's already filled the wood carrier on the porch, and it's nearly three foot high with more! I collect the bills from my barn coat pocket and move toward Jacob to pay him. He tips his cap and inquires about Florence. I fill him in on news of his arrival to Virginia. Jacob listens intently; the lines on his face revealing the hardship of seeing your only son go to war. His almond-shaped eyes still sparkle though his face has aged. I'm sure the relief of having Don home is the cause for this brightness, and I am joyous that this wonderful family has been reunited.

Jacob takes the bills but refuses to let me pay for the delivery. I protest, but Don comes forward and holds his hand in the air. He doesn't say a word, but I can tell he's insisting. I turn my face toward Don, but he's concentrating on collecting the wood ropes.

"Congratulations, son. You've made it back to West Springfield-- thank the Almighty Lord for it. Don, can you describe the state of the Virginia battlegrounds? Do you think other recruits have a chance of returning home?" Don's face drops, and I notice his hands become white, clenching the ropes as if they're his life line. He doesn't respond, hesitating for some reason, as he stares at the snow on his boots. Finally, after several moments, he raises his eyes, looks off into the distance and begins to talk.

"Mrs. Burke, I can't tell you of the things I've seen, but take comfort in knowing that Mr. Burke is in company with the bravest and most honorable men I've ever known. I would fight beside them any day, in fact I..." He pauses. "Never mind, your husband has the finest commanders--they'll look after him." He suddenly turns his attention to his father. "We've other deliveries today, we should be going. Good day, Mrs. Burke."

Don swiftly marches toward the woods and Jacob follows after offering a farewell embrace. As he departs, Jacob turn one last time and whispers, "Ellen, give Don time, he's only just returned and needs to settle into life here. He'll come round once he's been home a while, and he'll start talking. You'll see. Keep praying to the Almighty Father, it worked for us." Jacob breaks into a trot and heads toward the thick brush.

"Yes, Jacob I shall." I call after him." "Thank you for the firewood! Enjoy your blessings!" I'm startled at how troubled I feel after the encounter with the Ungers. It was not anything Don said that caused me to become alarmed; I think it was just his overall demeanor. I suppose I still see him as the same little boy who taught my wee ones how to catch bullfrogs by the stream. Jacob is probably right, Don just needs time to settle into civilian life.

The following week more neighbors and friends make their way to us. Thanks to fair skies filled with daytime sunshine, much of the snow melted, and it is warm enough for folks to travel. Mrs. Jenkins and her twins Madeline and Quinn call on Monday. They arrive with English tea and more delicious cinnamon scones! She also brings three canisters of strawberry jam. We've a lovely visit, the children run around the farm, and Mrs. Jenkins and I sit by the fire and enjoy some fine tea. I have many questions to ask concerning our farm. Mrs. Jenkins has managed her thriving land since her husband passed away nearly twelve years ago--the same year her twins were born. She's a strong woman and I value her friendship and her advice. Her visit is all too short. After tea, a brief chat and a cuddle with Grace, Mrs. Jenkins collects her children and bundles up for the trip home

Several days later Matthew Rooney stops by to bring us news of our gifted pig, Josephine. He seems nervous, fidgets with his hat, and shifts from one foot to the other. He also insists that we talk in private so he cleverly asks the boys if they would mind checking on his horse waiting at he bottom of our hill. He even brought a brush for them to use on her. When the boys are out the door, Matthew sighs and speaks softly.

"I have some news on Ol' Josephine, and I still can't believe what's happened. You see, Ellen, Josephine has been looking sluggish of late, and growing fatter, which is odd for an old pig like her. When I called Daniel in to check on her, he gave me the stunning news that she's pregnant. Can you believe it? My old Josephine! I thought certainly that she was past the age of bearing piglets, but I suppose I was wrong." Matthew raises his hands in the air, and his eyebrows automatically follow. "She's close now, and I think the piglets will be born any day. I've been thinking Ellen. I want you to consider sacrificing Josephine and keeping the piglets. She's old and the birth will be very hard on her. I know you could use her meat, much of it could be salted and stored. I'm only fretting on how the boys will take the news because I know they were eager to meet Josephine." Matthew pauses, waiting to receive my reaction. I understand that the boys are expecting to meet Josephine, but I think they will be even more thrilled to raise piglets here. I place my hand on Matthew's arm, and look into his worried eyes.

"Matthew, the boys will be fine. After the shortage of food during the storm, they will welcome the ham and sausage that dear old Josephine will provide. Michael will be over the moon with news of the piglets; they were his favorite on the Jenkins' farm. Thank you Matthew for this tremendous gift." Matthew's face relaxes and in the afternoon light I can see the deep lines on his forehead fade and the twinkle in his eyes reappear.

He says he'll come by later in the week to finish building the pen in the barn, stack it with hay and a proper trough, and bring Josephine to her final home. I can hardly wait to inform the boys that our first farm animals will be with us shortly.

Yesterday we saw the last of our unexpected visitors; it was Florence's oldest and dearest friend in West Springfield, Edward Fitzgerald. Edward and Florence arrived in West Springfield six months apart and met at the Town Hall while looking for farming work. Mrs. Jenkins was impressed by their mere stature, large, burly Irishman who knew how to cultivate land and to properly tend to farm animals. She hired them both, and together they expanded her farm, making tremendous gains in profit. Edward and Florence spent sixteen hours a day on the farm, and at the end of the day, they'd often share a good old pint before going home.

I recall one evening when I found them in the barn, brushing and feeding the horses before heading home. I heard them playfully betting on who would own his own farm first. Well, it was Edward who won that bet, for he met and fell in love with a lovely girl name Catherine, from North Hampton. Catherine's parents owned a thriving apple orchard and sizable dairy farm. Edward courted her for nearly four years and finally proposed to her on the very day that I gave birth to Jerry, May 16th. We've been dear friends over the years, sharing both joyful and difficult times together. Edward and Catherine are fortunate to have a healthy, strong union, but they've been disappointed by Catherine's inability to bear children. We naturally chose them as godparents for our children, and felt certain that in time they'd have their own, and we'd raise them together. Unfortunately, as the years passed, the hope for a full-term pregnancy waned despite efforts by Catherine's father to locate the finest doctors in Hartford and Boston. Over the years they've loved and cared for my children, but I feel their sorrow and regret from the inability to bear their own. Catherine and Edward have enjoyed prosperity and enduring love, but there'll always be a deep void in their lives.

Edward arrives just before sundown. Despite the mild weather Edward's cheeks are crimson, and I hope he isn't ill. It was probably the journey up the hill that caused his handsome face to flush. He is neatly dressed in a fine suit and matching cap. It always makes me smile when I see him in such lavish clothes, because I remember Edward in overalls and torn work shirts. I urge him to come in and relieve him of the sack of apples and pie he's brought for us. He removes his thick suit coat and cap and gives his long, wavy hair a good shake. He's still the same; how I wish Florence were here to enjoy this rare visit.

Edward wastes no time in offering his opinion on Florence's decision to join the war effort. He says he was shocked and troubled when he heard the news from my sister Mary in North Hampton.

"Why didn't he discuss this with me, Ellen? If I'd known he was discontented at the Jenkin's farm, I could have helped him. I would have loaned him money." Edward shakes his head again and runs his fingers though his long hair. "Ellen, where are the children? How are they faring in their father's absence?" Edward cocks his head to the side, his eyebrows rising in concern. I divert my eyes from Edward's and try to convey an optimistic response.

"The boys are getting on all right, they're busy here with preparing the farm and helping me look after Grace. In a few days time we'll be getting a pig and she's to have piglets. The boys are in the barn now finishing the chicken coup with Daniel Sheehan." Edward slaps his knee and says, "Daniel, well how about that! I must say hello to him after we finish our chat. Now Ellen, I want to know how you're faring?" I feel myself start to tremble, first my hands, then my lip, and then my whole body starts to quiver. I haven't shared my true feelings with anyone, and I mustn't start now with Florence's mate. I take a few steps to the fire and the warmth calms my tremors. I stall by asking Edward if he'd like some tea and busy myself with the fire. Edward merely nods and waits patiently for me to answer him. I muster courage and place my hand in my apron pocket, searching for my mother's handkerchief. I breathe a heavy sigh and then begin.

"I'm fine really. Of course I'm still adjusting to our new home and tending to the farm and children without Florence. It's difficult to manage, but I'm hopeful I will soon have a houseguest, my sister! I've written to Mary and asked if she would come stay with us until winter passes. I am in desperate need of a companion and another set of hands around here. But I'm all right, Edward. I worry for Florence, I'm sure you do as well." I look up and give Edward a resilient smile. He lowers his head and seems torn by what to say next. I feel we are both resistant to saying what is truly on our minds. Edward shakes his hair again and smooths it with his fingers. "Yes, I'm worried about him. I spoke to him a few months before he left and he said he feared the draft as much as I did."

Finally, however, he comes out with it, "Tell me Ellen, what changed in him?" Edward lifts his arms in the air but his eyes remain focused on mine. I swiftly turn toward the fire, as the same icy feeling penetrates my skin. My shoulders stiffen and draw forward as I listen for the kettle. The water is not boiling yet. I wipe my hands on my apron and suddenly tears are springing to my eyes. I can't speak because my throat is constricted. I lower my bonnet and mumble something that comes out as a low cry and tear off to my room. Edward does not follow me, he seems to understand my troubled state and gives me time to gather myself and check on my slumbering baby. I find my wash bin and flannel and gently pat the tears away. I want to share my anger and confusion with Edward, but I just can't because it would mean betraying my husband. If I unleash my true emotions, I know I'll plunge into a hateful rant, like a poisonous snake who'd strike out at its closest victim. Instead I gulp down my feelings and the words trying to escape. I believe Edward shares similar feelings but I'm certain he's sympathetic to his dear friend and will not react well to my spiteful, contentious words.

I take in several deep breaths and shake my hands, trying to suppress my volcanic emotions. When I feel the worst of my anger has subsided, I cover Grace's bare hands and return to the main room. Edward has been stoking the fire and has removed the kettle from the rod. I find my tin of tea and notice the apple pie Edward gifted to us. I am first to break the uncomfortable silence. "Edward, did Catherine bake this lovely pie? It looks delicious!" Edward immediately joins me and we both admire its light brown crust. Suddenly Edward's face breaks into a wide smile as he clasps his hands together.

"Yes, Catherine baked this pie for you, and I came to deliver it. Catherine would have come but she's been feeling a bit sick in the mornings these past few weeks..." Edward stops short, his face revealing the rest of his joyous news.

I gasp, "Edward, do you think, is Catherine with child?" Edward's eyes soften and his face turns a shade darker. His smile remains fixed upon his youthful face.

"Yes, Ellen, and the doctor says the baby is in good health. For now, I'm demanding that Catherine rest." Edward looks at me with the hope and fear of a man who's been in this state before and hopes to God it will work out this time. I jump in the air and Edward leans forward for an embrace. Tears of joy drizzle down my cheeks.

"Edward, this is delightful news. I will pray for Catherine and the baby. How I wish Florence were here to share this news. Please stay for tea. Daniel and the boys will finish up soon and..." just as

I am finishing my sentence, in walks Michael and Jerry with Daniel Sheehan behind them.

"Hello there, Mr. Fitzgerald. Mother, are you crying?" Michael asks, coming to me and placing his arms around my waist.

"No, dear. Edward just shared some wonderful news, and I am welling with happiness for them. Your godparents are going to have a baby!" I can't help myself, I rise and give everyone hugs and kisses, and the room swiftly feels brighter and warmer. After everyone congratulates Edward, Michael and Jerry tell us about the completion of the chicken coop. It's even prepared with hay and feed.

"Now all we need are chickens!" Michael declares as he leans his earnest face close to mine. Edward takes a few steps forward and leans down to look into the eyes of my boys.

"Well, now Michael, Jerry, I've had a little problem with my farm and I thought you might help." Edward scratches his beard, his hazel eyes twinkling in the flicker of the flame.

"You see, my chickens haven't been laying eggs of late. At first I thought they were ill or cold. However, I've come to the conclusion that they're too crowded in their coop. So, I was wondering if perhaps you could take a few from me so the others will have room enough to grow, run free, and lay their eggs properly." Jerry and Michael both open their mouths at this news and their eyes widen in bewilderment. Jerry's the first to recover, and he looks up to Edward with a serious countenance. Michael is less subtle, he jumps up and tugs at my sleeve. I place my hand on Michael's head to calm him and I turn to Edward.

"Edward, it's very kind of you, but I'm certain Florence would want me to pay you, so name your price." I try to make my voice sound authoritative, but I notice that both Edward and Daniel are trying not to smile. Edward raises his open palm in front of him and his face slackens, accentuating his high cheekbones.

"Nonsense. I won't accept your money. Florence is my best friend and I'm proud of him for acquiring this farm on his own, even if it means he must depart for a time. Florence can thank me properly when he returns. And by properly I mean he can buy me a pint of beer." Edward gives me a sly wink and then raises his hands in the air, sending his wisps of hair forward, covering half his delighted face.

"Who wants to collect the chickens? I hoped you'd say yes, Ellen, so I've brought them in my carriage. They're waiting at the bottom of the hill, I'll show you boys!"

Michael and Jerry holler in delight. They both rush to find their work gloves and I notice a brief smile exchanged between them. Before they collect the chickens, the boys come to us to thank Daniel and Edward for their help and gifts. Jerry turns to Edward and states, "You're the very best Godfather anyone could ask for. I'm gonna write to Father tonight and tell him you've given us our very own chickens. Let's go Michael, we got chickens!" Jerry's face explodes with joy as he runs to me for a hug, and then springs out the door with Edward right behind them. The three of them depart straightaway, leaving me alone with Daniel. I turn to him and tilt my head.

"You were not aware of this plan, were you Daniel?" Daniel lowers his massive chin and surveys the floor.

"What? No, Ellen. I knew Edward had plenty of chickens at his farm and I might've told him I was building a coop for you, and he might've asked me to meet him here today, But other than that, I know nothing of the situation. I'd like to call it a lovely coincidence!" I cover my mouth, overwhelmed at the generosity of these two friends.

"Oh, Daniel. Thank you for looking out for us. I'm without words to describe how blessed we are to have you in our lives. I only wish Florence were here enjoying this joyous time." Daniel comes to me and offers a final embrace.

After they've gone I think of the many acts of kindness bestowed upon us. I suddenly discover a quarter hour has passed, and I've been merely resting and daydreaming in this old rocker. I must get to work and organize our day tomorrow. I shall rise early and bake loaves of spice cake to thank our generous friends. Afterwards I shall journey to town to see Mr. Parsons about the deed and also collect my State Aid. We need this money now more than ever. With the pigs nearly here, the chickens in the coop, a cow to buy and crops to plant, I must have cash. I will do everything possible to make this farm flourish. I now believe this is possible with the help of our friends and neighbors.

I will visit the Postmaster and investigate why our letters are not being received in good time, and I shall try to schedule an appointment with a photographer to have our likenesses taken. There, that's quite a list of tasks. As hard as these times get, I feel strength coming from those dear folks who've gone before me, especially my mother, willing me to carry on. I shall do my best, I promise, I shall try. I take a moment to pray to God. "Almighty Father, I can't change what's happened to our family, but I can try to make the best of the situation. Please watch over Florence and please continue to help us here on the farm. I pray that our individual journeys will end in a common gathering place, here at the Burke farm. Amen."

Seamus Burke
March 1864
Ballinhassig, Ireland

Dear Ellen,

I received your letter but it came as no surprise that my son has made another foolish decision. We are sorry for you and the children and hope you are getting on okay. We don't understand this nonsense. Why would Florence join now, volunteering? He's no young man and he should be home looking after you. Florence has proven that he'd abandon his own family to get what he wants, believe me Ellen, we know of it.

I told him America was a bad idea because immigrants are nothing, and treated like my pigs here in Ireland.

How long will Florence be serving? What do you hear from him? I penned a note to John asking for more specifics as to where he is fighting and how bad it might get. Maura and I are troubled by this news, I know sacrifices are part of getting land, but his aspirations are irresponsible.

Let me know what you hear from him in your next letter and if you have any spare money from the State Aid. We could use some for our own use.

Take care of your kin and don't fret over Florence. He is a man who is going through life with his own good intentions in mind.

Seamus Burke

John Burke
March 1864
New York, New York

Dearest Ellen,

How are you getting on? What do you hear from my brother? It seems I have no influence over Union Army regulations, so I've abandoned efforts to pull Florence from his post. I am sorry, Ellen, I have tried to work every political angle and source, but there is a limit to my authority, and now I must place Florence's fate into the hands of God.

In this letter I have sent you a twenty-dollar note. We'd like to pay you a visit but Bridget has not been feeling well of late, and little Jessica's had a persistent cough. When the fair weather comes we will journey to West Springfield and assist you in any way you need.

My father has written to me and I hope he has spared you the spiteful words he shared in my letter. He clearly has not forgiven Florence for leaving Ireland and he does not know that his hateful words never left Florence's mind, finally causing him to make this miserable decision. I know this all too well. I wish I had done more to assist my brother. I thought he had abandoned the idea of landowning and was pleased with his life- I am sorry to have misread him.

Please take care, Ellen. I am certain those wonderful boys of yours are minding you and helping with the farm. Take care of baby girl. It's frightening with so many illnesses looming about this time of year. Bridget, the girls and I send our love and prayers to you.

Yours truly,

John Burke

Chapter 21

Ellen Burke
March 1864
West Springfield, Massachusetts

"She's here, Mother, Aunt Mary is here!" Michael says breathlessly and sprints down the slushy hill to greet her. My sister, escorted by a large man carrying her bags, is looking red–faced and weary from her travels. I rush indoors and ask Jerry to mind Grace while I step outside to greet my sister. It's a chilly afternoon, and I'm without my bonnet and scarf, but I'm so pleased to see Mary I hardly take notice.

"Mary, my goodness, you're truly here," I holler and pause to relish the moment. I delight in watching her eyes brighten with recognition as she spies Michael blazing toward her with open arms. My sister is here, thank God for it. Mary waves her right hand in the air and shouts back.

"Yes, and I thought the journey by carriage was rough, but this last bit tramping up an icy hill and whacking my way through brush, now that I didn't expect. Michael, oh my, get over here and give your Auntie a cuddle!"

"Hello, Aunt Mary, welcome to our farm," Michael says loudly. He spreads his arms out over the land, as if he's showing off his royal kingdom.

"Well, aren't you a little charmer, and look how big you've grown. The last time I saw you, you were no bigger than a toadstool, and now you're nearly as tall as me." Mary gives Michael a long embrace and then continues up the final incline to our little house.

"Wait till you see Jerry, he's nearly a man!" Michael says as he takes Mary's handbag and offers his arm. If only Florence could see his son acting as such a gentleman, he'd be pleased.

The anticipation is suddenly too much for me to bear so I run to my sister and wrap her in my arms. She's grown stouter since I'd last seen her, nearly one year ago, and it simply adds to the comforting embrace we share. She is here; she's come to me as I prayed she would. I've my lovely neighbors, my kind friends, and now I've my dear sister, I feel giddy with happiness.

"Oh Mary, it's so good to see you. Thank you for coming." I can hardly release her body, but Mary finally breaks the embrace and gazes at me.

"Ellen, you look thin as a rail, and as unkempt as a shaggy lion. I'm glad I'm here too. I've one inquiry, did Florence fail to notice there's no roadway to your new home?" Mary asks and turns to the overgrown hill she climbed. She burst out in a hoot of laughter.

I, too, regard the precarious rise Mary scaled, and then snicker at the absurdity of the site.

"Yes, he must've overlooked that slight detail." Even Michael senses our light moment; he laughs out loud as he escorts his Aunty to our front porch.

"Well now, I've nearly forgot my manners. Let me introduce you to Jack here," Mary says while catching her breath. "Jack's been a lovely coachman, as well as a good listener. I gabbed the whole way here about you, Ellen, and about James and Florence, in Virginia, and about your children, and my Emma. Jack, you must feel as if you know us already. I would've warned you about the final climb, but Ellen didn't mention it in her letter, and now I see why. Thank you for hauling my bags through the woods, and up the hill; I wouldn't have gotten here without you. I hope by the time you return for me, a proper road will be made. Now, how much do I owe you?"

As Mary settles the charge with her hired coachman, I see Jerry has come to the front door with Grace wrapped in a warm blanket. I give him a quick wink, and he smiles back, looking more relaxed than I've seen him in some time. He must've seen our light moment and is amused at hearing his forthright Aunty speak and counsel her coach driver. She warns him to tread carefully on the hill and reminds him to call on his mother, and be sure he replaces the shoes on his horses.

"Off you go then, Jack, I hope your journey back to North Hampton is a fair one."

"Thank you Madame Mitchell, it's been a pleasure assisting you. My best to your families. I do pray your brave husbands will return soon. Good- day."

We wave farewell as Coachman Jack trudges his way down the hill and out of sight. Mary turns back toward the house and I notice the red glow of the afternoon light is upon her face, highlighting her pretty features. She looks like one of the China dolls the Greenes' owned when I worked as their maidservant. Mary's cheeks are rosy, her nose perfectly round, and her deep blue eyes are wide and bright. Her hair is pinned neatly under her bonnet with only a few strands of stray hair blowing in the chilly breeze. We make our way to the porch and front door where Jerry remains, waiting for his turn to greet his Aunt Mary. Mary stops and looks up at Jerry, for he's a head taller than his stout Auntie.

"Jerry, is it you with baby girl? Oh my heavens look at you all grown and handsome too. Are you too old for a cuddle?" Mary leans forward, her hands on her round hips.

"No Ma'am, not yet," Jerry says as he walks toward Mary and passes Grace to me. Jerry leans into my sister's arms but I can see his face over her shoulder. He's wearing a look of relief, the same emotion I am feeling. He releases Mary and we all step inside the cozy house. Jerry has the fire blazing and he's thought to put the kettle on the rod. He's holding Mary's arm when he turns to her and says, "I'm happy you're here."

Now my irrepressible Michael adds, "Yes, and surely we'll receive twice as many letters from Virginia!" Mary nods, "Aye, that's true, Michael. Now before I snuggle the little one, I must find the Loo. Will you show me?" Mary is hopping from foot to foot. Michael finds this amusing, placing his hand across his mouth so his laughter won't be heard.

"Of course. It is just there," Jerry points his finger and Mary's eyes follow until she recognizes it. She nods. "Thank heavens there's a clear path to the loo because I'm getting desperate. I wouldn't want to soil my dress on the first day of our visit, now would I?" Mary gives a slight wink and we share a good laugh. Grace is beginning to get restless in my arms so I settle her on the rug next to Jerry. I lift Mary's hefty bag and purse and immediately drop them back down on the floor.

"Michael, will you please bring these bags into my room? They're far too heavy for me. How on earth did your Aunt manage, and what did she pack inside them?" I feel a warm, comforting feeling in my chest. It looks as if she's planning to stay for a nice, long visit. Michael obeys and mockingly appears burdened by the weight.

I begin preparing the tea and slicing the apple cake. When Michael returns he takes over for Jerry, playing a silly hiding game with Grace. I hear the two of them giggling together, what fun they have! Jerry comes to my side and assists with the afternoon tea. Just like his father, he is, always there to lend a hand without being asked. When my sister returns, I offer a brief tour of the house and we all sit together in front of the fire and catch up on each other's lives over this past year. Mary says her shop is faring well and that Emma is becoming one of the best dressmakers in Western Massachusetts. Her eyes light up as she speaks about her only daughter.

"She has a special passion for design and color. Her dresses are far better then anything I've ever made. She travels to Boston and even New York to locate the finest and newest material and fashion designs. I'm proud of her and James is relieved because ever since his folks passed away he's been debating whether or not to close the shop. You know James--he'd much prefer a store that sells hunting and gaming equipment. But now that Emma shows promise of taking over the business and making it even more profitable, we've abandoned plans to sell. Especially now that James has been drafted and our future is unpredictable." I nod my head in agreement.

"And your boarder Dana, how is she working out?" Mary dramatically places her hand on her heart and lowers her head. Michael and Jerry follow my sister's every movement, captivated by her emotional gestures.

"Well, our house is quite crowded and certainly more lively ever since Dana has moved in. She's a sweet young woman and a very good seamstress, but she's got troubles of her own and we're trying to lend a hand until she can get back on her feet." Michael and Jerry's eyes widen, willing my sister to go on.

"You see, Dana came to the shop a few week's past begging for work. She'd just arrived on a train from Hartford and said she'd never go back. I don't know all the details but Emma discovered that Dana is with-child with no man or family to help her. What was

I to do? The girl is Emma's age and in a terrible state. Thankfully, she is useful in the shop and she's made a nice companion to my daughter. Her baby is due in September and we're hoping she'll find a permanent place to rent by then." Mary finishes with a deep sigh. Michael's ears suddenly prick up.

"Aunt Mary, where's the lady's husband? Is he at war?" He reaches over to the table where his cake is resting, and takes a large bite. Grace is occupied with her rag dolls, lifting them, hugging them and then laying them down for a rest. Mary swallows her bit of cake with a loud gulp, and turns to Michael. "Well, you see …" Mary starts and I cut her off.

"Michael, it's not our business. Mary, you've always been generous with your home. I'll never forget the short time our family lived together with you. Dana is lucky to have found you and Emma." I swiftly change the subject so that Mary does not have to explain anymore to Michael. She is quite forthcoming with her words and he's far too young to understand this complicated situation.

"Michael, are you enjoying the cake? Would you like a sliver more?" Michael jumps up looking pleased.

"Aunt Mary, may I get you another piece as well?" Mary lifts her fork in the air, "Why not? Your mother is a brilliant baker. I've never had the patience for it and now a new, lovely bakery has opened just a half-mile from my house. I've no need to bake myself; I simply travel and buy treats without the work." Mary's eyebrows suddenly shoot to the top of her forehead. "Boys, I nearly forgot. I've brought presents with me. Michael, you serve another piece of this delightful cake, and I will find my gifts. Where'd my bag run off to?"

"I'll collect it Aunty," Jerry says and rises to put his plate in the washbin and walk to my room to retrieve Mary's bag.

Mary's eyes follow the boys, and she shakes her head as she smiles,

"Ellen, you've certainly trained these children properly. I must say I've never met boys as polite and thoughtful as yours." Jerry returns with the overloaded bag, "Ok, now. Ah, here is a new rag doll for Grace, Emma sewed the dress herself just last week." Grace recognizes her name and looks our way. Her grin widens as she greedily seizes the new doll, looks it over, and then gently places it in line with the other sleeping dolls. Mary reaches into one of her bags and pulls a large sack from it. "Jerry and Michael, I have a bow and arrow set for you that used to be your cousin Emma's. Have you ever used one?" The boys gasp as they reach for it, amazed at their gift. Michael looks to me. "Mother, look at this! May we give it a go?" He's completely forgotten his manners, talking to us with his mouth full of cake. I signal for him to swallow his food and try to give a positive outlook on this dangerous gift.

"Uh, I think you should have a lesson first. Maybe Daniel Sheehan has experience with this weapon," I say and feel a bit of anxiety as I examine the sharp point on the arrows. Mary speaks up immediately,

"Nonsense, Ellen, it's me who'll teach them. Boys, your Uncle James may have worked his whole life in the family dress shop, but he considers himself a sportsman. I knew from the very beginning that if I wanted to get his attention, and spend time with him, that I'd need to learn to hunt and use weapons. James was amused at my interest and soon taught me to string a proper bow and then to shoot straight. In my best day I could shoot an apple off your uncle's bald head! I learned to use a rifle too, but I was never proficient at shooting animals. I didn't have the heart for it. Your Uncle tried in earnest to interest Emma in hunting, he'd take her out into the woods every Sunday. Unfortunately, she was more delighted with gathering wild flowers and chasing butterflies. She showed no desire to work a bow and arrow-- or a rifle. That's why I thought you boys might enjoy this set; it's almost new."

I am stunned. "Oh my! "Mary, you never cease to astound me with your talents. I want you boys to wait until your Aunt gives you proper lessons before you remove those arrows from the pouch. No wonder your bag felt weighty, and your poor coachman had to cart it all the way up our steep hill! I hope you tipped him well."

Mary fires back, "Hill, you mean that miserable crag, don't you?" Mary throws her head back and laughs. I'm reminded of my childhood and the constant playful banter, the secrets we've shared, the heartening times we've experienced. I've been fortunate to have special relationships in my life, but none have surpassed the precious bond with my dear mother, my candid sister and my darling daughter, Grace. I suppose it's true that a sisterhood exists beyond the realm of our human world, and I feel certain that our souls will remain connected even in the afterlife. As my mind drifts back to our little front room, I see that the cake has been eaten, and that the boys are gathered around Mary, still enthralled with the bow and arrow set.

I begin tidying up and send the boys out to the barn to feed the chickens and check on the piglets. I've not had a moment to speak to my sister without constant breaks and questions, and I'd like to relax before the dinner preparations begin. The boys rise and thank my sister for her gift, then pull on their caps and coats.

When the boys have gone and Mary and I are alone at last, I sit down beside her while Grace plays with her dolls between us. Our conversation begins lightly, with news of each other's neighbors, our children's growth, and finally we touch on our husbands at war. James was drafted over a year ago, but Mary knows he wasn't upset with the news. In fact, she believes he was relieved that he would have a break from managing the dress shop. He is a dutiful son, but now he's been placed in the position of using his skills for hunting and strategy. Mary says the only regret James had about being drafted was leaving his two great loves. Although his absence has been difficult, Mary and Emma are managing all right, and James feels confident he will return home soon.

When it is my turn to confide in Mary I confess that I'm nearly at my breaking point because I fear that Florence will be killed and I'll be left to tend this farm and raise the children alone. I begin to weep, my tears coming fast. I place my head in my sister's lap. I cry for myself, and for the shameful resentment I feel at having Florence leave me again. I want to share my true feelings aloud about how livid I am, but words will not form in my mind. After my tears abate, I lift my head, and my sister looks at my face and pulls me close to hers. She wipes away the last of my hot tears. "Ellen, I think I know what you could use right now." I sniffle.

"You do, what is it?" Mary raises her hand in the air and slowly heaves herself off the rug.

"Sit there. I've brought you a gift," Mary says as she sifts through her handbag. She finally finds a present bound tight with rags and string. I rise to help, but she stops me and says to sit while she gets it prepared. I move to Florence's rocker and my aching eyes become mesmerized by the flicker of the fire. I feel drained but relieved to have released the turbulence inside me, and as I turn my eyes to the rug again, I smile inwardly as I regard Grace. She's silently fallen asleep on the rug, her dolls beneath her. Oh, my baby girl, you are good indeed. Mary turns from the cupboards and walks toward me.

"Here we are, Ellen. Two glasses of apple brandy made in North Hampton. Drink up, sister." Mary hands me a glass of the liquor and notices Grace snoring lightly on the rug. "Is Grace asleep right there on the floor? Oh my, Ellen, that's the sweetest sight I've seen in some time. Would you like me to move her or should we leave her be?"

"I think she looks content right there. Let's sit beside her and share the warmth of the fire. I move to the ground and Mary clamors beside me."

"Well, okay," Mary raises her glass and toasts, "To our husbands, our brave men of war. May they be a comfort to each other as we are for one another, and may they return in good health."

I clink my glass with Mary's and take a long sip of my Brandy. I haven't had spirits in a long time, and this is sweet, warm and comforting. I thank my sister for the perfect gift and slowly drain it over the next half hour while we chat. My spirits have been lifted and I choose not to discuss my animosity toward Florence. Mary's only just arrived and I've already displayed quite a bit of emotion. For now, I'll keep my inner-struggle to myself and hope that I find more comfort and confidence with Mary at my side.

When Grace wakes, my sister rises to attend to her as I begin warming her milk and heating the pork stew and cornbread I'd prepared early this morning. Old Josephine was slaughtered last week and we've a bounty of pork meals: ham, sausage and best of all, bacon. Mr. Sheenan and Mr. Rooney did the slaughtering, and they're still in the process of smoking and salting much of her good meat.

I'm gaily humming as I pour the soup into the large stockpot hanging above the fire, and half-listening to my sister whisper to Grace in a maternal, loving manner. Then suddenly I hear a knock at the door and jump back, startled by the loud sound in our tranquil house. I quickly compose myself, wipe my hands on a dishtowel, and walk to the door to greet our visitor. To my surprise it is Don Unger, the young soldier. He is wearing a matching cap and scarf, and his face looks handsome in the faint pink glow of the early evening. I'm sure the glass of apple brandy made me sound a bit more cheerful than the last time he was here delivering wood, but I can't help hide my surprise at his unexpected visit.

"Well, hello Don, welcome, please come in! What brings you here this late in the day?" Don casts his eyes to the ground and reaches a gloved hand into his jacket. He retrieves a letter and holds it out for me to take.

"Good evening, ma'am, I'm here to deliver a letter for you. My Daddy asked me to drop it by your place on my way to the Stickney's for a wood delivery. I'm afraid I can't stay and chat. I hope this letter finds your husband well," Don tips his cap and immediately turns and hurries off toward the thick woods. I holler a thank you to Don and close the door swiftly because the cold air is making me shiver.

"Mary!" I call, "I have received a letter from Florence. Come here with baby girl and feed her the bottle whilst I read it. Let's pour one more glass of Brandy and read the letter in private before the boys return from the barn."

Mary shouts from my room, "Alright, Ellen, I'm coming. I'm taking my time with your beautiful girl because she is smiling so brightly, reminding me of my Emma when she was an infant. I can't take my eyes from her and I'm afraid I'll put a pin through her tiny baby folds."

"I think she's taken with you as well, it's as if she instinctively understands we are sisters! Come, let us take our libations and sit by the fire and read this letter."

Florence Burke
March 4th, 1864
Camp of the 37th Regiment

My dear wife and children,

In earnest I have commenced the life of a soldier. The day after I sent my last letter we were ordered to pack for a march. Some of the boys here are pleased that we're drawing closer to the battlefields, but I am not. I've become accustomed to the daily routine of training, marching, cleaning, cooking and parading, but now it seems we are to put these skills to the test.

We left camp about 8 o'clock Saturday morning, each of us fully equipped with forty rounds of cartridge, a haversack filled with hard tack, pork and coffee, a canteen of water and a knapsack filled with clothing, a load for a horse. We were forced to march quick time eighteen miles to a place called James City where we bivouaced at night in an open lot. It is there that I slept under the stars, wondering if you or the boys were looking up at the same brilliant sky.

Sunday morning we marched again about 9 o'clock and advanced about 10 miles where we stayed on the South Bank of Robertson's River Hill until Tuesday evening, when we were ordered back to our old camp again. We only marched about a mile in the dark, in mud knee deep, and then we were ordered to bivouac on a hill in an open lot, mid a snowstorm. What a miserable night we passed in the mud and cold. It's times like these that send my spirits drooping, for I miss the warmth and comfort of my family beside me.

This morning we started at sunrise for our old quarters which we reached about dark after a horrid march of 25 miles, and such a jaded set of men were never before seen in the Army of the "sixth corps or any other corps" of the Potomac. The Sixth Corps is the one we belong to, and men who have been in the Army of the Potomac ever since the war began say it was the hardest they have yet seen. Strong, brave men from every Regiment in the Sixth Corps were seen played out and straggling the whole length of the march, but thank God I came through safe with the company, though a tired and weary man. I pray my fate is not to collapse on the side of the road or die of a simple affliction from a blister or infection. At present, I am in good health, so please don't fret.

On my arrival at camp I found a letter from you containing your well-known features and that of the children. Mingled tears of joy and sadness welled up to my eyes. Joy at seeing through the medium of a picture the features of those I hold so near and dear to my heart, but sadness to think they were not true nature itself, that they might speak to cheer my drooping spirits. But thanks be to God the sight of them, though mute, shall even be a beacon to urge me on to duty.

You say you killed the pig and hope I may yet get the chance at eating the ham. I hope the same for James...I think a good slice of ham with a few eggs would come in good play about this time. I am very glad to hear that Mary Mitchell is with you and I hope she will stay there with you until I get home. It's hard to believe little Emma is old enough to manage the dress shop on her own, but James says she's getting on fine. James is in good health and he's been encouraging to me on the long marches. I wish I had James's experience and confidence, for he is a true Union Army soldier and those who have fought beside him say he's one of our best. I hope to remain close to him when the time comes for us to engage in fighting.

I have just received another letter from you with five dollars in it and was very thankful for it but you need not send any more till I send for it. I forgot to say in my last letter that I never wrote to my father as I suggested I would. I can't summon the strength, and all that will come from my pen are harsh, vexed words. I wonder if you've heard from him; please let me know what he writes about my decision to volunteer. You wanted me to send five dollars to my parents, but I can't see it, and when I get paid I will send the money to you and you can do as you like but I am little thankful to them for the favors they've shown to me, or to you or to the children. You can use your own discretion about sending them anything.

I have written to John, but offered no explanation for my actions. I told him I enlisted and will hopefully complete my duty by September. I asked him to look out for you while I am gone, and to pray for my safe return. I hope he is not disappointed in me. Please let me know what he writes to you.

Tell Mr. Sheehan thank you for his help with the chicken coop and tools for the farm. I am hoping to have a little money when I get home so I may repay my neighbors and so we can have some comfort for a while. I will close by wishing you a good bye for this time and give my best love to the children and I will try to send a likeness in my next letter. Please write again soon.

From your true and affectionate husband,

Florence Burke

Chapter 22

Ellen Burke
March 1864
West Springfield, MA

"Are we ready, children? We must leave or we'll delay Mrs. Jenkins." I say and anxiously look around the house for any last candles to snuff or lanterns to turn down. The fire has dwindled from breakfast, and it looks safe to leave unattended. I place the wide screen in place and turn to my sister.

"Thank you for seeing to Grace. I think if we leave now we'll be on time to meet Mrs. Jenkin's carriage at the main road. You look lovely, Mary. Your bonnet and dress coat are stunning."

"Why thank you, Ellen. I suppose there are some benefits to working as a seamstress! Baby girl here is bundled and prepared to visit the house of the Lord. I've stowed a clean nappy and milk bottle in this basket in case she gets fussy during mass. I also filled a baby bottle with apple brandy for me in case the priest becomes long-winded!"

"Mary, you haven't?" I look to Mary and she waves her hand at me and breaks into a snorting laugh. The boys follow suit, and soon we're all walking out the front door with laughter in our wake. The morning is bright and crisp, but the ground appears to be covered in a thin layer of snow and ice that will be treacherous for our walk down the hill. I probably shouldn't have agreed to the invitation from Mrs. Jenkins, but I know Mary will be more comfortable travelling by carriage, and I desperately want to attend Sunday Mass.

I knew this morning would be trying even though I woke at the crack of dawn with Grace. She hasn't been sleeping well in her tiny closet. I know she misses my nightly cuddling and warmth, but Mary needs a place to sleep, and mine is our only available bed. I shall try her old crib at the end of my bed tonight, and see if it helps to settle her so she might sleep more soundly. Since the weather is not as severe, and the drafts are not as widespread in the house, I think she'll be alright sleeping in her crib. Michael's been pleading to have Grace sleep in the loft, but she's still too young to sleep the night with her big brothers. Also, I don't want to expose her to any sickness the boys may carry. I've done my best to keep her free from disease this winter, taking the extra precaution to wrap her tight at night and to boil water since many diseases in West Springfield seem to come from contaminated wells.

At last we depart and plod down the overgrown hillside towards the main road. Jerry is carrying Grace in his arms, I am toting a hamper filled with a warm sweet potato pie. Mary is holding a basket of Grace's necessities and has her arm intertwined with Michael's, trying to balance herself on the uneven, slippery path. I am pleased we allowed time enough so we could safely make our way to the meeting point.

I'm eager to attend Sunday worship with our fellow neighbors. We've not been to a service since the middle of December, and I feel desperate to hear words of comfort and strength. I also want to speak with townsfolk who have loved ones fighting for the Union Army in Virginia. I want to know what they hear and what news they've obtained on the state of the war.

Since receiving Florence's latest letter I've been feeling a terrible guilt at being cross with him. He is in imminent danger now, and I can sense a different tone, a new fear, an altered state of vulnerability. Florence is a brave man, but knowing he's soon to enter the battlefield can make even the most courageous man sick with fear. His prior letters were light -hearted and connected to matters here in West Springfield, but now, with his marching orders, Florence is forced to immerse himself into a soldier's life and expend his efforts on keeping himself alive. I'm amazed that he still manages to inquire about the state of our family, our friends, Mary and even Josephine, our deceased pig. I suppose thinking of life back home is one way to cope with the reality of being in a perilous war. I'm certain Florence is questioning his decision to join, his decision to put his life on the line for land, and I cannot let him lose heart. He needs his strength and will to defend himself and come back to me. I feel the anger and resentment drain from my body like a wet towel being constricted and wrung dry. With each step down the thick hill, I feel a weight vanishing from my shoulders, and a new energy surging into my heart, igniting, waiting to catch fire.

"Mother," Michael hollers, interrupting my secret thoughts. "I see Mrs. Jenkins--just there!" He releases Mary's arm and waves in their direction.

The horses come to a halt a few feet ahead of us. Mrs. Jenkins is driving the carriage and her children are tucked under the fine white canopy. I introduce Mary and then we make our way onto the back of the carriage. It's a fine way to travel since it's protected from the elements and the wooden seats are supported with thick cushions and bountiful pillows. We sit with the two Jenkins children, Madeline and Quinn, and my boys talk excitedly to them about Old Henry and the other animals.

Oh, my, we've made it. I exchange a smile with my sister. Mary seems pleased to be travelling in such a luxurious manner. I've always wondered how she manages to keep her sense of humor through times of trouble. I regard her now and recall the same look of contentment she wore when she announced that she was leaving Ireland for good, at just twenty years of age. I admire the fine woman she's become, but will always remember the strong-minded, rebellious young woman she was in Ireland.

When Mary announced her departure, my folks were shattered. They begged her to reconsider, offering to lighten her work on the farm so she could pursue other interests. Mary, however, would not relent. She said she was determined to follow her dreams in America because she felt stifled in Ireland. I listened to Mary's fervent rationalization, remaining quiet, for only I knew her true reason for leaving.

My sister had kept a secret relationship with a young man who was, unfortunately, a Protestant! Mary knew that my father would not approve of their union. We'd been raised in a strict Catholic household where no mention of any other religion, especially Protestant, would be tolerated. Although Mary and her beau were discreet, I knew something was stirring because my sister went missing on Saturday afternoons, and she'd commonly return home late from trips to the town center. I also noticed Mary was paying more attention to her appearance. As soon as her chores were completed she would shed her work dress in exchange for neat, pressed day dresses. Once or twice I even caught her sneaking out of the house in fancy church clothes.

The young man named Andrew courted Mary for nearly two years and I know she believed he would soon propose. Much to her regret, Andrew did not do so because he feared my father's reaction to his Protestant religious beliefs and he did not want to cause a rift in our family. He promptly ended the courtship. Mary was simply devastated.

Weeks passed and Mary tried convincing Andrew that God would bless true love of any faith, but Andrew would not bend and Mary could see their love was not as strong as she had imagined. Mary was angry and began to think how senseless it is to live in a country where religious beliefs are a dividing factor, and a union between them would never be tolerated, even though both are Christian. Mary made up her mind to leave heartbreak behind, to accept a maidservant position with a wealthy family emigrating to America, and to bid our family farewell. My Ma and Da were distraught, but they saw the determination in Mary's eyes. Tearfully they saw her off at the docks of Cobh. Mary promised she would keep in touch with our family, and she would send money when she was paid. I can recall the ache in my heart at watching my older sister sail away. However, I also remember thinking she was the bravest woman in the world.

Now, as we make our way to Sunday service, I look at my sister in her present state. She's made a good life here and it's in America where my sister finally found true love. She met James soon after her arrival and he assisted in finding her good-paying work in his dress shop. Mary began as apprentice and eventually progressed to the position of head seamstress. She quickly learned how to sew, tailor, create original patterns, and even use a foot-pedal sewing machine. She was also charming and witty, so James (and his entire family) soon fell in love with her, and she with him. James and Mary were married six months later, with only the groom's family in attendance. Still, Mary claims it was the happiest day of her life. I smile and think: only my sister Mary could twice fall for a Protestant. But, this time there was no uproar. This time Mary knew God was winking from Heaven and blessing this union. My thoughts are swiftly interrupted by Michael's inquiry.

"Mother, are we having our noontime meal here after church?" His eyes rise, hoping I answer yes. I turn and scan the faces of Mrs.

Jenkin's children, and then lock eyes with Michael again. All the children share the same bright look of anticipation.

"I believe the Jenkins are staying after, and we are travelling with them, so yes, we will take our meal here. I've made a sweet potato pie, I hope it's well received." Michael claps his hands together, his face shining with delight as he smiles from one child to another. I see Mary, too, is beaming and smacking her lips together.

"Oh, Ellen, I'm sure no woman in this town can cook a sweet potato pie like you. It smells delightful and it's making my belly rumble. How long does this Mass commonly last?" Michael snickers in amusement. I do not. I widen my eyes and raise one eyebrow. Mary quickly reads my body language and nods her head in my direction.

"Of course the reason we are here at church is to pray to God to look after your Uncle James and your Father, and to thank Him for our daily gifts and for bringing us together. The meal afterward is simply a nice way of connecting town folk, and I look forward to meeting your family friends." Michael's face turns crimson, trying to hold back his laughter. In the light of the carriage window his freckles stand out, making his face look like he's been sprinkled with cinnamon.

"Of course, Aunty Mary, same with me." His mouth forms a devilish smile and he giggles again into his scarf. Everyone shares the lighthearted moment and suddenly we feel the horses slow to a trot and then come to a complete stop.

As we gather our things and make our way out of the carriage, I feel a sudden longing for Florence. This is the first time we've gone to church without him, and I feel troubled, like something's gone missing. I must try to keep my head raised and be thankful that we are here this morning. Mrs. Jenkins ties her horses to an iron ring attached to the granite posts, and joins us under an oak tree.

"Oh, my, we made good time, we are early. Thank you, Ellen, for giving us reason to make haste this morning, and allowing us to arrive before the first reading." I offer Mary a little wink knowing how difficult it had been to get prepared in time, and all the time Mrs. Jenkins was feeling the same way. Suddenly Michael is tugging at my cape. "Mother, I see Little Dan over there. May I go say hello before mass?" A moment later Madeline is jumping in her pink woolen coat, asking if she too, can talk with a friend a bit before the church service begins. Mrs. Jenkins and I decide that all the children may see their friends as long as they safely place the baked goods in the rectory and come to find us after the first sound of the bells.

Mary, Mrs. Jenkins and I remain outside. Grace will have to sit still long enough during the mass, so now its best to have her observe all the hustle and bustle of folks arriving to church. Mrs. Jenkins begins talking about the upcoming spring planting and how her land is prepared for it. She says she's ahead of schedule because she's hired four new farmhands. She squints into the morning sun and lines around her eyes deepen. Her face softens for a moment as she addresses me.

"Ellen, how's your land coming? Have you worked out what you plan to grow?" I pause a moment before answering. My land isn't nearly prepared; we have only three rows cleared and we're not even certain what we should plant and which crops will reap the most profit. I must find out the cost of seedlings because I still long to own a cow for milk and dairy products. I bite my lower lip and wish that Florence would return my letter with advice on planting. For now, I'm a bit puzzled. I finally manage to respond,

"The children and I have made illustrated plans on how we'd like to use the land, we just need to be sure it's within our budget and meets Florence's approval. I believe the soil to be fair; I've tried in earnest to describe the land to Florence so he may advise us on plantings and fertilizing. He's the real farmer you know, and the boys are eager to do as their father wishes."

"I see, good for you Ellen. Mary, I hear your family owns a dress shop! I have recently purchased some fabric from the Mercantile and would love your opinion on its merit. Well, now, look who's coming this way, its Daniel Sheehan." Mrs. Jenkins takes a step backward and allows Daniel a place in our little circle. I look over Grace's wool hat and try to see Lara in the crowd of the congregation now gathering at the steps of the church. I can't find her so I turn my attention to Daniel.

"Good morning, how are you?" He wears a tight grin but takes a moment to properly greet Mary and Mr. Jenkins before responding to me. He looks massive in his wool dress coat and cap, his large square jaw twitching as he bends down to offer a welcome kiss to us. When he is finished with the formalities Daniel's eyes dance between us as he raises his hands.

"I am well, thank you. It's so good to see you all and I'm pleased you've made it to church this morning." Before I could inquire about Lara and the baby, Daniel speaks up, "Lara wanted to come this morning but she's been feeling a little off and is planning to rest while little Fiona naps this morning. Oh, Ellen, before I forget. The reason I came straight to see you is that I have a letter for you from Florence. I intended to bring it by this afternoon, but here you are, and I've the letter right here in my coat pocket," Daniel places his large hand into his coat pocket and retrieves it. I gasp with delight.

"Thank you for collecting this letter from the Post, Daniel. Please give my best to Lara and tell her I will call on her later this week if she's feeling better." I glance at the letter and squeeze it tightly to my chest. Mary notices this gesture and pulls me to one side.

"Ellen, go there behind the carriage and read your letter before church. The boys will be eager to see it later, but go on and read it in peace. I'll take Grace and Mrs. Jenkins can carry this here basket. Do you mind?" Mrs. Jenkins nods her head swiftly. I survey the faces before me.

"Really? Okay, thanks." I feel myself shaking with anticipation, much like I recall feeling on Christmas morning. I so want to hear news from Florence.

Mrs. Jenkins takes her pale pink glove and shoo's me like a pesky dog.

"Go on, Ellen. We'll meet you inside with the children. You only have a few minutes before the bells rings, so hurry." I dash off to the carriage and find a sheltered place to open my letter.

Florence Burke
March 6th, 1864
Camp of 37th Regiment

My Dear wife,

Your kind letter came to me in due season and I was overjoyed to receive it. I am sitting on a cold log at present, tending to the fire as I write this letter to you. Most of the boys have retreated to their tents, played out, hungry and overtired from our late raid last evening. I believe our Calvary succeeded in doing a good deal of damage. They burned three large mills filled with grain, blew up six cannons belonging to the rebels, tore up several miles of rail road track, captured five hundred horses, took about fifty prisoners and nearly a hundred niggers and returned to camp without loss to our side. As a farmer, it troubles me to see the destruction of land and feed, and as a son of God it agonies me to witness the pain in a man's face when he is captured or wounded. I must bear these trials however, because war is strategic, and destroying the rebel's vital supplies, tearing up their transportation and stealing men lessens their ability to counterattack and gives us room to push forward. I hope to God that this tactic is being used in all Union Army regiments so this cruel war will be won before too long.

I dreamt of you last night and thought I was home and we were together with Mary Mitchell. We were taking a sociable glass of beer together. But, I woke to find myself still on the sacred soil of Old Virginia. I hope on receipt of this you will avail yourselves of the opportunity of drinking to my health in a good old beer.

How are my lovely children? Is the baby creeping yet and are Jerry and Michael working hard on the farm? From your detailed description of the land, it seems we have a good chance of turning a profit this first growing season. I want you to not plant any more than you can manure well and not plough deep. The upper field seems a good spot for potatoes, corn and turnips, and the lower right field seems fit for lettuce, cucumbers, carrots and those sorts of vegetables. Behind the barn is a good place for your own crops; find good prices on seedling and plant what you will need for cooking. Let the rest of the land lay idle till I get home. It seems you've been making the land ready, and I imagine the three of you, with baby Grace on your back, tilling and plowing the land in the red glare of the early morning sun. My eyes have just begun to fill with tears wishing I could be with you to take the plough off your shoulders and place the straps over my own. Ellen, I am sorry I've left this burden with you; my heart aches knowing I am here and not at home with you. The one great hope is that I survive this war, then we'll have years together to grow our farm and watch the children blossom as well.

I had my picture taken which I will send you today. It is rather dark but I suppose you will know it and appreciate it according to its merit.

I will close by bidding you a good-bye for this time and receive this in love and kindness to yourself and the children and all that inquire for me. From your true husband, Florence Burke

I am all out of postage stamps and can't get them here. Please send a few in your next letter.

Yours Faithfully,

Florence Burke

Chapter 23

Ellen Burke
March 1864
West Springfield, MA

"Good morning, Liam." I step through his heavy door and the raw wind comes with me. I heave the door shut and brush the soft snowflakes from my bonnet and cape. Immediately I am assaulted with the pungent odor of slaughter, animal hide and fresh meat. I try to ignore it, for it is the butcher's chicken parts that make our stews and soups hearty and delicious. I see Liam behind a huge hanging carcass, his red hair is thinning at the top, but his build's not been altered since I've known him these past sixteen years. He's six feet tall, strong as an ox, with wide shoulders and protruding muscles on his arms and legs. His head is enormous, like that of a giant's. Most of it is forehead, and below that are his round blue eyes and his bulbous, circular nose. Only his lips are thin and pale, making him look like a jack-o lantern with a smile. Liam pokes his prominent nose around the hanging meat, his whole face brightening as he greets me.

"Good day to you, Mrs. Burke." Liam searches the area behind me. "Where are your children?" He rakes his hands across his stained apron and examines them. I wish he'd wash them in the basin, but I suppose they'll just get soiled again with the next patron. I turn my attention back to him.

"They're home with my sister Mary. She's come from North Hampton to stay with me for a spell. Her husband is fighting in Virginia with Florence as well, and we've decided to band together while we wait for them to return." He nods his head, then tilts it to one side.

"Aye, what do you hear from Florence? How is he getting on?" Before I reply Liam turns and faces the wall where I notice he's hung a picture of a Union soldier on a rusty nail. "This is my nephew Benjamin who's been in Georgia fighting for six months. He seemed to be getting on all right but we haven't heard from him in two weeks and we are scared he may be dead or taken prisoner." Liam takes a few steps towards the picture and traces his hand on the outside of the frame. I am frightened by his news, my body suddenly has gone stone cold. I reply nippier than I intended.

"I'm sorry, Liam. I pray you will hear from him soon. Florence seems to be fairing well, his Brigade has yet to lose any men and I am thankful for it." I'm shivering with dread now, and the putrid smell of dead animal is sickening me.

"Have you any spare chicken parts today? I've no biscuits to trade, but I have twelve fresh eggs. If you'd prefer, I can make the trade at the Mercantile and bring you cash." He offers his hands for the basket.

"The eggs will do just fine. Let me get the parts I've saved just for you, Ellen." He smiles and his eyes reveal the generosity and friendship we've always shared. Now with the common fear of losing those we love in battle, we are bonded as we pray to God that the men will return to us. Before Liam retreats to the ice shed, I remember one more inquiry I have for him.

"Thank you. I was wondering if you know of anyone in town who would be interested in trading my good hay for a cow?" He rubs his chin a moment, and to my horror, he leaves behind brick-red residue. The smear on his face is more than I can bear and I turn away for a moment and stifle the heaving of my stomach.

Suddenly the door opens and an older man enters, his heavy boots echoing in the silent shop. Liam greets him warmly as I try to compose myself. "Hello there, Blaine. I'll be with you in a moment." Liam looks in my direction. "I'll collect your chicken parts while I think about the hay you want to trade." I cannot shake the bilious feeling in my stomach and know I need to find fresh air or I will surely lose my breakfast. I take a few steps to the door and brush against the old man whose hollow eyes bear down on me.

"Pardon me sir, I, I must leave. Please tell Liam I'll return shortly."

The old man tips his hat and then just as I am reaching the heavy door he lunges forward in front of me and shoves it ajar. I am surprised by his nimbleness, especially when I get a good look at his bony face covered cheek to cheek with gray stubble. He smiles and I see that he has several teeth missing which causes his upper lip to curve inward. He shakes his head and thin wisps of silver hair are tossed about.

"Yer pardoned ma'am, but I couldn't help but overhear you might be fixin' to sell yer hay. My son is lookin' fer hay, he has been fer some time. May I ask how much you got and how much yer thinkin' of selling it fer? Oh, I've forgotten my manners. My name is Blaine Elden." Blaine stretches his veiny hand towards mine and I pause a moment before accepting it. I don't want to be compelled to entertain a trade with this man especially since I have yet to work out how much my hay is worth and how much I should trade for a cow. I finally decide the best path to take is to stall. I bow my head instead of taking his hand and tell him I am not prepared to sell or trade the hay at present because I am determining how much I will need myself. I mumble a good day as I swiftly step through the open doorway and out into the cold, cloudy day.

Despite the overcast conditions, it feels refreshing to be outside, to breath in the fresh air and to smell the dew shimmering on the grass and stones. I'm trying to shake off the vile sights at the butcher, but what did I expect? It is a butcher shop after all. As I walk along the sidewalk passing the shops lined on my left, my mind starts to replay the encounter with Mr. Elden. I can't put a finger on it but I think it was something in that old man's eyes that's unnerved me. He was brash and a bit dishonest looking, but he did no harm other than overhear my conversation with Liam and inquire about my hay. Still, I certainly hope I did not raise his expectations of acquiring my hay.

I must ask Mrs. Jenkins how much hay I should trade. For a girl who's lived her whole life on a farm, I should be more knowledgeable about prices for farm items. I am humbled by this experience and will continue forward with a more clever approach. I will make lists and have prices, and sell items and plant crops. Dear Mother, I reflect as I sink my hand into my coat pocket and grasp my comforting handkerchief. I have so much to think about in establishing this farm, and all my thoughts are consumed with the safety and well being of my husband at war, and my family here at home. Please help me as I try to manage on my own. Thank you.

"Look out there, young lady!" I jump back as I see a man hauling several large buckets on a wide, wooden pole on his shoulders. I nearly got knocked down by one of the buckets swaying in the wind. How did I not see him? Oh, dear, he looks cross.

"So sorry!" I stand off to one side as he makes his way by me mumbling to himself that folks should mind their way. My heart is beating quickly now. To avoid being struck on the head by maple syrup buckets or any other item, I concentrate on walking and temporarily hush my inner thoughts. Two steps later I think I hear my name.

"Ellen, is that you?" I turn and see Daniel Sheehan coming from the direction of the Mercantile. "Did you almost get clobbered by the bucket? You're walking like you have your head in the clouds!" I feel my cheeks turning hot as I look up at Daniel's face. He's regarding me with a serious stare and his hands on his hips, making me feel like a little girl being scolded by her strict father. I try to brighten the mood.

"Yes, hello Daniel. What a pity you had to see my near collision with the maple, but I've got my wits about me now, I trust. Hard to believe it's already time to tap the old maple trees. isn't it?" I quickly change the subject. "Tell me, how is Lara and little Fiona?" Daniel shakes his head and I see his face breaking into a smile. He lowers his head to the ground and drags his boot across the stones, making a grinding noise against the cobblestone. He seems to be thinking. Finally he turns his full face to me.

"Ah, you know, the baby is keeping her up at night and wearing her down, but it is expected with a new little one, right? I've inquired with the doctor here and he's prescribed some medicine to help her along. Are you heading home now, may I join you?"

"No, I still have more items to attend to. I'll see if I can get a lift with Matthew Rooney if he's working at the Town Hall today; if not, I'll walk. Having Mary here to watch the children is a blessing. It's much easier to get my errands done without hauling Grace around. I think Lara would feel the same." Daniel nods and suddenly his eyebrows rise and his eyes widen. His face becomes animated as he speaks,

"Oh, Ellen, did you hear that Don Unger is to be wed? Remember the O'Connor girl, the one he was courting before he enlisted? I spoke to Jacob just yesterday. He told me his heart is torn because he's pleased for the wedding, but Don wants a speedy ceremony so he might rejoin his regiment for another tour of duty." I gasp and feel the blood draining from my face. After I allow a few moments for the shocking news to sink in, I turn to Daniel.

"Why would he re-enlist when he's just returned?" Daniel gestures with his shoulders, lifting them to his chin, and sinking them back down.

"Jacob didn't say. He and Amy are as stunned as we are. He only said Don's been having a hard time adjusting to civilian life. He's been having night terrors and feels he needs to be back with his Regiment." The news of a young man volunteering to go to war for a second time makes me immediately think of the women he will leave behind. I feel so sorry for Amy and his fiancé.

"The war is gobbling up the good men from our town, Daniel, and I wish to hell it would end. I, I…" My voice wavers and I feel tears threatening to spill from my eyes. I avert my eyes from Daniel and lower them to the ground. I hear him heave a loud sigh and then I feel his large arm around me. He tucks his head down and whispers into my ear, telling me it will be all right, and that Florence will return safe, like Don. I accept the comfort of my dear friend, but only momentarily for I don't want to be seen blubbering about in town. Daniel and I part, he heading home and I off to the Town Hall to find Matthew Rooney. I hope to finally settle this matter with the deed. We have had several cancelled meetings with the councilmen, one emergency absence by Mr. Parsons and at least two delays by Mr. Day's lawyers. Matthew and I will not tolerate this any longer. He's told me to bring Florence's trade agreement to town and we will both approach Mr. Day and Mr. Parsons. If we're not given a deed then we will go to the newspaper and have them print Matthew's letter on unfair deals the Town officials are giving to Irish Immigrants. I only wish I had communicated to Matthew that I would be coming today. Well, I suppose it's a chance I must take.

I climb the many granite steps and open the large, wooden door. I'm momentarily blinded by the dark inside, as I haven't realized how bright the afternoon has turned. When my eyes finally adjust to the darker interior I search around the building for the library where Matthew volunteers on those days he's in town. It shouldn't be too hard to find a room with stacks of books. I make my way to the end of the hall and find a receptionist sitting in the foyer. Behind her is a vast room with dark wooden tables. This must be it. I inquire about Matthew, and to my disappointment, he is not working on this day. I thank her and turn toward the exit, wondering to myself if my family now has access to this library because we are landowners. What else might be available to us now? I have never considered the benefits of Florence's trade because I've been so consumed with anger and resentment. I see now that besides owning our own farm, Florence was trying to improve the lives of our children. With the deed comes entitlement, to many benefits still unknown to me, and my dear husband made them possible. I feel a surge of heat in my chest, rising to my face, threatening to spill down my cheeks. I choke them back, realizing I must finish my errands and walk home before the day escapes me.

As I make my way out of the Town Hall and into the chilly day, I remember I must stop at the Postmaster's to mail a letter to Florence for the boys, and a letter to James from Mary. I also want to send stamps in the boys' letter, so I hurry across the street and hear the chime of a clock when I enter the small office. I check the time and see that it is 3p.m. I have been gone for hours! I must finish my business here in town and return home. I hope this will not take too long. I gaze around and notice three unfamiliar patrons waiting in the queue if front of me, and one feeble man entering through the doorway. He takes his place behind me and soon I can feel his stare boring into my back. It's not long before he addresses me.

"Excuse me Ma'am, ain't you the lady selling the hay?" I don't want to start another conversation with this man, and I've already told him I'm not ready to sell. I wonder for a second if he isn't following me? I hope it is a mere coincidence that we both have errands at the same places. Turning ever so slightly toward him, I murmur, "Not now, sorry." I realize I should have chosen better words because he immediately asked if his son could come out to my place and have a look at the hay because he's been looking everywhere to get good hay. He was rambling on how his son needs it for his cattle farm, and that he'd come with a carriage to haul it. Finally, I could not bear to hear this aged man beg any longer. I turn around and look into his bloodshot eyes. "I'm sorry, sir. I spoke the truth earlier when I said I am just beginning to take inventory of my farm needs and I want to discuss any deal with my manager. I'm sorry I cannot help your son, but please respect my position." I hear the low ting of a bell and to my delight I see the Postmaster waiting for me to come forward. "Oh, it looks like I am next, good day, sir." I walk briskly to the counter to buy stamps and mail my letters. After I pay Mr. Shurman, the Post Master, he holds up his index finger indicating me to wait, and he returns with a letter from Florence! I eagerly grasp the letter and thank Mr. Shurman. When I raise my head from the letter I notice Mr. Elden is still regarding me. His eyes travel over me in a way that leaves me unsettled.

I quickly exit the building and make my way to collect my chicken from Liam's Butcher Shop. I want to get as far away from that strange man as I can. I am sure he would not have the gall to follow me home, but the sun is beginning its afternoon descent and I am unnerved by his boldness. I wouldn't sell cow dung to that crass man, or his son for that matter. My mood is lighter now that I have a letter in my possession. I swiftly return to the butcher Shop and collect my chicken parts and find the main road out of town. I can't help but turn back a few times, but fortunately I see no one following me. I do, however, notice that the weather is turning. The wind has picked up, the sky is several shades darker, and the sun is casting an orange-red glow just over the tips of the trees. I cannot walk faster, but at least I have my shawl for cover if it rains. I suddenly feel a tug in my lower back and realize I have aggravated my back. I take smaller steps and toss the bag with the chicken parts over my shoulders. This walk usually takes forty-five minutes in fine weather, but with my sore back and heavy load, it will be much longer. I should have left town earlier! Just then I hear hooves coming toward me from behind. I step to the side of the road and notice the horse and buggy is halting to the left. I feel paralyzed in my position, not sure what to do or if I am even capable of running. When I finally get a look at the driver I see that it is Jacob Unger. I release the tension in my shoulders, and breathe a sigh of relief. I certainly gave myself a fright! I shake my head and smile toward the moving carriage. Jacob calls his horses to a halt and looks over the reigns.

"Afternoon, Ellen. What are you doing out here so late? Let me give you a lift home." He jumps from his seat and insists that I come with him. I consent to the ride knowing how fortunate I am that my neighbor is going in my direction. Jacob takes my heavy sack and places it on the wide seat and then offers a lift as I struggle onto the large step of the carriage. When I am safely aboard Jacob comes around the side and hops back up. We are off. He clicks his tongue to propel the horses just as cold rain falls from the heavily bloated clouds. I take my shawl from my shoulders and carefully wrap it over my bonnet. My hands are turning white and I wish I'd thought to pack my woolen mittens. Jacob and I ride in silence for most of the trip, but as we near my hill I feel compelled to inquire about Jacob's son Don. I begin as politely and as positively as I can muster.

"Jacob, I've heard that Don is to be married, is this true?" The wind is blowing the icy rain straight into our faces now. I duck my head and Jacob pulls his cap further down on his forehead. He's looking straight ahead but I see the strain in his face, the worry lines on his left cheek. His face contorts even more the moment before he speaks.

"Yes, it's true. Have you also heard that he's set on going back to Virginia to join his Regiment?" Jacob looks in my direction and I nod in assent. "Amy and I are shattered. We don't understand why he'd go back again. He loves Kristin, and we hoped he would rise out of his gloom after he proposed, but he hasn't. I think he feels shamed at leaving his fellow soldiers, especially now that the spring campaign has begun. That's probably why he acts so odd around you, Ellen. He feels he should be in Virginia fighting alongside brave men such as Florence." Jacob squints his eyes at the dirt road ahead. It may be he's attempting to block the rain pellets, or perhaps the dim light hinders his view, but I believe he may be squinting to keep his tears at bay. Poor man. I take his arm and give him a gentle pat.

"I know how you feel. I too, struggle to understand how Florence could enlist and leave us. However, as time wears on I'm discovering his intentions were indeed to benefit our children, and nothing less. I'm sure Don has his own good reasons for re-joining. He'll be of no good use here if he doesn't see this through. I know it's terribly painful for you and Amy, and of course for his fiancé Kristin, but some things just must be." I hear my voice tremble, and I pause. Jacob brings the horses to a halt and places his gloved hand over mine.

"Aye, Thank you Ellen. Let's hope Lincoln's new commander Grant will succeed in overcoming the Confederates. He's a proven leader, taking hold of the Mississippi River a year back. He's the main reason Don wants to rejoin, but it troubles me because Grant's aggressive approach will surely produce heavy casualties." A cold shiver travels down my spine. I rise, unsteadily as Jacob comes around to help me climb down. He collects my chicken parts and offers to walk with me through the thick path, but I insist I am rested and can manage on my own.

However, the rain is adding a layer of gray to the shadowy sky, and it makes the thick path darker and eerier. I rush through it, tripping occasionally and catching my hood on an odd pricker bush. As I reach the crest of the hill I spot Michael exiting the barn. I wait until he sees me, then I wave my free hand in the air. He immediately stops and waves back, his cap and scarf blowing in the wind. Suddenly Michael begins sprinting towards me and I see he is carrying a basket of eggs.

"Michael!" I holler, "slow down, my love. You don't want to crack a single one of those brilliant eggs." Michael doesn't hear me over the wet wind. It doesn't matter because he's soon at my side, his cheeks bright, his freckles pronounced, and his eyes glimmering in the last of the day's pink light. Before I can give him a cuddle, he's already spilling out the day's news.

"We've had a good day here on the farm, Mother. Aunt Mary's been telling stories of when you and she were little, and you sound like you were a pesky little sister. Oh, and Aunty Mary burnt our noontime meal." Michael's giggling so hard he has to take a break. I place my hand on the small of his back and lead him in the direction of our home.

"Thankfully, Jerry made us ham sandwiches." He continues, "Aunty Mary is a keen seamstress but a very poor cook." Michel slaps his knee again, having a good laugh. I agree. I inquire about Grace and ask if the other chores were completed. Michael lists the many items they've looked after in my absence and when we finally make it to our front door, he seems out of breath. Suddenly the door flies open and Jerry is standing there, eyebrows raised, his hair in its usual state of disarray. He looks past me to the dark- grey sky and lowers his head.

"We've been worried about you, Mother, what's delayed you?" Before I can respond he comes to me with a timid hug, and takes the chicken from my cold hands. He must have been concerned because he's looking at me with narrow, bird-like eyes. Poor Jerry, he's such a love. I am weary and still need to make my chicken soup, but first I need to lift his spirits.

"Jerry, you needn't fret over me. You know I'm not a speedy traveller and I had many items to attend to. Collect the large pot and fill it a quarter full with water. Michael, find Aunt Mary and Grace and we'll gather around the fire and read Father's new letter!" Jerry responds immediately.

"Yes, straightaway."

Michael turns to me, a wide smile emerging on his little face.

"But Mother, baby Grace is sleeping and Aunt Mary has gone to the loo!" He explodes in yet another fit of laughter.

John Burke
March 1864
New York, New York

My Dearest Ellen,

I received yours of the 7th yesterday. Bridget and I are thankful for your quick reply. A few days back I received a letter from Florence but it was brief and vague. I have written to the West Springfield recruitment officer and he responded with what I expected; that Florence indeed collected commutation pay, the most horrid part of Lincoln's Draft law, to earn money for his land. I cannot say how disappointed I am in hearing this. I only hope the man he traded with is a good man, worthy of the gift of security and freedom.

You asked for my opinion on the war. I am conflicted with my feelings at the moment. At the start those of us in Tammany Hall were in favor of the war to preserve the Union. We hoped it would create work and new opportunities for the Irish immigrants, and at the very least, we expected that the Irishmen who volunteered to join the Union Army would gain respect from American servicemen.

But now Lincoln has changed the intention of the war; he says we're fighting for Emancipation. Well I can tell you that New York is divided, and not in favor of the war. The wealthy republicans want to keep their slaves and the Irish Immigrants fear they will lose work to the freed blacks. Tensions have been high ever since the bloody draft riots, for the Irish and other immigrants refuse to be degraded by any man, black or white.

My dear Ellen this is precisely why I am so tormented by Florence's trade. It's everything I am fighting against! The Government is sparing the rich and prominent and thereby insinuating that the lives of immigrants and the poor are unimportant. How dare they pass judgment on a human life? It disgusts me. I walk with a cane now since my injury in the draft riots, but I believe I walk taller than most of the filthy rich bastards in this city.

I'm sorry to take such a hard stance on this issue, Ellen, It's just that it is so near to my heart. But I suppose what is done is done and I must accept it. I only wish Florence had talked to me first because I would have counseled him in a different direction. I know he's tried to procure a loan, and find extra work in town, and that failed, so he must have thought this was his only choice. It seems a desperate one and I feel for you and the children. Please know that you have the full support of Bridget and me in New York, and if you need something, please ask.

I've some news, Ellen. Bridget stands beside me as I deliver it to you. Bridget is with- child once again, and we are to have a new baby in October! She's not been well, but it doesn't seem to affect her spirits. We hope, by the grace of God, that Florence will return home, and you can bring your children here to meet their little cousins. It's long overdue. Please tell Michael and Jerry to be brave.

Your Affectionate Brother-in Law,

Jonathon Burke

Chapter 24

Ellen Burke Late
March 1864
West Springfield, MA

"The ceremony was brilliant! The bride was lovely, perhaps a bit too slight, but what a handsome couple they make," Mary remarks as we exit the church. The cold air feels invigorating and despite the low temperature the sun is shining down, as if putting a veil of happiness over the union. Mary's correct, the ceremony was perfect, and I nod and put my arm around her as we walk to the carriages. However, I can't help but notice there is a lingering sense of melancholy in the air, probably because I know that the bride will not be united with her husband for long. Don, dressed in his full Union Army uniform, will be leaving for Virginia in two day's time. My heart is heavy thinking of Jacob and Amy Unger, what a pity to see their only son leave for war once again. I can't help but wonder how handsome and strong Florence must look in his blue jacket, polished buttons, and Union Army cap. Although I have received a dark photo of his likeness, it would be wonderful to see him in plain sight.

As we search for Edward Fitzgerald's carriage, I pause a moment to take a deep breath of air. Even out of the church, away from the crowd of guests I feel constricted. I know the homespun corset Mary made for me is not helping matters. I feel uncomfortable and long to remove it. However, I could never complain after Mary spent two weeks designing, sewing and hemming these fine dresses. Since I have not worn such elaborate attire since my days of working parties at the Greene's Estate, I have forgotten just how difficult it is to move and breathe in them. As if sensing my discomfort, Mary turns to me.

"Ellen, you're looking a bit pale, are you alright?" Mary's eyebrows rise above her wired rims. She looks lovely in her sky-blue dress and matching bonnet. Her face is glowing and the pretty features of her eyes and cheekbones are accentuated by the make up she's brought from North Hampton. Mary smeared some on me as well, but I wiped off most of it because I thought it made me look too harsh. But I can see that Mary is in good spirits. We've not been away from the farm very often, so I want to be sure we enjoy this special occasion. I pull her arm close and whisper into her ear.

"I am just fine. I haven't owned a fashionable dress for some time you know, so the corset, and wide crinoline takes some getting used to! Thank you for making me this lovely dress, Mary, I hope we can both wear them again when our husbands return from war."

Mary smiles and her eyes glimmer in the sunlight. "Come now, I'll loosen your corset at the reception. I must say I did some fine work on your dress. I am pleased with the silk material I found at the Mercantile and the color is brilliant with your ginger hair. I knew there was still a beautiful, young woman in there somewhere, I just needed to brush the dust off." Mary tilts her hooded head to the cloudless sky and lets out a deep belly laugh. It's true that I am feeling comely for the first time since Florence left. I am not sure if folks will recognize me at the reception! My dress is truly fashionable, tight in the waist and wide at the bottom. I had to beg Mary to adjust the neckline twice because she made it so low that I blushed in the mirror. She complained, stating that short sleeves and low necklines were the fashion, however I told her that it was not necessarily the case here in West Springfield, and I would not wear the dress without a shawl. She relented on my dress but made hers so low it caused Michael to gasp and ask if her bosom would freeze.

As I think of the children, I wonder if they're getting on with Catherine Fitzgerald. She offered to watch the children for me since she's feeling better now that she's entered into her second trimester of pregnancy. Edward hardly lets Catherine leave the house, but she reasoned with him, explaining that she needs practice tending to a baby, and the older boys can help with the tough bits. Edward finally gave in and offered to be our escort for the wedding.

We meet him at his carriage and he tucks us in for the ride to the Ungers' place. Mary and I enjoy the royal treatment, looking out the window, passing familiar homes and farms, basking in the comfortable carriage. Mary removes her crocheted gloves and lifts her head to look at me.

"Ellen, did you notice only one other woman had a looped overskirt at the bottom of her dress?" She tilts her head to the side, as if framing the dress in her mind.

I purse my lips together for a moment, trying to follow Mary's train of thought.

"Mary, I'm afraid I don't understand what you are asking. Are you referring to the tailoring of the dresses? Remember, I am a farmer's wife, not a seamstress or even fashion-minded," I laugh, and wave my gloved hand back and forth. Mary sits up straighter, no longer interested in the outdoor view and gestures with her hands on her dress.

"I am speaking about the dresses I saw worn today by the women of West Springfield. Did you notice most of them were solid in color, some with brilliant hues, but their colors were uniform straight down to the bottom hemline? Well, we had a young girl from Italy named Gianna working at the shop in North Hampton for a time. She taught the European trend of looping the overskirt here, and there, and in several places around the bottom, thus revealing another matching or contrasting color underneath! This makes the dress far more interesting and unique, don't you think? I noticed only one woman wore a dress of this style and I wondered where she bought it." Mary crosses her arms, and her eyebrows lower, reminding me of a crusty old judge. I feel the carriage coming to a halt, and before Edward opens our door, I speak to Mary, telling her if anyone can find out where the dress came from, she can. I also whisper to please be mindful of her low cut dress because surely the priest will be here at the reception. Mary lets out a shriek of laughter and waves her hand as if shooing me away. Suddenly Edward opens the small door and places his handsome face into the carriage.

"Hello there, ladies, it sounds as if the celebration has already begun, I am pleased you're enjoying yourselves. I trust the journey was a fair one? May I help you down and escort you to the reception?" Mary and I exchange smiles and carefully make our way out of the carriage. The sun's now falling, but it's casting the most brilliant light upon the town in the clearing way off in the distance. I can see the church steeple, the white roof of the Town Hall, and the copper weathervane on the mill. The three of us pause a moment to take in the view.

I've never been to the Unger's house or been this far from town, and it's lovely. Jacob seems to have done well in the sale of his sawmill last year. I am not surprised to see how grand and new their house is here on top of the steep hillside. I turn to Mary, and give her a nudge. She was certain the reception was going to take place in a small farmhouse, where we would be overdressed and cramped, but this house looks vast enough to accommodate all the guests and more.

Mary raises her shoulders and eyebrows at the same time, and I see her mouth opening as we enter the ivy-covered front gates.

"What a charming house," she says and we agree. We enter the doorway and I notice the kitchen is three times the size of our little house. It has been decorated with colorful flowers and bows, the greenery giving the house a warm, festive look. I breathe in the bouquet of sweet scents emanating from the dried herbs ornamentally hung from the ceiling. I look around and admire the charming woodwork and two wide, grand cookstoves. No wonder Jacob is proud to have the reception right here in his home; it's the perfect place for a celebration. As we make our way into the drawing room, I stop to talk with many of my neighbors and introduce Mary to those who have not met her. Mary's eager to mingle and she's a wonderful conversationalist at any occasion, so I never have to fear she will need tending to. We part as we both become involved in separate lively discussions. I find Mrs. Jenkins and she tells me all about the organization and preparations for this reception. I notice Mary has traveled to the buffet table containing luscious foods such as dried figs, olives, European cheeses, thick cuts of meats and rich sauces. I'm pleased to see Mary indulging in such delights because we eat quite humbly at home and Mary's never complained. I notice her crystal wine goblet has been filled generously and I only begin to quiver when I spy her engaging in conversation with our priest, Father Stephen Hornat. At this point I politely end my conversation with Mrs. Jenkins and cross the room to have a word with her. I hasten my steps because Mary is known to invoke controversy, especially given her past experiences with religious matters. I'm relieved when I finally reach them and discover Mary's talking about my boys and how she loves to watch them interact with Grace.

She pauses as she notices my arrival. She takes a large sip from her goblet and places it down on the hearth. I greet Father Hornat and offer my hand.

"Good afternoon, Father, what a lovely ceremony today. I'm pleased you've met my sister. You may recall that she's visiting while Florence and her husband James are fighting in Virginia." Father Hornat bows toward me and gently lays his free hand over mine.

"Yes, Ellen. I've had the good fortune to meet up with Mary again, and she tells me you and the children are managing all right on the farm, and that her grown daughter is running the family business in North Hampton. I am pleased you've had a companion. Tell me, what do you hear of Florence and James?" I tell Father Hornat that Florence is keeping his spirits up, and trying his best to be a brave and honorable soldier. Mary, now enjoying a plate of figs and beets, gives details of their duties, and I conclude by asking Father to pray for them. Father Hornat nods his bald head and shuts his eyes. Just as quickly he opens them and a look of excitement crosses his face.

"Ellen, Mary, I've something for your husbands, and for Don Unger as well. I had a visit from the Bishop of Massachusetts last month and he gave me several gospel pendants to distribute to Union soldiers. They've been blessed and have a lovely engraving of Saint Adrian on them. I can only pray that these pendants will give your husbands strength and protect them from harm." His lined face looks solemn as he pulls two beautiful silver pendants out of his coat pocket. Mary puts her plate down and reaches her hands toward the gift.

"Oh, my!" How lovely and kind... Now Father, I am not sure if I mentioned that James is a Protestant man..." Before I can intercede Father Hornat raises his hand and smiles.

"Mary, saints are worshiped by all Christians. Saints are men and women who are examples of great holiness and virtue. They're considered to be able to intercede with God for the persons who pray to them. This pendant is a Saint Adrian pendant, and he is the patron saint of soldiers. Your husband is a Christian man, but if you think he's all right on his own then I can surely gift it to another soldier." With that, Mary nods her head back and forth and gratefully accepts the pendant. We admire the gift and I am filled with hope for the first time. This pendant will surely keep Florence safe and he'll come back to me.

A few moments later we hear a clinking of silverware to crystal and we see Jacob Unger gathering everyone's attention. The crowed rooms become quiet and still, except for the subtle sounds of champagne flutes being distributed by well-dressed servers. This must be the wedding toast! As guests collect in the large drawing room, Mary and I find ourselves standing in the grand doorway with an excellent view of the bride and groom and the proud parents. Jacob and Kristin are beaming, holding each other, and whispering gently into one another's ears. Finally Jacob taps his glass one final time and the murmur of folks stops at once. Jacob raises his glass and begins a lovely toast about young love. He's an eloquent speaker, using florid descriptions and emotional words. He expresses his joy at watching their relationship blossom and grow, like spring flowers, pure and graceful. He speaks of them separately, calling his son valiant and loyal, and exceedingly loving. Jacob's face softens as he speaks of Kristin, calling her beautiful, kind and ever patient. He looks Kristin in the eyes and tells her to keep good courage until Don arrives home safely again. He then raises his glass and asks us all to do the same--to toast the couple all good health and happiness. Mary and I both find ourselves wiping tears from our eyes; however, it is the conclusion of the speech which catches everyone by surprise.

Jacob turns to his wife and son and raises his glass one last time. He clears his throat and I notice his free hand has found Amy's. Is his hand shaking? Perhaps he's nervous but begins again.

"Don, you're my only child and to endure the pain and worry over your service in the Union Army is more than my heavy heart can bear. I managed once, but I fear I cannot a second time. A father's duty is to protect his child and I cannot do that whilst you are at war. I've made a decision that gives me peace and comfort." Oh, no. I feel something ominous in the room and my chest is beginning to constrict. I see tears forming in Amy's eyes and their clasped hands have both gone white. Before I can turn and exit the room I hear Jacob's final haunting words.

"Late yesterday I went to Mr. Parson's office and volunteered to join you in service as I, too, will become a soldier of the Union Army!" Jacob's last sentence is spoken in a loud, determined voice, and I see him standing there resolute as if he's already under a General's command. Within moments, the reception becomes a chaotic scene. High pitched voices of shock fill the air; folks are clamoring toward the family, Kristin is sobbing and Don stands stunned, glaring at his father. Through all the commotion, I lose sight of my sister but I never take my eyes off Amy. I am shocked by the way she remains calm and stoic. She must have known Jacob was going make this announcement, but I still can't imagine taking it with such grace and dignity. I suddenly feel smothered by this calamitous scene. I need fresh air. I search for Mary or Edward but cannot distinguish them in the mingled crowd, so I turn and find my way through the kitchen to the doorway.

Outside, the air is crisp and cold, and I find a shaded corner at the side of the house. Suddenly I'm shaking all over. My heart is beating swiftly and it seems it would burst if not for the tight corset wrapped around it. All that goes through my mind is the hatred I feel for the war, a war that is taking our good men and tearing apart families. When will it end? I must control myself now or I will certainly fall apart. There's enough heartache in the house right now, I don't need add to it. If I hurry back now, no one will know I've gone. I lift my head to the sky and admire the twinkling of the stars. I pray for Florence, hoping he's resting in his tent, safe and sound. I take a deep breath and make my way back into the reception. Music is playing from the back of the house, the windows are glowing with orange and yellow lanterns, and it looks as if the disturbed mood has lifted inside the Ungers' grand home. For this celebration is now a wedding reception and a hero's farewell.

Florence Burke
March 13th, 1864
Camp of the 37th Regiment

My Dear Wife,

I received the letter from you and the children and I was exceedingly overjoyed to hear from you as I always am. I also received the five stamps and two dollar bills of which I am most appreciative. As I enjoy tip top health so you must not fret a bit about me.

My dear wife, it is for you and the children that I am worrying about day and night, and I wish you would let me know in my next if you got the State aid, and how much it was. I hope that you may receive enough money to get the cow and hire a few farms hands to do the plowing and planting. I dream that the children will be able to return to school full time one day soon and they'll have an opportunity to receive a proper education. Speaking of the children, please tell Jerry I thank him for his kind words. I know he'd be fighting beside me if he were old enough. Tell Michael I've learned to load my rifle in good time. He asks how it is done. Tell him I bite the end of the cartridge and tear it off with my teeth, then I pour the powder into the muzzle of the musket, and crumple up the cartridge, stick it in the musket and shove it home with my ramrod. That's how it's done.

We wait here in an open cornfield for our marching orders. Last night we were woken and told to pack our things and break down camp, but just as we were nearly done, the orders were countermanded and we had to make camp all over again. You would be surprised that I have become something of a cook. I have learned simple recipes and I make the thickest, moistest cornbread the Union Army has ever seen. I am pleased that I have found a useful purpose, for all the young soldiers seem to brighten when they taste my food.

It commenced to snow and blow yesterday afternoon and continued till near daylight this morning when it finally cleared off. Today is as pleasant as ever and the sun came out and is fast melting the snow away. You asked about what kind of bed I have; well I have some pegs driven into the ground lifted about a foot high with two bars across way. I spread my rubber blanket on them, roll myself in my blanket, place my overcoat on top, lay my head on my knapsack and try to imagine I'm somewhere else besides Virginia. Often times I wake and think it's time to stir Michael and Jerry, that it's time to complete the chores around the farm. But it's not long before I recognize I'm not in West Springfield but in a muddy tent with a young Union soldier.

You haven't told me if you've sold the hay or how the piglets and chickens are faring. As for the cellar, I agree you should hire a man to make it bigger. Contact Mr. Doyle and ask for his price.

You can do just as you have mind to about answering John's letter; please yourself about it and it will please me. I haven't written him another letter because he's digging into how I got myself here and I can't bring myself to tell him the truth. He's certain to be vexed, but he knows I have my reasons and that I must do what I feel is right to benefit my family. When I received word from you that John and Bridget are to have a new baby I fell to my knees, overtaken by the joyful news, saddened that I am here and not at home with you to celebrate. It looks as if spring will be a true season of awakenings; plants and crops will be reaping, and our dear friends and families will be giving birth to little ones.

I am going on guard for the first time and it is getting late so I must close. Give my love to Mary, Daniel, Matthew, the Unger family and all the neighbors with the largest share for yourself and the children. So good-bye for this time.

Your True Husband,

Florence Burke

Chapter 25

Ellen Burke
April 1864
West Springfield, MA

"Mother, how long do you think the war will carry on?" Michael calls from my room. He's sitting at Florence's tiny desk, penning his father a letter. We've finished tidying up from dinner, and now we're winding down for the evening. The house is quite still; Mary is resting before the fire and Jerry is checking on the animals in the barn. I tip toe into my room and point to Grace in her crib. She is not fully asleep, but her eyes are wavering, and she looks ready to give in to slumber. Michael scrunches his face, mouthing "sorry." He rises from the chair and comes toward me. I lead him out and as we enter the main room we hear a low rumble. Michael is the first to see Mary snoozing in Florence's rocking chair. Her head is facing the ceiling, leaving her thick neck exposed, and she's making quite a racket. Her snores sound like a saw slicing through dry wood. She's worn out from our trip to the Mercantile and the many chores here at the house and farm. I find the Irish blanket and gently place it over her. Michael playfully covers his ears and rolls his eyes. A smirk comes to my face and before I begin to address Michael's question about the war, Jerry bursts through the door. His face is ghost white and he's running so fast he stumbles on Grace's rag doll on the floor.

"Mother, someone's near the barn. I saw a man. I couldn't tell who he was but he saw me and I ran here. Hurry, bolt the door!"

I pause too long, stunned. Jerry turns back around and places the iron bolt into place. Mary's suddenly awake, eyes wide, wondering what the commotion is about. I take Jerry by the arm and try to calm him, for I can see he's trembling and afraid.

"Jerry, are you sure you saw a man? Was it a neighbor perhaps?" Jerry shakes his head wildly. No! I feel a rise of panic in my chest. I'd never expect that a stranger could find his way here. What does he want? As I try to sort out what to do, I see Mary and Michael are gazing through the windows, trying to make out any movement in the darkness. Jerry's gone to the fireplace and has grabbed the fire poker, placing it into the bright red center of the flame. I know what I must do.

"Jerry, give me the fire poker. I'm going out there to see what this is all about. Get your coat and follow behind me. Mary, stay here with Michael and guard Grace with your life. Michael, go find as many lanterns as you can and place them in the windows. I want this prowler to know we're awake!"

If only we had a rifle. There was one back at the Jenkin's farm but when we moved here I left it out of concern the boys could injure themselves. What if I made a fake rifle with a log and a brown cloth? But I realize I haven't time for that. I quickly don my coat and give Jerry a small hanging lantern. I whisper to him that the plan is to scare the man off, not to confront him. I tell him to remain behind me, and to run back to the house if things get dangerous. He nods, but does not utter a word. I see he is breathing hard, but his narrow eyes tell me he's determined to protect our property. As we open the door Mary warns us to be careful, and I respond with a forced smile, reminding her to bolt the door behind us. Outside the air is bitter and it is menacingly dark and quiet.

Once our eyes adjust to the pitch-black night, it is easier to move forward with our dim lantern. There is no sign of the moon this evening, and even the stars seem dull and sparse. We take three more steps toward the barn when we hear a stirring near the empty outdoor chicken coop. I turn toward the coop and in the shadows I see the silhouette of a man, standing there with his hands on his hips. I can't see his face in the darkness, but I can see he's wearing a bandana and has a very long beard.

"Good evenin' Ma'am." I gasp and stand directly in front of Jerry. "I heard ya might have some hay for sale, so I reckoned I might come here and see the lot." From the sound of his voice, I think he's a young man. I squint my eyes to try to make out his face and see if I can spot a weapon on him, but it is just too dark. I'm stunned into silence, not sure how to respond. Jerry's standing beside me, so close I can feel his teeth chattering. He reaches for the fire poker and I release it to him, wondering how we will overtake this prowler.

"Get off our property. You're trespassing! You got no business here!" Jerry waves the poker in front of him causing the shiny metal to flicker in the light of the lantern. The stranger must see the motion because he takes a step backward, rustling some branches on the ground. I stand firm, shoulder to shoulder with Jerry until we hear movement again.

"I told you my business, boy, now I'm aiming to leave." Heavy footsteps fade to slight tapping but they're not travelling in the direction of the woods, instead he's running around to the side of the barn! Something in the rough man's voice sounded familiar; was it the dodgy old man I'd met in town? Yes! Could this be his son? He certainly has the same temperament and disagreeable tone. If he's fixing to steal our hay, how will he manage that alone? I shiver as I wonder if there are accomplices hidden in the woods. Or perhaps he's just scouting out the lot of hay and is planning to come back and steal it later. Fury and fear grab hold of me, but I know I must protect my family and property. I turn to Jerry who is craning his neck to see where the man has run off to.

"Give me the lantern and poker and head back to the house, Jerry. I think I know why this man is here and I must talk with him." I reach for the lantern and for a moment Jerry's face is lit up and I see he's just as infuriated as I am. His eyes have a fiery glow and his face is crimson. He hands me the rod and the lantern and then tears off in the direction of the barn.

"No!" I bellow, but he is gone. A new sensation of terror fills my veins. I hear Jerry hollering for the intruder to get away from our barn. I scramble behind him with the lamp and the poker, praying the man will not harm my son. I cannot see even a few feet in front of me but soon I hear a skirmish of some sort, followed by the muffled cries of my son. All fear behind me, with the adrenaline of a mother grizzly bear, I holler "stop," I repeat this over and over until I am certain my cries can be heard all the way in town. When I finally grow silent, I track the sound of loose dirt being grounded beneath boots, and I believe Jerry is being dragged toward the house. I shine my lantern towards the walkway and I see faint moving shadows. When I finally reach the house I can actually see the outline of Jerry and the taller man behind him. The intruder has one hand over Jerry's mouth and one hand holding Jerry's arm behind his back. A sharp pain fills my chest, but I approach with no caution or intimidation.

"Let go of my son," I say flatly. I am still walking towards the ever growing shadows, when I hear the scoundrel growl.

"No woman talks to me like that. I think I need to teach you and yer son a lesson!" The man takes one step toward me, pushing Jerry along with him. I am nearly close enough to see their faces, just a few steps more. I hold the lamp up high and prepare to wield my fire poker, but just as the light is about to capture the intruder's face I hear a door slam behind me. I turn quickly to see Mary lifting her arms apart. The next thing I hear is a high-pitched yelp, followed by more loud moans. I draw close enough to cast a dim light near the wailing man, and what I see sickens me. Bright red blood is pouring from the side of his head, some of it splashing onto Jerry's shoulders. Jerry is free, but seems to be paralyzed because he remains in the same spot. The trespasser, however, is howling and holding his torn ear with both hands and jumping up and down as if trying to escape the pain. Suddenly he dodges to the left and runs out of sight, cursing and spitting on the ground. I run to Jerry and lead him into the house. Mary's in the doorway, her eyes fixed behind me, another arrow readied in her bow. We make our way into the safety of our house; Mary taking the last opportunity to address the trespasser,

"I grazed your ear this time, son, but if you ever come back, the next arrow will be through your heart!"

As soon as the door is bolted, Mary and I embrace. My head sinks into her wide neck but I hold back tears threatening to spill from my eyes. I raise my head and look over my sister's shoulder. I see Michael congratulating Jerry for his bravery; Michael's eyes are wide and he's treating his brother like a hero. His hands are on Jerry's shoulders; his eyes are scanning for possible scrapes or blood. I release my sister, thanking her for coming to our rescue and move to Jerry so I might scrutinize his face as well. He appears to be unharmed except for a few scratches around his hairline. I tussle his blonde curly mop and give him a long hug and kiss his cold cheek.

"Well done, Jerry." I pat his head then walk to my room to check on Grace who sleeps undisturbed, thank heavens. I draw the lantern close to her face, observing her pale skin, sweeping blonde wisps of hair to one side. I watch for a moment as her light eyebrows rise slightly, then fall as she responds to my touch. Her head does not feel as warm as it did last night, and I've hardly heard her cough today. Miraculously, all appears well. I reach for my handkerchief and grasp onto it, saying a quick prayer to my Mother. Just as I am replacing it in my pocket I hear Michael's voice calling me. I turn and make my way back to the main room where I see Mary and Michael looking out the windows again.

"Where's Jerry?" I search the room, craning my neck to look up at the loft. Michael points his index finger out the window and Mary rushes to the door as we hear light footsteps approach. Jerry comes running in carrying two dead hens, their necks broken, blood pouring from their beaks.

"That awful man killed our chickens with his bare hands! He's gone now but he's frightened the animals and left these two dead." Jerry holds them up, their necks dangling forward. Michael bursts into tears calling out for Lenny and Gracie, his prized hens. I pull him close to me and cover his head so he doesn't have to look at them.

"Why would he kill our hens?" Michael's face is wet with tears. Mary clicks her tongue and places her hands on her hips. She joins me at Michael's side and places her thick arm around his narrow shoulder.

"Michael, that man is evil. I should have aimed my arrow at his leg so he couldn't escape." Mary's eyes meet mine, and I'm warning her to watch her temper.

"We must report this to your Sherriff, Ellen. He can't get away with this, terrorizing us on your farm and killing the fine hens. I never did get a good look at him but he shouldn't be too hard to find, a bandit with one ear!" I ask Jerry or Michael if they'd seen his face, but neither of them did. Nor did I. I take the chickens from Jerry's hands and bring them to the wash bin. At least we'll have plenty of meat for soup. I know that we're all unnerved by tonight's unexpected events, so as I begin to pluck the chickens I ask Mary to read a few psalms from the Bible. Quite remarkably Mary opens the Bible and finds herself looking at the story of David and Goliath. The boys listen intently as I ready the chickens and boil water in the kettle. While I work I can't help but ponder the terrifying encounter in my head and worry the intruder might return to seek revenge. What happens if he brings a gun? Will he return later tonight? The hair on my back stands on end as I think about what to do for protection. I will not discuss this with the boys because they'll be frightened, but I must speak with Mary. We can borrow a rifle from Mrs. Jenkins, but we'll need practice in using it. What of tonight? I'm afraid the animals are on their own in the barn, but besides the bolt, how will we protect the children if that crazy lad returns? I mumble to myself, thinking, as I pull each feather away from the pink skin of the hen. Finally, as I ready the carcass for the rod, I know what we must do. Mary and I will take turns standing guard here. I will keep hot water boiling over the fire, and use it to throw on any trespasser. We will also need to have lots of tea on hand for it is only 8:45p.m. It will be a long night, but when the sun rises we'll go to town and report the crime and perhaps we'll look into getting that rifle at the Jenkins' farm. I only wish we could also protect the farm animals, but I'm surely not going to allow the boys to sleep out there. As if reading my thoughts, Michael raises his body from the floor where he's been listening to the Bible story. His eyes are wide and his face is bright.

"Mother, I just had the most remarkable idea! Why don't we get ourselves a watchdog? It could sleep in the barn and protect the piglets and chickens. I would make it a comfortable bed in the hay. I've always wanted a dog, please Mum!" Michael turns his head to the side waiting for my reaction. I must say I would have never thought of a watchdog. I turn from the hot fire after placing the rod in place.

"Well, Michael, you've come up with a clever solution. Tomorrow I must see Mr. Doyle about fixing this tiny cellar, and I know his son Graham breeds dogs. Briard's I think. We'll see if he has any for sale. Now boys please prepare for bed. Aunty Mary and I will be up for some time turning the chickens and making a delicious soup. We may even make a spice cake for a treat. Now off you go."

Mary's eyebrows rise as she looks toward me. I place my finger over my mouth, willing her not to question our late-night cooking. The boys give us one last cuddle and go off to change into their dressing gowns. I take the kettle off the rod and pour two strong cups of tea. Mary takes the thick cloth and turns the rod over, rotating the chickens. We take our tea, and have a seat in front of the fire. I need to tell Mary all about the man I met in town, and we need to make our strategy for this evening's watch. If Florence and James could see us now, two women reporting for duty, prepared to guard their home and family.

Florence Burke
April 13th, 1864
Camp Near Brandy Station

My Dear Wife,

I am taking the favourable opportunity of writing these lines hoping to find you in good health, as I am not at present. My health is pretty bad these couple of weeks. I hope I receive a letter from you soon, as it will cheer my drooping heart and I'm sure I would feel as well as I ever did.

I have been gone from camp about eight miles on picket duty and it snowed and rained most of the time while I was gone making it the most disagreeable time I ever experienced. Standing and waiting on the peak of a hill, in the crook of a snow-covered tree, alone, truly tested my will. And it snows again today. When we have a snow storm of any amount here which is quite often these days, it makes but a little odds with us whether we stay in or out of doors for the tent we have leaks badly and we get but little wood except the chips we burn. My little Bible's even disintegrated in the dampness.

Dear wife I have sent fifty dollars home to you. I directed it to Mr. Parsons to be forwarded to you. I am afeared it is lost unless you tell me you've received it. If I don't hear from you by the 20th of the month, I will inquire here with the mailman. You should know that it is not the money that makes me feel so bad but thinking of you and the children is coming down as a load on my heart. Is baby Grace recovered from fever? Has she been to see Dr. Winterkorn? I pray night and day that the children are safe with you for I know I left you with a weighty burden, perhaps far too much.

When you write let me know all about the baby and the boys. Write soon, we do not know the day we will leave here. We were all ordered to pack our clothes and send them off to Alexandria, which I did except for my coat. With General Grant now in command, we will be forging toward the enemy, with the Massachusetts 37th Regiment in the front lines, and won't be able to carry them. I have gotten to know many of the boys in our Calvary and I dare say we are nothing but farmers, but all of us have heart and loved ones back home who we hope to reunite with. Ellen, my beautiful wife, please keep good courage, I will return to you. For you are the bravest, most clever woman I have ever met, and you've made me a father to three brilliant and loving children. Write to me as quick as you get this. No more at present.

Yours Faithfully,

Florence Burke

Chapter 26

Ellen Burke Late
April 1864
West Springfield MA

The golden yellow sun is seeping through the rafters as I kneel in the hay, praying to God that Grace survives her sickness. It is very early, and my baby is finally settled, if only my mind was as well. I have a familiar feeling of unease, and this barn, with the cascade of brilliant rays falling around me, seems an appropriate place to speak to Him. I've come here to survey our tools, for today Daniel Sheehan and Edward Fitzgerald are coming to plow the field. Instead, I've found myself using the barn as my cathedral. From the ground I look up at the high rafters, where the light from the cracks resembles crystal chandeliers, and the row of lanterns hung on the stalls looks like an altar. I wonder if this is how the Virgin Mary felt as she gave birth inside the cold, lonely manger. My handkerchief touches my lips as I bow my head, concluding the prayers. I must be tired because in my head I hear a chorus of angels singing "Halleluiah." Could this be a sign that my baby will recover?

I finally rise stiffly, one leg at a time. I stow my handkerchief in my coat pocket and make my way to the side of the barn. There I see our rakes, picks, shovels and hoes. I look to the loft and make an estimate on how much hay we have for sale. I know we have more than we need, and although I was planning to trade it for a cow, I'd settle for a guard dog. Ever since the prowler appeared we've all been on edge in the evening. However, we're much more prepared now that Michael's had some lessons with the bow and arrow and Jerry and I are training with a rifle. Last week Edward Fitzgerald took Jerry out into the woods and to my astonishment, Jerry returned carrying a rabbit on a stick!

I suppose we're learning how to adapt here on our own, but I still feel vulnerable to things I can't control, like illness and councilmen. Matthew Rooney has taken my papers from me and insists that he will have the Councilmen conclude this deal with a proper deed, proof of payment for the taxes and an agreement to make a roadway when the ground thaws. His threats to take this matter public have yet to yield results. Instead, indifference and procrastination have ensued. I am no further along now than I was when Florence left four month's past. I am filled with frustration over this matter. Matthew insists the paperwork will be signed the day after Mr. Day returns from his latest trip to New York City. All I can do now is wait.

Just like the Sheriff said to do, wait. He promised to send his deputy to the Elden place and search for his son, but he didn't think we'd find him. The deputy agreed that he was probably long gone, licking his wounds and dodging the authorities. I had to remove Mary from the office when she asked the Sheriff if she could borrow his badge. She said she'd like to take a look around herself because, really, how hard could it be to find a one- eared criminal!

We then walked to Mrs. Jenkins farm to borrow a rifle so we'll have one here at the house. I explained my reasons for needing protection, and her eyes widened when I mentioned the name Blaine Elden. Apparently Mrs. Jenkins was friendly with Blaine's wife Katy before she up and left town for Boston several years past. Mrs. Jenkins said Katy was constantly complaining of her husband's problem with drink and unemployment, and that he'd swatted and cursed at her from time to time. Katy took her son away, but he returned recently and has been causing trouble around town. The father and son pair are disgruntled because no one in town will hire them to work. After meeting Blaine I can't say I blame anyone. But since we've no hard proof that it was Blaine's son who crossed our property and killed our hens, we must wait to see if a scoundrel turns up whose ear has recently been pierced through.

I shake my weary head and focus on the morning chores. I must make a hearty meal for my friends and neighbors coming to plow our land today. I am staying behind to tend to Grace, and to try to sort out a way to rebuild our cellar. Early this morning I heard a rumbling noise and I discovered that the rocks along the back wall of the cellar have given way and half of the tiny cellar has caved in. I rescued the smoked ham and chicken parts from beneath the rubble, but two bottles of milk and five glass jars of canned fruits and jams were shattered in the collapse. I must tidy up the mess and find a way to support the remaining wall. The cellar is vital to us; we must have a place to store our provisions. The icebox holds so few items—It's hard to believe I'm faced with another burden here in this house. I feel a surge of heat emanate from my neck but instead of steaming over this, I open the door and let the cool breeze carry my wrath away.

It's a raw clear morning, but I can see tiny buds appearing on trees and purple crocus sprouting from the ground. Spring is upon us, and I hope that once the plowing and planting are done, the boys may return to school. Florence is pleased the boys have a fondness for farming, but he wants them to be educated so they can make better lives for themselves. Because of his trade, Florence made it possible for them to receive a higher education, for only landowning citizens in West Springfield are granted the privilege of education beyond the primary years.

I enter the doorway, pushing my way through with the two filled water buckets. I place them near the cellar and turn to see Mary rocking Grace before the fire. I bid Mary a good morning and inquire about Grace's health. She whispers so not to disturb the slumbering boys,

"She's a bit warm still with runny stool, but she's been smiling and I think she's feeling better." I exhale and I feel my shoulders relax.

"Good. Thank heavens. She is probably all right. I think it must have been the excitement of the past few days that has gotten my mind fretting." While Mary remains in the rocker with Grace, I set about making biscuits that we'll have with our fresh scrambled eggs and sausage. I heat a small amount of milk for Grace, hoping she will take it without a fuss. I must keep her in good health. I must keep our family together.

Florence Burke
April 19th, 1864
Camp of the 37th Massachusetts Regiment

My dearest wife,

I received your letter of the 10th and the boys' letter of the 11th. Please thank Jerry and Michael for their letters and the stamps. Staring down at their words, knowing they penned them alone, makes my heart beat faster. I cannot express enough my regret for not being home with them, leaving them without a father. Each day it is clearer and clearer that my gamble may have been too much, that this war is not near its end, but gaining a new momentum propelled by the campaign for reelection by Abraham Lincoln.

We remain here in camp awaiting our next orders. These days pass slowly because boredom and fear are causing men to stir trouble and act out. Yesterday during a friendly game of wicket one soldier accused another of cheating and a clash broke out among ten men. All of them were reprimanded and some lost pay.

I've received some troubling news from home, Ellen. It was written in a young soldier's letter, the few lines had no name, but we think we know who's done it. He writes that Daniel Sheehan resides at your house 2 or 3 times a week and regular every Sunday and doesn't leave until 12 or 1 o'clock every night and sometimes he stays until morning. He also said he saw for himself you kissing Daniel on the Main Street of West Springfield. I don't believe it but I beg of you to write to me and tell me what it started from. I wish to God he kept his damn stuff at home. Dear wife, I am quite certain it is that Elden man who's spreading these rumors. He was an enemy of mine when I was home and perhaps it is the way he wants to rise trouble between you and me. He's always blamed me for not getting hired by Mrs. Jenkins. He thinks I swayed her decision, but actually she didn't hire him because he's an unreliable, untrustworthy drunkard. His son is surely the man who killed your hens upon the snow. If it ain't true don't say anything to anybody but write to me and let me know all about it.

The last letter I got from you told about the cellar caving in and if this is true I would not wonder the house would cave. Please have Ed Begley take a look.

I am agitated with all the reports from home, from you and from neighbors. Please let me know the truth of it.

I pray baby Grace is over her sickness, and I pray all of you stay in good health. We must keep good courage and get through this.

I must bid you good-bye for this time.

Yours Faithfully,

Florence Burke

Chapter 27

Ellen Burke
May 1864
West Springfield, MA

"Mother, Grace isn't moving! Come quick!" Michael's high, shrill voice sweeps into the main room where I'm preparing a wash bin. Without hesitating, I release the boiling tea kettle from my hand, it lands hard on the floor, toppling over and losing its lid. Hot water streams down the floor, soaking the braided rug. I hardly notice the mess because I'm in a state of terror, moving as fast as I can to attend to my baby girl. When I enter my room, the air feels cold and raw. Michael has Grace in his arms. He holds her up to me, his eyes filling with tears, his lips trembling in fear. I notice the blankets surrounding her are oddly still, as if he's carrying a doll, not my wiggly baby. Dear God, please don't take my baby! I feel a shift in my mind, and suddenly my emotions are stowed and I am thinking clearly and rationally.

I take Grace from Michael. He takes a step back, his wet eyes searching mine, wondering if I feel the worst of her symptoms. She's burning with fever, the heat is seeping through the blankets. Before I examine her further I order Michael to find Jerry and have him run to the Begleys' house. He's to get Edward and meet us down the hill with his wagon. I also instruct Michael to fetch Mary from the barn immediately. Michael tears out of the room, hollering at the top of his lungs, crying out for Jerry and my sister, barely comprehensible. Silence now looms around me as I slowly peel back the blankets around Grace's face. Her sunken cheeks are stone white, her red-rimmed eyes are shut, and her chapped mouth is pursed. She looks sickly but still could pass as an ordinary infant enjoying a deep, heavy slumber. I continue to unwrap her blankets, willing my baby to wake, but there is no movement. With her covers removed I now untie her dressing gown. Before I slide the neckline down her milky white chest, I see a red, blotchy rash appearing everywhere. The rash is scattered, but appears to be connected by tiny red dots, as if trying to consolidate and consume its victim.

"No, no Grace, wake up, please..." My voice trails off as I draw her near to me and listen for breathing noises. I hear labored, faint breaths which give me hope. I once again squelch my emotions and begin gathering her clothes and readying my baby for the journey to town.

"Has the fever returned?" Mary comes barreling into the house, with Michael following on her heels. Mary's out of breath as she runs to me and wraps one arm around me.

"Yes, and she has red marks on her chest. Help me gather her things, and Michael, will you find a flannel and take it to the well. She needs a cold cloth for the fever. Come Mary, let's get her to the doctor. She's still breathing; we must save her." I can't raise my eyes to Michael's because I must stay focused on Grace. He turns to go, heaving large breaths of air, sick with worry. My eyes do catch a side-glance at Mary. Her eyes are lowered and teary, her shoulders shutter in quiet despair.

From that time on, events seem to unwind in slow motion, and I'm no more the rational woman, but one plummeted into a dream- state. Grace did not live to see the doctor; she died in my arms along the roadway. Typhoid. I knew the moment it happened because suddenly my handkerchief became moist in my hand,

and my entire body became warm and tingly, a sensation I recall from my mother's passing. Somehow, though, I recognized subtle differences stirred from losing my mother and now losing my baby. With my mother's passing, I remember feeling terror and emptiness, but with Grace's death I feel a sense of relief and peace. Perhaps it's because I know Grace is departing to a beautiful and safe place. I close my eyes and I see my mother's arms around her, holding her, caressing, and loving her. Grace's tiny blue eyes open once again and she flashes her brilliant smile, sending white light between them. My two angels are together in heaven, and if it weren't for the boys and Florence, it would please me to join them.

I pass the next few days in bed. Not with fever, as the typhoid illness isolated its wrath upon Grace alone. The doctor prescribed sleeping medicine and I take them willingly because in my dreams alone is where I can find my entire family together, my parents, my brothers and Mary, and Florence and the children running together through the green grasses of Ireland. We run towards the steep cliffs and marvel at the ocean, a vast body of water that forms the waves of time and carries the tides of years. In between the deep sleeping hours, I wake and Mary feeds me broth or serves me sweet tea until I become unconscious again, on my precious green isle. I vaguely remember Jerry reading a letter from Florence while I am partially awake; Florence the soldier seems lost and confused at my writing lapse, but I shall not worry about him now as I am in another dimension and time. I am in the green valleys of my childhood, a safe and naive place where war and death cannot invade. Somewhere around the third day of continuous sleep, I wake with Michael at my bedside.

"Hello Mum, are you back for good now?" He whispers. I look at him through cloudy eyes. I can make him out just well enough to see his eyes are swollen and red, and his face is drawn and thin. He needs his Mum.

"Yes, my love. I'm back. I needed time to rest and heal. I'm stronger now and feel more at peace with your sister's death." At that, Michael grips me very tightly, places his head on my chest and sobs uncontrollably, soaking my blankets with his boyish, salty tears. For days he's held in his emotions, receiving guests and mourners whilst I lay here in bed. Mary and Jerry must be exhausted as well, and I must relieve them. I take Michael's face in my hands and promise him we'll be all right. I assure him I have returned with my whole mind and soul, and that I will care for him and his brother as we celebrate the life of his sister. Michael listens and lays his head back down upon me, I look up and see Jerry standing in the doorway, his eyes anxious and despondent. I signal for him to enter and he cautiously comes forward, offering me a kiss on my cheek. I take his strong hand in mine and find his eyes.

"Jerry, I'm sorry to have temporarily left you. However, I'm feeling better and I think I'm able to carry on. Thank you for all you've done these past few days." Jerry's eyes begin to well with large tears, and soon his eyes seem to be swimming in them. He swipes them away and clears his throat.

"Mother, what I don't understand is why the good Lord would take our baby girl? Isn't He supposed to show mercy? It's bad enough that our father is gone to war! Why...? " Jerry's throat constricts, and his face reddens displaying his outrage. Michael's chest continues to heave, in small spasms, even though he's fallen into a deep sleep upon my chest. I tighten my grip on my elder son's hand.

"I know it seems unfair, Jerry, and I feel the same as you. However, none of us knows what God has planned for us. Perhaps he wanted to protect baby girl from the hardships here on earth, she's so tiny and vulnerable. I feel at peace knowing she's with my Mother and Father in heaven, and someday we will all be reunited with them. You and your brother, you're strong, and hardy, and together we will remain here and build this farm. I'm rested and convinced that our life will continue, and we will make it as brilliant as we can. I suppose we've received loads of food these past few days, what day is it anyway?" Jerry nods and tries to form his lips into a smile, but they remain flat, unwilling to bend.

"It's Wednesday, the third of May. And yes, our friends and neighbors have been calling on us, day and night. They've brought fruits, meats, breads, pies and other sweets. We've enough food here to feed the whole town of West Springfield. I only wish our cellar hadn't caved in because we've no room to keep it fresh. The icebox is overflowing. Even Aunty Mary hasn't been eating, so it's just piling up on the floor."

I feel Michael's heavy breathing on my chest. I suddenly have a surge of strength. I hoist myself into a sitting position on my bed and cradle Michael's upper body with my hands. I slowly ease out of my bed and lay Michael's limp body back down to rest.

"Jerry, it's time to put that food to good use before it spoils. Let's have an afternoon meal fit for a king! Today we shall no longer mourn. Today we shall celebrate the short life of our baby girl. "Where's Aunt Mary?" Jerry heads to the door, but turns to respond.

"She's out in the yard reading letters from Uncle James and Emma. We received a new letter from father too, but he seems troubled, so I kept it from Michael. He doesn't know what's happened here, we must write to him soon." I raise my hand to Jerry's soft face.

"We will son, in good time."

Florence Burke
April 25th, 1864
Camp of the 37th Regiment

My Dear wife,

For God sakes do end my misery, write and let me know the reason you have been so long delayed to write to me. Have I in any way, either by word, deed or action given you just cause to be vexed and neglect me in this manner? If I have I beg you let me know how I may try and prove to you that I am innocent of any such intention. If I have written anything to you to make you angry, or feel bad, if I have, I have done it not with the intention of causing any bad feelings but only wrote what I have to warn you to be on guard against scandalous reports, for almost everyone in the army is hearing something bad from home.

But, you know me well enough to know that whatever I may hear I would not believe or pay attention to, but only wish you to be on the sharp lookout for Elden and his son or any other neighbor that may have occasion to speak ill of you. I know you've resented my decision to join this war, and you have the right to be, but please know that I have been faithful to you and our family, and I am certain you have been as well. For God sakes Daniel Sheehan is my best friend, I would never think of you messing about with him. Please write to me and ease my mind that you still love and support me. I will have nothing to live for if you abandon me. I pray in good time you will see that I tried to do right by our family, but with our marching orders imminent I am not certain of my future.

A man was caught trying to desert by one of my tent mates last Friday while on picket. Never have I seen a man so terrified. He kept his head to his chin as they marched him in front of us, his hands tied behind his back. We hear he's to be branded with a "D" and returned to the Regiment when he recovers.

General Grant reviewed our corps yesterday. What a sight to see the man in Command, a common looking soldier, dressed entirely as we are in the Blue Union Army uniform, looking like he needed a shave and a bath. Some of the younger soldiers weren't impressed by his positive words, but I, being significantly older, rushed to greet him and hear him speak. He was much more soft-spoken than I imagined but he seemed confident we'd defeat the Rebs if we listen to our orders and stand our ground. He thanked us for our service and called us men of honor. I am trying to take these words to heart, though I feel a deserter as my mind and heart are fixed only on returning to you and the children.

This morning we have orders that all letters must stop for thirty days and it troubles me greatly. We are on the march. I am in low spirits to go into battle without hearing from you and the children for so long, and I worry that something has gone amiss. As this may be the last letter you may ever get from me I hope, Dear Ellen, that you will try to take good care of yourself and the children and may the good God watch over you and them. If I am doomed to fall on the field of battle and we are destined to never meet again on earth, may we be so prepared that we will meet in heaven.

If I live to see the 3rd of next September I expect to be home with the Regiment, their time being out at that date and one of my tent mates wrote to Governor Andrew who answered that the recruits would end with the Regiment. I sent you all the money I have got but eighty cents. I borrowed twenty cents and with the dollar, I got the picture taken so I am left without a cent to buy tobacco. Dear Ellen, this may be the last you ever hear from me but trust in God and all may yet be well. I pray I will see my boys grow to men and plant a hundred kisses on dear baby Grace. Farewell, Dear Ellen, perhaps forever, but hope not

Yours Faithfully,

Florence Burke

Chapter 28

Ellen Burke
May 1864
West Springfield, MA

I rise slowly from my bed and automatically check the empty crib. The bare wooden bed remains a painful reminder of my loss, but I do not feel ready to move it just now, because I ironically muster courage and strength from gazing at it in the morning and praying at its side at night. Mary worries that I am not moving on whilst the cot remains in our shared room, but I assure her that its presence is a blessing and a comfort to me as I heal from Grace's passing. I make my way into the living area and lay a new fire in the fireplace. I pour water from the bucket into the kettle and place it over the roaring fire. I yearn for this special time of day, the time I used to share alone with baby girl. I take a moment to look out the window but the sun has not risen yet so it is dark and bleak. On the days following Grace's death I wondered how the sun could keep rising each day, as if I expected darkness to continue looming over us as we mourned. But that is not so, days keep passing and the sun keeps rising and setting.

The house is quiet save for Mary's snoring and an occasional sweet sound of murmurings from the boys. I rest in Florence's rocking chair, with Grace's small blanket wrapped around my chest, and I wait until the tea kettle boils and steam billows from its spout. This is my new routine and the place I find some peace in the vast area of my broken heart. I'm far more at ease here alone before the fire than at night, racked with nightmares of Grace crying for milk-- and waking to find only an empty crib. This is terribly hard to bare.

I must write to Florence but I have been unable to do so as I fear writing these words makes them everlasting. I also fear his reaction. My poor husband is about to be sent to the battlefields and now he'll hear the news of his baby girl? I want to give him strength, but how can I when I can barely cope with this myself? I long to see Florence, just for a few days so we may grieve together for our baby. We made her, we loved her and our loss should be equally shared. I try to temper my emotions for the sake of the boys, but if Florence were here I would be able to lean on him, seek comfort in his huge chest and long arms, and release my tears until he kisses them away.

The terrible bitterness from his departure has left me now and all I want is to see him again and heal with him. I shall find the courage to pen him a letter and perhaps the outpouring of my words will free some of the pain I feel inside. I only hope that this news will not distract Florence, because I need him to protect himself in battle and return to me. I pray that he will be kept out of danger. I cannot lose another… No! I will not even think about that. He must return and I will manage a way to carry on without Grace. I will write him now. I will speak of our baby's beauty, her contagious smile, and the warmth and comfort she offered me this past winter. I will offer Florence words of encouragement and love…praying he returns.

Jonathon Burke
May 1864
New York, New York

Dear Ellen,

It was with great sadness that we received your letter. Words cannot express the sorrow we feel for you at the loss of your beloved baby. We send our heartfelt condolences to you and the boys.

Has Florence been informed of this tragic news? I fear his Regiment is on the move and he may not be able to receive letters from home. I am not certain if this is good or bad for his sake.

I wish Bridget and I could come to West Springfield and attend the service for Grace, but Bridget remains unwell and I am overwhelmed with work here in Tammany Hall. With Lincoln's new push for recruits, he's offering commutation rates at $350 to $600 a volunteer, and I must be certain these immigrants are receiving them with proper paperwork in good time.

We plan to visit no later than the summer, but in the meantime Ellen, take care of yourself and the boys. Try not to fret because it may cause you to become ill yourself. Bridget has been troubled as well, grieving for you, feeling frightened about bringing another innocent baby into the world. She thinks we've lost the ability to keep our children safe and protected, and she certainly does not want to raise them in a nation divided. She weeps at night, praying for young Grace's blessed memory and for the war to end and for peace to prevail.

I have been following news of the Army of the Potomac, and they are marching south towards the Rapidan River, prepared to engage the Rebs in battle. It seems the Union Army far outnumbers the Confederates, so let's pray to God that they are victorious and do not suffer large numbers of casualties. The newspapers here are reporting that Grant's strategy is to win the war by mere attrition alone, that he feels he can outnumber the Rebs and diminish their supplies until they eventually surrender. I hope to God that his plan is successful.

I plan to write to my brother in a few weeks time after I am certain he has heard from you. I am offering my prayers and support for both of you. I will do everything I can to see to it that Florence comes home. I have written to many of his commanders asking their support in keeping him safe, but I know in the throes of battle, men become dispersed and everyone is minding his own safety. I know he is with James and his experience should serve Florence well.

I shall close, sending you our greatest affection and love.

Jonathon Burke

Chapter 29

Ellen Burke
May 1864
West Springfield, MA

I'm sitting in a small, dim-lit room with cigar smoke wafting around my face. My chair is hard and cold, causing my back to become stiff. Across the six foot mahogany table are the councilmen, Mr. Parsons, Mr. Day and my friend Matthew Rooney. Mrs. Parsons is present too, but she stands in the corner, not wanting to sit and wrinkle her new, elegant dress. I shift in my seat until the last of the signatures are scrawled upon the legal document. I lean forward, hoping to expedite the matter.

"Thank you, my husband will be pleased this matter is settled at last." I rise from my chair, not wanting to remain in the miserable office any longer than I must. I've paid the taxes, collected our deed, received approval on the roadway and signed the legal trade, now I want to depart. I hear Mr. Parsons and Mr. Day whispering to Matthew Rooney, apologizing for the delay in this matter. Shouldn't these cantankerous old men apologize to me? Oh, why do I even bother fretting over them.

As I collect my paperwork and place it in my basket, I feel eyes upon me. Mrs. Priscilla Parsons has left her husband's side and stands in front of his desk, donning her gloves. She has a smug look on her face, as if she's accomplished some important task. I'm not sure why she was invited to this meeting anyway;

apparently Mr. Parsons wanted her here to sign as witness. I can't bear to make eye contact with her, I've had enough of her false sympathy. Then I notice she's coming towards me. Oh no! I swiftly turn my head, hoping to deter her from addressing me directly. It doesn't seem to work because I hear her high-heeled boots pause before me and I can make out her fancy blue dress in my periphery. Bloody hell! I press my lips together and it takes all the strength I have to raise my head in her direction. Just as I thought, her eyes are narrow, the lines between her eyebrows deepen, and her red lips are frowning. She reaches her white-gloved hand to me, resting it on my own.

"Dear, you're quite fortunate to own this land given your position. You must be very proud of your husband, he's done right by you." She leans her head toward me until her wrinkled mouth is near my ear, and whispers, "All my husband ever gives me are trinkets and such. He can be quite a bore." Mrs. Parsons offers me a quick wink as if I understand her complaint.

I clear my throat to speak but words fail to come, so I just nod, feeling numb. Suddenly I am aware of Matthew pulling on my arm, leading me out of the dim office and down the wood -paneled corridor. I feel heat rising in my cheeks, just below the surface of my skin, and hot tears forming in the corners of my eyes. Matthew heaves the Town Hall door open and ushers me through.

"Are you all right there, Ellen?" I realize I am walking briskly, and Matthew is half limping, half running beside me. I'm hurrying because I don't want to explode with anger and cause a scene in town. Poor Matthew is trying to keep up with my pace, and now I see he is puffing and his face has gone red. I slow down, and take deep breaths, trying very hard to collect myself. Suddenly I spin around and stop Matthew in his tracks. I take two large long breaths and finally find my voice.

"What do you say we share a pint, Matthew? My business is settled, and in good time. The boys are in school for a few more hours, and I'd like to thank you for your help." I am surprised by my own spontaneity; this is not my usual manner. Matthew shoos me with a wave of his hand.

"You don't need to thank me, I was happy to help. I would be honored to accompany you to Porters, but I could never allow a young lady to buy me a drink. Come, let's go and sit down. You can tell me what Mrs. Parsons said to trouble you. I thought I spotted steam coming from your ears!" Matthew flashes me a smile, and although I am still vexed, I can't help but return his grin.

Matthew and I enter the tavern and straightaway Nathan leads us to a fine table dressed with a yellow tablecloth topped with a vase filled with spring flowers. My spirits are lifting, and I take a deep breath, knowing this trade is finally settled. I am eager to inform Florence; he must know that we are official landowners. Nathan breaks into my thoughts inquiring after Florence and the boys. I remove my bonnet and raise my eyes to meet Nathans.

"Thank you for asking after Florence, he remains in good health. He's in the throes of battle now with many of our West Springfield men, so I haven't heard from him in a spell. The boys are back to school. Reluctantly. They'd rather be home looking after the crops and animals, but the planting is done and Florence wishes for them to return to school until the harvest." Nathan nods but does not press further. He simply rubs his chin, takes our order, and dashes off to the bar. I take a deep breath, taking comfort in the delicious aromas of beef stew, fresh bread and beer. Matthew's found a newspaper on one of the empty stools and is browsing the articles. I can see the first page of *The Republic*, and as expected, it's coverage on the war. I was just beginning to read the headline, something about "battlefield carnage hitting home in Western

Massachusetts" when Matthew abruptly folds the paper and places it back on the empty chair.

"Nothing interesting today, Ellen, Springfield journalists are useless, writing about baseball, fishing and spring fashions. Oh, here are our drinks. Thank you, Nathan." I raise my eyebrows, knowing Matthew is trying to hide some sort of news from me. If I was not already worn out from dealing with the highbrow councilmen, I would press Matthew to read me that article, but I cannot bear any more forbidding news. I came here to have a drink with my friend, and I would rather pass the time talking of lighter subjects. I must remember to purchase a newspaper on my way out of town. I reach my hand out for my beer and notice a miniature pink rose has been left behind my glass. I gaze toward Matthew but he nods and points a finger in the direction of the bar. I spot Nathan, washing glasses and talking quietly to three guests sitting at the bar. When I finally catch his attention he excuses himself for a moment and comes towards our table.

"Ellen, the rose is for you, in remembrance of your baby girl, Grace. I'm very sorry for your loss, I remember how beautiful a baby she was, and I remember how she slept soundly here a few months past." Nathan lowers his eyes and I am touched by this sweet gesture. I grasp the delicate flower in my hand, and images of Grace whirl through my mind, her soft pink cheeks, her tiny hands and feet, thin wisps of blonde hair, ocean blue eyes and most impressive of all, her dazzling smile. I wonder for a moment if she has taken her first steps in heaven. I blink away the fresh tears welling in my eyes.

"Nathan, thank you for this perfect symbol of my little girl. It is as pretty and as fragile as she was. I shall press it and keep it with her blanket and dolls. Thank you my friend, you don't know how much this means to me." Matthew hands me a fresh handkerchief from his coat pocket. I can see that he's become emotional as well. He collects himself and orders two bowls of cabbage soup and bread. Nathan releases my hand slowly and sets off behind the bar to the kitchen to prepare our lunch. I find my own handkerchief and dab at my eyes.

"Well, I didn't expect that. Matthew, would it be silly of me to believe that this is a sign from my mother, or Grace or even God that they are together in heaven?" Matthew doesn't speak but covers his weathered hands over mine and looks into my confident eyes. "I feel them near me, Matthew. I can almost hear them cheering for me, urging me on. My mother would not want me to concern myself with the patronizing words of Mrs. Parsons, or the dismissive tone of the Councilmen. She knows that I can persevere, and I finally feel I have the strength and conviction to do just that. I must stand strong for my boys and for Florence. I truly believe I've changed these past few months and that I'm become more spirited and resilient." Matthew releases my hands and slides my beer toward me. He takes his own mug in his hand and raises it in the air.

"To Ellen Burke, a woman to be feared!" I beam. Feared, I think I like that. I should have known my fiery red hair and Irish heritage would some day show itself. I raise my glass to toast his and take a long swig of my pint.

Florence Burke
May 1864
Cold Harbor

Dear wife,

I am sending this letter to you with Ed Begley jr, who was wounded and sent to hospital. I'm hoping he'll mail it from there since we are still no longer able to send or receive letters. I pray it reaches you because I have so much I need to say. The first is concerning our little Grace. My heart is all but shattered at the news of her untimely death. I am filled with a grief I've never felt, and I regret that you and the children have to bear her death without a father to mourn with.

Dear Ellen, I take full responsibility for putting my family in this merciless situation. I thought my intentions of joining were pure and selfless, but now I see they were reckless and unfounded. I should never have signed up and left you with such a burden, but I truly thought the war was to end soon and that our family would be greatly benefited by the land. I was wrong, Ellen, and now our baby is gone! I am so sorry, I can only imagine the toll this is taking on you and the boys. I sit here in a river of tears wishing I could turn back time and be with you or wishing the Union Army would allow me to come home to mourn.

It seems that Lee is not surrendering, Ellen; in fact, he seems to be gaining momentum. We've suffered numerous casualties, and the morale here is very poor. I have no choice but to continue because our commanders need every man possible, but I promise you that I am fighting like a new man. I have a blazing fire inside me, a scathing anger, the tirade of a wounded lion!

We are in some God-forsaken Wilderness and there is confusion, desertion, desperation and terror. We are building narrow trenches instead of camping and it is here in the mud that I am penning this letter. Please continue praying for me. James is next to me, providing some comfort and urging me to release my wrath on the Rebs.

I want to close by saying a prayer to you and the boys. Father, please take baby Grace into your Kingdom, and keep her with you until we meet her in Heaven. Please keep my beautiful wife well, and help her to heal during this time of grief. Please watch over my dear boys, Michael and Jerry, and let them know that their father loves them beyond all things. I pray that our family will be united together again. Thanks be to God. Amen

Dearest Ellen, I now know my gamble was not a sound one. Please understand I never wanted to put baby girl in harm's way! I must live to tell you this in person, to apologize, to mourn, to live, to reunite.

We are between raids, pausing only to collect the wounded and bury the dead. I will fight come daybreak, but every other moment is reserved for thoughts of my family.

Yours Faithfully,

Florence Burke

Chapter 30

Ellen Burke Late
May 1864
West Springfield, MA

The spring flowers are in full bloom atop our hill making it look less woodsy and more naturally landscaped. Treetops are filled with bright green leaves, the tall grass is splattered with vibrant colors from numerous varieties of wild flowers, and the rough texture of the large stones and dirt piles shape and distinguish our land. The beauty of our scenery sometimes brings me back to Ireland and my days as a child there, but since Grace's death I have been afraid to let myself go there, frightened that I will not return. It's hard to appreciate the lovely summer-like weather and the blossoming of new buds when I still mourn my dear baby. However, I have placed her little soul inside my own and know she is with me as I look across the field, surveying our crops. It has been a superb growing season with fair weather and adequate rain for irrigation. I am thankful for that. With our bills paid for and money coming in from Florence's State Aid, I have managed to buy a cow (named Gillian) and I'm in the process of hiring two farm hands. Michael traded weekly fresh eggs with Mr. Doyle for a working dog named Rosie. He and Jerry are thrilled with the lively dog, feeding and caring for it without my nagging.

I hear rustling from the woods. Rosie appears from the barn and tears off toward the footpath. Moments later I see Michael and

Jerry, pails and slates in hand, climbing through the brush. I wave to them and smile as Rosie has licked and welcomed them home and now trails behind their heels. When they finally approach I offer them each a cuddle and take their pails from them. Michael runs off with Rosie, eager to complete his chores so he may have a slice of ginger cake. Jerry lingers beside me, telling me about his day.

"Mother, today Michael and I were moved into the third row of the classroom and we were given textbooks to use to follow along with our teacher, Mrs. Siff. She says we're in a new program, and it's the same level as Madeline and Quinn Jenkins! We can take exams and advance into courses that will prepare us for college. Michael was not thrilled-- he's useless at reading, but his letters are improving. I know this is Father's doing so I promise to work hard. I think I want to be a lawyer." I am overwhelmed with gratitude when I hear this news. I feel a stab of pain in my chest knowing I am the reason he feels responsible for Grace's death and for our troubles here this winter. However, the benefits of his trade keep growing: we've a deed to our land, our farm is thriving, our children are in school and may continue on to higher education and we now share in the rights and privileges of citizens of West Springfield. I simply cannot allow Florence to believe his enlistment failed. I must pen a letter to him immediately and let him know that his selfless act is finally apparent and that we support and love him for it. I only fear that he may fall on the battlefield never knowing our admiration toward him. I turn to Jerry.

"Please help Michael with the chores and make your sweet Aunty a cup of tea. She's sewing in my room. The orders from her dress shop are piling up, and she's doing her best to work from here. I'm afraid she must return home soon. I suppose it's time. She's been a lifesaver to us, but she must get home to Emma and the shop. We've been so fortunate to have her here..."My voice trails as I imagine parting with my dear sister. But I finally feel confident that I can manage alone. Jerry remains still, his eyes following mine to the floor. I clear my throat and shake off my gloom. "Right. Now I need to write and deliver a note to Mrs. Unger. She's receiving letters from Don and Jacob's, and I must find out how they're coming through." Jerry's face suddenly grows pale and his eyes well with tears.

"Mother, did you not hear? Mr. Unger and his son Don were both killed at Cold Harbor. My teacher read us the report from Virginia. Their bodies lie side by side beneath an old tree log." Jerry lunges into my arms and I hold him, letting him cry. I want to press him further but I don't. When did this happen? Why didn't a neighbor or friend inform me? My mind is racing as I try to process events from the past few days. I hold onto Jerry's waist even tighter as he dampens my shoulder with tears. Oh, bloody hell! Was that the article in the paper that Matthew Rooney was shielding me from the other day? It must be. I never did make it to the Mercantile to buy a newspaper. But why hasn't Daniel or Ed Begley come to me with this news? We haven't been to town since I finished our business at the Town Hall, and now that I think about it, we've not seen Daniel or Mrs. Jenkins' or anyone in a few days. I wonder if my dear neighbors are avoiding me, trying to spare me from this tragic news?

I lower my head and feel Jerry's warm ear against my cheek. I pray for Amy Unger who's lost her husband and son. I pray for Kristin. She's lost her brave, young love. I remain still and cold. I pray for Florence. Please God, watch over my husband. Let him return to us! A new determination grips me and I feel a rush of heat sear through my veins. I will write Florence, sending thousands of words of love and gratitude. I will send a record of the boys' marks in school, trinkets from the farm, and photos from our past. Lastly, I will send Florence a new Bible and written words from his adoring sons. I will find a way to reach him, I must...

Florence Burke
June 11th, 1864
Cold Harbor

My Dear and loving wife,

I once more take my pen in hand to let you know I am still living, thank God for it. I have not received a letter from you in weeks, our mail being still suspended. What weighs on my heart the most is the thought of dying and leaving you without a final good bye. I hope in receipt of my letters you understand that I have thought this enlistment through, and I may pay the ultimate price for wanting land in haste. I am vexed that you and the boys think poorly of me. Please forgive me.

Please try and get a letter through to me. Some boys are receiving them and no one knows for sure just how that happens. I want to know your feelings toward me Ellen, please write openly for I want to know the truth. Let me know if your back troubles you or not, let me know how you and the children are getting along and let Jerry and Michael be paid by their mother. I will send them a present when I get paid again. There is now 4 months due to us but I don't know when we shall get paid because we are so close to the enemy. The Confederates are only 100 yards from our entrenchment.

I can't describe the fear on this star-filled night, lying here in my filthy trench. There are hundreds of men surrounding me. I can hear the enemy when it is quiet; they are praying, singing hymns, and talking quietly just as we are. I often think how foolish and cruel this war truly is, boys and men killing each other so the states may become united. I find myself praying for both sides, praying for their families, praying death comes without suffering. I know the terror of the battlefield has affected my state of mind, but I promise you I will try and defend myself and return home to you. Home is the one word that draws me out of despair, out of Virginia, and I pray I will be there soon. I don't know if Mary is still with you but if she is tell her James is well. He may get moved to heavy artillery, but I hope not. I'm sure by now you've heard that The Ungers' have been killed. It was a courageous moment for both of them and I take comfort knowing they died together.

We have been on the move for several days now, away from Cold Harbor, heading toward the James River. I have lost all my clothes on the march, the road being hot and I could not carry them. All the boys share the same fate, and we only have what we wear.

You commonly hear it talked up North that the Rebels are starving, but you would think they are well fed as they fight and don't turn back. Grant seems to think we will conquer the Rebs if we stand our ground and press on, but these full frontal attacks are leaving countless good men here on the battlefield. I cannot describe all the unimaginable details at present but I will in some other letter. Ed Begley, Jr. is back from hospital.

Keep good courage and do not be fretting as I am doing the same hoping that I will see you once more. Good-bye.

Yours Faithfully,

Florence Burke

Chapter 31

Ellen Burke
June 30th, 1864
West Springfield, MA

Our house is still, not even a cool breeze passes through the open windows. The fireplace is barren, for no one has the desire to lay wood and bring it to life. Breakfast plates remain in the bin, soiled; only the flies feed on the scraps. This morning we received an unwelcomed guest, and since that time we've lost our simple routines, each member of our family is shattered.

Mr. Parsons made the miserable journey to our little house. The very man who sent Florence off to war came to inform us that he would not be returning. My dear husband is dead, killed in the trenches before St. Petersburg. I did not react to the news as I always thought I would. I simply thanked the Councilman for coming in person and turned toward my room. I believe Mary talked at length with Mr. Parsons, asking for details, inquiring about his possessions, and whether or not his body will be returned. I cannot imagine my husband, lying in a trench, victim to the summer sun. I know I cannot remain in solitude for long, so I comb my hair, rouge my raw lips, and return to the main room.

Mary and Jerry have gone outdoors to weep, while Michael alone lies on the floor, wrapped in his Father's dress coat, clutching our very last letter. Mr. Parsons received it along with the news that Florence was among the latest casualties from the 37th Regiment.

The letter was written two days prior to his death. I slowly make my way to Michael, kneeling by his prone body. I can hear the heaves of his grief as he sleeps fitfully on the floor. He wakes with my touch and turns his tear-stained face toward me. His eyes are red and swollen, his freckles hidden beneath his gloom. He looks to me and then to the letter in his hand and lays his head down hard on the floor.

"Mother, I can hardly move. I keep falling asleep, and when I wake I think Father is home with us! Then I remember he's never coming back, and all we have left of him is this letter and it's ordinary, no different from the others. " Michael heaves loudly, sounding as if his chest will burst. I agree that his letter shows no signs of awareness that his life is near its end, no idea that a bullet would soon be aimed at his skull as he stormed the Reb's heavily defended trenches. But I disagree that it is ordinary. I am thankful to God that Florence finally received our letter, the money we sent him, the Bible and most importantly our grateful and loving words. He died knowing we supported him. Michael shifts and to my surprise I see he's lying on baby Grace's pink blanket. I want to lie with Michael and sob and complain that there is no mercy or justice, but I know that will do him no good. Instead I pull him toward me and stroke his fine brown hair.

"Michael, darling. I know your heart is hurting. Mine is too. But please remember that God has a plan for us, and perhaps our plan is to grow this farm in your father's name. He acquired this land for us and we must make it come to life. We've already collected farm animals, we've ploughed and planted our crops and we're tending to them so they'll grow. We've proved that we can manage here on our own, and we'll do so until it's our time to reunite with your father and sister in heaven. As soon as I release my words Michael's chest spasms and he covers his eyes with his hands. My poor little boy is confused and scared. He's far too young to deal with his emotions. Suddenly Michael releases his hands and throws them in the air.

"But I haven't even stopped missing Grace yet. Sometimes I imagine myself playing with her on the floor, making her laugh, seeing her reach out to me!" Michael's face flushes with anger. He turns and leans his tortured face into mine. His lips are quivering. "How will I ever stop missing Da? I loved him so much, and he said he'd come home. He promised!" Michael buries his head in my chest. Indeed Florence did promise to return and I am not sure how to respond. Finally, words of wisdom come to my lips.

"Michael, if it was within your Da's power alone, he would have returned to us. We know this because he's said it in his letters. He tried his very best to protect himself in battle but it proved too difficult. Now we must mourn his death, but realize Michael, that your Father is a hero. He gave his life so we'd have a better one. Let's work hard on our farm and make it prosper; it's the best way to celebrate his life." Michael stops his crying for a moment. I look into his face to be sure he's all right and I see he's wearing a look of deep concentration. Suddenly he's wrapping his arms around my neck and I feel a new energy surging through his small frame. He turns his head toward my ear and whispers, "You're right, Mother, Da told me he'd return a hero. He did keep his promise." As I remain still, trying to hide the emotion taking over my body, Michael stands up and wipes his eyes so he can see. Without a word he opens the front door and I hear him calling to Rosie as he exits. Jerry is collecting eggs in the barn and Mary is sitting under a blooming apple tree penning a frantic letter to her husband James. I now feel I can set free my emotions but to my surprise, tears refuse to flow. I take my handkerchief from my apron pocket and squeeze it tight, praying to God to take my husband into his hands and reunite him with his young daughter. I thank my mother for giving me strength, finding the words to heal even when I feel

I've none to offer. I realize for the first time that I am a survivor, and if it is God's will for me to live here alone with my boys, then I shall do just that.

Mary is packed and has been preparing for the journey home for several days now. I will insist that she hire a carriage tomorrow. There is no more that my dear sister can do here to help; for we must learn to manage on our own. It's time for Mary to be with her daughter and to return home to her business. I know she longs to hear word from James. I pray he is safe and finds his way back to her.

I must collect myself and lay a fire. I shall make tea and perhaps some scones, for the procession of friends and neighbors should begin very soon. Before I begin these tasks I take hold of my handkerchief and rest briefly in Florence's old rocking chair. I open my other hand clutching Florence's last letter. Florence will no longer have to live in fear for us or for his own life, for he has been put to rest. May he sleep peacefully. I open the letter and read his final words.

Florence Burke
June 16th, 1864
James River, Virginia

My dear loving wife, I received your kind letter this morning with the money in it-50 cents. I also got the letter you sent me enclosing one dollar and postage stamps. Thank you for it. Have you received the miniatures of the children and of yours I sent you from Brandy? I am returning them to you in case anything should happen to me. My dear, I thank you for the new Bible. I have reread the passage about David and Goliath. God saved David in the Lion's den, so I pray too that I shall be spared. I am relieved that you have forgiven me and you've not forgotten about me in this God-forsaken place. Your words and those from our boys are cherished. I keep the letters in my chest pocket.

Last night we crossed the James River on a large, rickety pontoon boat. It seems we're marching south, toward Petersburg. Grant aims to cut off supplies and starve the Rebs into submission, or force them to fight in the open. He still commands us to press forward trusting that our superior resources will besiege Lee. I've more respect for the Confederate Commander though, he's resilient and tactical, and refuses to back down. He sends his men into battle without shame; I suppose it is what a great commander must do. I'm not certain who's claiming victory in these battles of late. As reported, there are heavy casualties suffered on both sides. My vitals here are hard tack, coffee, mush and beef jerk. I have my haversack, and the clothes I wear, though my boots are falling apart at the seams. I have grown thin, and I'm in need of a scrub, but I remain in good health, thank God for it.

Dearest Ellen, all I want you to do is keep good courage and mind the children and keep them in school. That is the wish of an absent father to his family. My love to you and the boys, goodnight.

Yours Faithfully,
Florence Burke

Seamus Burke
July 1864
County Cork, Ireland

Dear Ellen,

It is with great shock and sorrow that I received John's letter informing us of Florence's death. I hoped it wouldn't happen, and I am very sorry for it. I am in poor health at present suffering from an infliction in my chest. I remain in bed and it is here that I've reflected on my life. I know my time here is nearly up and I feel compelled to share with you words that I wish I'd the courage to say to my late son. Had I been more clear thinking in my younger years I'd have repaired our relationship and been a true father to Florence. Instead, pride and stubbornness kept my words sealed within my mind.

As I lay here in agony, with many regrets. I see now that Florence was much the same man I am, and I feel responsible for his death. Like Florence, I put my family at risk by remaining in Ireland during the famine in the hopes of acquiring my own land and freeing myself from a life of tenant farming. I instilled in Florence the need to do whatever it takes to prosper, even if it meant sacrificing his own life. I wish I told Florence that he'd succeeded in America, he's done far more than I ever did. My son made a brilliant choice in leaving Ireland, bringing his brother to New York where he's thrived, following his true love and establishing a lovely family in Massachusetts. I'm sorry he's gone now and I'll never be able to tell him he made his Da proud.

I know my words are very late and my behavior over the years unforgivable. Please know that Maura and I send our greatest deepest regret at losing our son, your husband and Michael and Jerry's Father.

Affectionately yours,
Seamus Burke

Chapter 32

Ellen Burke
October 1864
West Springfield, MA

As I walk through the neat cornrows, picking the last of the late harvest ears, I feel nervous and weary. I couldn't sleep last night, tossing and turning, replaying scenes from years past and fretting over today's proceedings. It is a chilly afternoon and the air is heavy. It feels like it could rain any moment. I look to the sky and watch the dark clouds pass overhead, as if they're setting the mood for this foreboding day. The children and I are dressed appropriately in somber mourning clothes. For today Florence's body is to return home to us.

We've made good use of these melancholy outfits, wearing them for an elaborate military service hosted by the town of West Springfield, and again donning them for a private funeral service here on the farm. Mary sewed these outfits herself using fine silks for my long, black dress and black linen for the boy's trousers and blazers. The expense for proper mourning clothes was dear but worth it when we discovered that we'd be walking in a procession led by Union military officers, a marching band and even a bugler. It felt like a parade with thousands of folks and their children lining the Main street, waving their Union flags and throwing confetti. A woman in the crowd came forward and handed me a beautiful bouquet of fresh flowers, and offered the boys tiny Union flags to wave. It was all a bit overwhelming, but by no means somber. It was more of a celebration for the hometown heroes who gave their life to save the Union. But it was obvious to me that this was also West Springfield's political strategy for raising fresh recruits. Patriotic banners were hung on storefronts, the marching band played patriotic songs such as "When the Saints go marching in" and Union colors and uniforms adorned the townsfolk. The boys wore proud faces that day; there's plenty of time for sorrow.

Our private ceremony was delayed until August because I wanted the roadway to be cleared and completely finished before allowing carriages to make their way to our house. John and Bridget and their two girls were among the first guests to arrive. Bridget's feet were swollen and her belly was protruding, but she never complained. Her new baby boy would arrive a month later. Mary and my niece Emma arrived shortly after, followed by Edward, his very pregnant wife Catherine Fitzgerald, the Sheehan family, Mrs. Jenkins and her twins, Matthew Rooney and Amy Unger. The boys and I spent a week preparing for the service, making foods, decorating the barn with wild flowers and old cornstalks and collecting tables, chairs and dining items from neighbors. Michael and Jerry built an ornate cross, engraved it with their Father's name and Regiment and a dedication. We gathered on the Northern tip of our land, on a flat rise overlooking our farm. It was there that the cross was placed, right next to the gravesite of baby Grace. I remember a warm wind blowing from the trees behind the clearing, and the heat from the sun reflecting off the granite surrounding this lovely site. With John delivering the eulogy and Father Hornat presiding over the service, the day was passed in collective grief, praise and reminiscence.

I hoped that I would have a sense of peace once the services were carried out, but to my displeasure, I did not. I kept having this nagging feeling that perhaps he was still alive in a Union

Hospital or a prison camp, or hiding out as a deserter. I know that my thoughts are irrational given that eyewitnesses in the Regiment saw him enter the Rebel trench without exiting. Perhaps if James had been by his side and seen Florence's death then I could accept it and move on. But James was reassigned to heavy artillery. He was firing off a cannon half a mile away.

I have been writing to the Union officers in Washington, hopeful that his body is recovered and returned home to me. This seems to be the only way I can move ahead. My wish came true just two weeks prior when I received a letter from a man named Mr. Alexander. Reading it in the privacy of the barn, I wept.

L. Alexander
September 22nd, 1864
Washington DC

Dear Madam,

Your favor received this morning in reply I will inform you we shall be ready to exhume bodies from the battlefield immediately after the first of October. The charge for exhuming and disinfecting in the airtight coffin and travelling including express charges to Springfield Mass will be one hundred dollars. You can deposit the money with express agent at Springfield and request him to telegraph us. Please send full particulars as regards to the name, regiment, company and where buried. In short, all the information you may have.

Yours truly and respectfully,

L. Alexander

Chapter 33

Ellen Burke
October 18th, 1864
West Springfield, MA

"It's here Mother, Da's body has arrived!" I hear Michael calling in the distance; he must be on the other side of the barn. His voice echoes through my head, as though he's hollering from miles away. I remind myself to stay collected for the children. I do not have the luxury of taking my handkerchief in hand and escaping back to the green valley of Ireland. I must see this through. A light rain has begun to fall, further hindering the view in the distance. I do see Michael though, he's running from the barn, searching for me. Beyond him I can just make out the black, somber-looking carriage that transported Florence's body. It rests in front of our house like an ominous dark cloud.

My mourning dress has begun to look polka dotted as the raindrops hit me in random spots. I should don my shawl but I do not feel cold. In fact, a warm feeling of excitement is racing through my veins. I did not expect this sensation, but I suppose it's impossible to predict how I'd feel given this unthinkable situation. I step from the cornfield and walk swiftly across the grassy pasture. Michael finally notices me and begins to jump up and down, pointing his small finger toward the carriage. He seems to be excited as well. I believe he and Jerry are eager to see their Father in his Union Army uniform and perhaps collect a cuff link or a tiny piece of material from his clothing. I am hopeful they can find some small article that will serve as a remembrance and comfort them as my mother's handkerchief has done for me.

I've waited for this moment but now that it's so near to me I feel anxious and a bit frightened. I've seen the portrait of my husband in his uniform looking strong and well, but seeing him lying inside a coffin, his body surely broken and rotted, may be more than even I can bear. I shall have the first look at him and decide whether or not it's fitting for the boys to do the same. I pray it will be. They long to see their father one last time before he is buried, to thank him for his bravery and sacrifice.

As I approach the carriage, I notice Jerry is there speaking with the military officer. I am surprised the official is not wearing a Union uniform. Instead he's dressed in a formal black suit and his head is covered with a tall, black top hat. If he'd been sporting a black beard I'd think Abe Lincoln himself were here delivering my husband's body, but he appears to be an older gentleman wearing a serious countenance. He greets me with a tip of his hat and inquires whether or not I am indeed Mrs. Florence Burke. After we complete the formalities, I sign the legal documents and take my receipt in hand. I'd forgotten the dear price I paid for this service but I would've paid even more to see Florence returned to his land.

The official (who never offers his name) walks solemnly to the carriage and stands before it. He collects his ledger and ticks off tiny boxes with his pen. Finally he unrolls a scroll and begins reading from it, like a politician prepared to make a declaration. I look into his face but it's devoid of emotion; his tiny wrinkled eyes shift left and right mechanically across the page. Michael and Jerry take their places on either side of me and I take a moment to regard them. Jerry stands tall and proud, he's clearly putting on a brave face. Michael takes my hand into his and leans his sodden head against my arm. This must be grueling for the boys. I wish this official would just get on with it.

When he finally concludes his speech, stating that the Union Army has followed protocol and preserved the body in the best manner possible, he furls the scroll and stows it in the carriage. He motions for me to follow him, and I turn and kiss the boys. I'm shaking now, finally feeling the rain pouring from the clouds, making my dress heavy and cold. The official lifts the casket off the back of the carriage with a rope pulley. It finds its way to the ground without a sound, landing on the soft, wet grass. I take a deep breath to try and control my quickening heart, then I stand over the casket as its lid is gently pried open.

I'm not sure who was more shocked, the official or me, because the lid suddenly slams shut and we both go pale. I cover a hand over my mouth and shake my head wildly. Who is this? The official frantically opens the casket and places his head in the box to examine it closely. Before I can even make sense of this and try to explain it to my frightened children, the official is beside me apologizing for the mistake. He swiftly collects his ledger and flips through its pages, searching for the error. His face crumples and he's mumbling something about how this has never happened before, and he's looking desperate. If I hadn't been so shocked and disappointed I would have felt sorry for him.

All at once I am filled with a sensation of anger, but that soon changes to a feeling of release and lightness. I turn my face into the rain, and begin to smile. Jerry cannot stay silent any longer.

"What is it Mum?" His eyes are wide and his lips are tight, preparing for the news. I shift my eyes downward and offer another sideways smile, what is the meaning of this? I take the boys' hands and lead them away from the frazzled official and the erroneous body, and head up towards our gravesite. When we reach the memorial plateau, we kneel in the wet grass and I tell them that there's been a mistake and that their Father is not in that casket.

Michael lets out a loud gasp and sits back on his heels. He lowers his chin to his chest, and closes his eyes.

"Are you quite sure?" Jerry's face twists in confusion and disappointment. I nod and remarkably, I feel my face brightening. "Yes, I'm certain. The soldier in that box is colored... Boys, I think your Father is having a laugh in heaven right now, and we should join in."

I rise, feeling lighter than an angel despite my wet clothes. Tiny bursts of laughter travel from my chest and up to my lips. The boys are still in shock, deflated by the news. They remain by the gravesite, praying for their Father. I move a few steps further and reach into my pocket for my handkerchief. I clutch it firmly and start to twirl. The rain has stopped and my wet dress flaps like a vast sail luffing in the wind. I am laughing into the breeze, realizing that I am free at last from grief's imprisonment. When I finally stop and catch my breath--I open my hand. I can only presume it was the heat and pressure in my fist that scorched the cloth, because it becomes dust in my hand. I flatten my palm and watch the tiny particles of fabric dance on my skin before sailing off into the wind, scattering across our farm.

The End

Author's Note

Florence Burke's gamble did pay off. Although I was unable to discover what became of Ellen Burke and Jerry Burke, I do know that Florence's son Michael married Margaret Foley and gave birth to several children including Florence William Burke, who attended Brown University and Boston University Law School and ultimately became a judge; William Burke, who attended Tufts University and became a prominent Boston dentist and professor; and Francis Burke, who also attended Brown University and worked for the government in Washington, D.C. All of Michael's eight children were educated, successful, and considered true Americans.

Michael Burke is also the grandfather of my father, Michael, a beloved teacher and head of school and most importantly, the person who inspired me to write this book. I am Ellen, and I will never forget my Irish roots and the sacrifices of those who came before me.

Below is the Deed to the land-traded by Julius Day and photos of the Burkes.

The 19 Civil War letters I found in my attic are the basis for the storyline in this historical novel. I tried to remain as true to their characters, events and life as much as possible. To view some of the original letters, go to www.ellenalden.com.

Original deed to Florence Burke's land

Immigration photo taken at Staten Island 1848

Florence and Ellen's baby girl 1864